T0285535

BETTY FRIEDAN

# Betty Friedan

## *Magnificent Disrupter*

RACHEL SHTEIR

Yale
UNIVERSITY
PRESS
New Haven and London

Yale University Press books may be purchased in quantity for educational, business, or promotional use. For information, please e-mail sales.press@yale.edu (U.S. office) or sales@yaleup.co.uk (U.K. office).

Set in Janson type by Integrated Publishing Solutions.
Printed in the United States of America.

Library of Congress Control Number: 2022951535
ISBN 978-0-300-22002-5 (hardcover : alk. paper)
A catalogue record for this book is available from the British Library.
This paper meets the requirements of ANSI/NISO Z39.48-1992 (Permanence of Paper).

10 9 8 7 6 5 4 3 2 1

*Frontispiece:* Betty Friedan relaxing in California shortly after her sixty-fifth birthday. (Photo by UPI/Bettmann via Getty Images)

ALSO BY RACHEL SHTEIR

---

*The Steal: A Cultural History of Shoplifting*

*Gypsy: The Art of the Tease*

*Striptease: The Untold History of the Girlie Show*

For Esther Shteir

## CONTENTS

# *Introduction*

This book takes its subtitle from the words of former House Speaker Nancy Pelosi. In 2006, not long after Betty Friedan's death, Pelosi used the phrase "Magnificent Disrupter" to describe several American heroines who had just died—Coretta Scott King, Rosa Parks, the San Francisco activist Mary Helen Rogers, and Friedan. These women, Pelosi thought, combined visionary achievements and a commitment to "tirelessly" fight against injustice, whatever the cost. She considered the phrase an essential ingredient to patriotism and social change.

Maybe more than other magnificent disrupters, Friedan unsettled those around her. An often-told anecdote illustrating her public ire is set at a dinner party at the home of her younger brother, Harry, in the 1980s. Someone asked her: "Can you explain the feminist movement to me?"

She lit into the asker. Later, walking to her car, Harry said,

"Betty, why did you do that? I've sat at your dinner table a lot of times and I never said anything so offensive to your guests."

"But Harry," she replied, "there aren't any idiots at my table."

Since Friedan's death, the practice of either ridiculing her or making her disappear continues, carrying forward the portrait cemented twenty years ago in the last round of full-length biographies. In the popular 2020 television series *Mrs. America*, Tracey Ullman played her as a mean-spirited, irrational cartoon, recalling a phrase from Daphne Merkin's 1999 *New Yorker* review of Judith Hennessee's *Betty Friedan: Her Life* and Daniel Horowitz's *Betty Friedan and the Making of The Feminine Mystique: The American Left, the Cold War, and Modern Feminism*—"icon without portfolio." Hennessee disliked her subject. Horowitz's influential book (which largely ends in 1963) argues that if Friedan had not exaggerated her role as a housewife and played down her years as a labor journalist, she could have linked the Old and New Left and saved second-wave feminism from shattering on the rocks of multiculturalism, on the one hand, and conservatism, on the other. This perspective, while important, minimizes the Left's disregard for women's rights. In 1983, at the height of the feminist backlash, Gloria Steinem recalled the actress Lee Grant telling her that she'd "been married to one Marxist and one Leninist, and neither one took the garbage out."[1]

Even more striking is the embrace of the cliché that Friedan's unfeminine looks and aggressive style crippled the famous, best-selling writer whose weathered face, like that of Lillian Hellman, defied retrograde categories of attractiveness. By contrast, this book argues that Friedan developed her harsh affect to protect herself from her parents' definitions of what a woman should be, from men comparing her to their mothers or calling her "mieskeit," the Yiddish word for ugly, and from her own insecurities. She joins feminists who raged and who wrote unsparingly and analytically about crises of femininity, the home, and the family as sources of contradictions, female oppression, and yearning. She writes alongside and in front of many twentieth-century feminists incensed about gender inequity: Simone de Beauvoir's riff about the "Sisyphean" agonies of housework's "endless repetition" in *The Second Sex;* Shirley Jackson's subversive stories about performing that work; the sociologist Arlie Hochschild's 1989 phrase "the second shift," documenting how society obligates women to shoulder both domestic duties and the paycheck. She emerges from a domestic landscape, a country of daughters struggling in the immigrant cultures of the American Midwest at a time of financial opportunity and fragility, of prejudice, fear, and assimilation.

Friedan never stopped fighting to make society regard women as "people too," as she wrote in 1960. "The gut issues of this revolution involve employment and education and new social institutions and not sexual fantasy," she once wrote. She would likely be disappointed by our failure to address those "gut issues" and by our "cancel culture" world, with its 24/7 sex scandals commanding more attention than persistent class and gender inequities.[2]

To find the Magnificent Disrupter, I did new research and new reporting, including more than one hundred interviews. I was fortunate to access newly opened archival collections and scrutinize several caches of private papers, with an eye to correcting unnuanced judgments about her alleged classism, racism, and homophobia. Friedan was no saint. But she was an oracle and an iconoclast, ahead of her time, the American activist with a Russian soul, the artist of moral and intellectual fervor, driven by a desire to change herself and others. She imagined herself under the shadows of history and eternity, acting with remorseless courage. She said things (about women, about

Jews) that many people did not want to hear. As Daniel Friedan, her oldest son, said about her: "I think of the words attributed to Archimedes: 'Give me a lever and a place to stand and I will move the earth.'" Betty Friedan moved the earth.[3]

# 1

## *A Prophet in Peoria*

Although Betty often explained the writing of her momentous book as a reaction against her unhappy mother, Miriam, her relationships with her male forebears are important too. Her maternal grandfather, Sandor Horwitz, was crucial to her life's work as was her father's brother, Uncle Ben. To understand their biographies—her family's roots as Midwestern Jews—is to understand her triumph and limitations. Born in 1867 into a family of eminent Hungarian rabbis, at age six Horwitz lost his parents to cholera. In 1885, he made his way to New York alone. After three months as a street peddler, he moved to St. Louis. He learned English, graduating from high school in 1892 and starting studies at Missouri Medical College, specializing in "genito-urinary diseases." He tutored Jews in German and Hebrew, read the Torah, participated in synagogue life, and joined both Jewish and non-Jewish fraternal orders, a balancing act typical of first-generation Jewish immigrants.

Though never ordained, Sandor briefly moved to Richmond, Virginia, to work as a rabbi, then returned to St. Louis, where, in 1895, he graduated from Missouri Medical College.[1]

On August 7, 1896, Sandor married Bertha Horwitz, a distant relation who had arrived in the United States around ten years earlier from Hungary. They moved to Peoria for a decade, where Sandor worked as a surgeon. Betty's mother, Miriam—their only daughter—was born there on February 21, 1898. In 1906, they briefly returned to St. Louis, but two years later, Peoria hired Sandor as City Physician and the Horwitzes set up their household at 410 South Borland Avenue and raised Miriam with the help of a live-in German maid.[2]

Betty loathed Peoria as a child and only conceded in her fifties that she felt "rooted" there. She spent the first half of her life defining herself against a place she would describe as more Southern than Midwestern—by which she meant segregated. Yet when Sandor Horwitz first saw Peoria, he was drawn to the small, bustling city 170 miles southwest of Chicago. It would not be until the 1920s that New York theater producers coined the show biz slogan "Will It Play in Peoria?" with a sneer in the question. At the end of the nineteenth century, Peoria thrived. It housed a major manufacturer—Caterpillar—over 50,000 people, booming distilleries, and the largest Jewish community outside of Chicago, around 2,000 immigrants from Eastern Europe and Germany. These Jews—professionals, merchants, distillery owners, politicians—could attend one of two downtown synagogues: the Reform one, Anshai Emeth, or the Orthodox one, Aguda Achim. Sandor helped rebuild Anshai Emeth after a fire and assisted at the Sunday school as he developed a robust private practice and served the city. Described as a "local man of eminence" in *The Jewish People of Peoria*, he fought for modern medical ideas, such as quarantines for patients, penicillin for the madams and prostitutes in the red-light district who might be afflicted with syphilis or gonorrhea, and a clean supply of milk for Peorians.[3]

The tension between home and opportunity in Miriam Goldstein's life shaped her famous daughter. Betty recounted frequently a story about her mother that she linked with the genesis of *The Feminine Mystique:* Sandor Horwitz forbade Miriam from attending Smith College in Northampton, Massachusetts, then among the finest schools for women in the country. In 1914, he did let her attend nearby Bradley Polytechnic Institute, a combination of high school and junior college. She studied literature, sang in the chorus, and joined the French and German clubs and Delta Kappa. During the summers, she had an active social life, hosting luncheons and sewing circles, and traveling to St. Louis to see friends and relatives. She graduated in 1917.[4]

That summer, not long after America entered the Great War, Sandor joined the medical corps. He served as a lieutenant colonel at the Jefferson Barracks, Missouri, 179 miles south of Peoria. Miriam and her mother would visit him. When, the following year, the war ended, he returned to Peoria. By then his pretty, smart, and socially ambitious daughter had begun working as a stenographer, first at Newman Stratton Company, a regional distributor of automobiles, and the following year at JW Franke and Sons, a printer. However, according to family lore, she next did something uncommon for someone of her gender, class, and era. She began working at a newspaper, probably the *Peoria Evening Transcript*, becoming the editor of the woman's page.[5]

Shortly after that, Miriam met Harry Maurice Goldstein, nearly twice her age, a stocky jewelry merchant with a kind face, who would be Betty's father. Betty never wrote about her parents' initial encounter, but she believed the moral of her mother's life is that women of that generation could not both marry and have a career. As for Harry, he had a coming to America story not unlike that of Miriam's father. Born in Russia in 1881, the oldest of thirteen children, Harry arrived in St. Louis (the same town as Sandor Horwitz) with his family in 1896. Betty remembered Harry saying that he lived in a tenement "near Edna Ferber or was it Fannie Hurst, or both."[6]

Sometime over the next few years, Harry left school early and moved to Peoria to strike out on his own. At first, he sold shirt collar buttons from a peddler's stand. Soon he sold diamond ones. By 1908, he had saved enough to buy a store, Goldstein Jewelry Company. The store struggled. But it soon began to flourish, and Harry relocated to bustling South Adams Street. The so-called "Tiffany's of Peoria" became successful, selling china, including Spode and Wedgwood, as well as crystal, watches, clocks, and diamond and gold jewelry. In 1914, Harry was making enough money to send his youngest brother, Ben, then nineteen, to Harvard Law School. (Their sister, Sarah, had taken a secretarial job to get him through college.) Ben would graduate from law school in 1917 and the following year, Goldstein Jewelry Company moved again, a block away, to a large storefront with a gorgeous mahogany interior, silk curtains, and beautiful electric lights. In 1920, *Jewelers' Circular* called it "one of the handsomest [stores] in the country."[7]

In photographs taken after his marriage to Miriam, Harry looks distinguished, jowly with thin white hair and a mustache and round glasses. But Sandor Horwitz saw Harry as a mixed blessing. Eighteen years older than Miriam, he was well-read, but he was a first-generation immigrant with only a seventh-grade education. He owned a business, but he spoke with an accent, which Miriam later ridiculed, to the discomfort of their oldest daughter. He was also a widower whose first wife, Edna Lidwinoski, died in 1911, a year after the wedding. Further, Harry, like many Peorians of his day, gambled. Since Edna's death, he'd lived in the Jefferson Hotel, sometimes joined by his brother, Ben. Harry played in a regular poker game, "the knights of the round table," with vaudeville stars like Fibber McGee and Jack Benny, when they were in town for one-night stands at the Rialto and the Hippodrome Theatres.[8]

The Horwitzes sent Miriam away to break up the romance, but it didn't work. Perhaps in marrying Harry Goldstein, Miriam attained certain freedoms after all. She stopped working when the couple married on February 3, 1920, about six months after women got the vote. The jewelry merchant and his young wife honeymooned in California. For the next twenty-three years, Miriam volunteered, raised a family, exercised, entertained, and helped out with the Goldstein Jewelry Company. She regretted stopping work but, as she told a reporter years later, it "was not considered ladylike."[9]

Harry wanted a boy, but their first child was a daughter. Bettye Naomi Goldstein (she dropped the "e" at Smith) was born February 4, 1921, at Proctor Hospital in Peoria. From infancy, she suffered from poor health. According to Betty, a nurse predicted she would not survive more than two weeks. She had bow legs for which she wore iron braces until the age of three. However, she began to talk almost right away. Five decades later, her mother recalled that her eldest "always spoke in grammatically perfect sentences."[10]

The birth of Betty's sister, Amye (she would also drop the "e" later), in 1922, made Betty unhappy. She would never be close to Amy, who had naturally curly hair, mimicked her mother's mannerisms, and was exceptionally neat. Amy would complain that years later, Betty dismissed her as if she were afflicted with the feminine mystique, or said she barely remembered her. As for Harry Jr., the boy her father wanted so badly, born in 1926, she ignored him too. "You know Harry you got the same brain I do but you're not using it," she said. The stubborn, independent founder of second-wave feminism emerges from a home anchored by gender polarities and sibling rivalries. "She didn't play with dolls like her contemporaries," her mother said.[11]

A photo taken of Betty, age five, shows a girl whose hair is cut in a bob wearing a loose-fitting dress with a white Peter Pan collar tied at the neck with a ribbon. This girl, who looks at the camera with the same gravitas she would later summon when talking about politics or her famous book, already displayed her legendary bad temper. At around the same time as the photo was taken, she hit a boy on the head with a hoe.

During Betty's first nine years, the family had money, which Miriam spent freely. The Goldsteins employed several domestic servants. Isabel, a Black nursemaid whom Harry Jr. found "kind," looked after the children, and a chauffeur drove them to school. Betty emerges from upper-middle-class society, swaddled in material comfort and stability, the product of immigrant striving and the economic opportunities of early twentieth-century America. Yet she also comes from Jazz Age Peoria, a city of contradictions. Its population swelled from 70,000 to 100,000, but it never became a true metropolis. Peoria was one of the few Illinois towns that was not a "Sundowner Town"—it did not impose a curfew on Blacks after dark—although the Klan appeared in the region. With the distilleries closed during Prohibition, "the whiskey capital of the world" became notorious for crime and bootlegging. In 1955, Betty wrote about how people used to drive through the red-light district "on a dare." Yet Peoria in the 1920s also housed a large entertainment hub, with nineteen theaters, including ornate, Italianate movie emporiums and vaudeville houses, like the Palace Theatre on Main Street, and the Madison, on Madison Avenue. Betty "hated having to go to the movies" there with her parents on Saturday night. Sometimes she did go with friends, to classics like *City Lights* with Charlie Chaplin or *Monkey Business* starring the Marx

Brothers. She liked Myrna Loy, Bette Davis, Merle Oberon, and Norma Shearer but she loathed the goody two-shoes Shirley Temple. If she went to the movies *en famille*, Harry Sr. pointed out the moral afterward.[12]

Geographically, Peoria was split between the Bluffs and the Valley. The Bluffs, a group of neighborhoods on the cliffs overlooking the Illinois River, comprised the wealthier districts. For the first years of their marriage, Miriam and Harry lived in the Valley, not far from the Caterpillar plant and the distilleries and breweries. In 1924, when Betty was three, they moved to a three-floor brick house at 105 Farmington Road in West Bluff. Just before the Crash, they almost moved to a more affluent part of West Bluff, with Prairie style houses—including one designed by Frank Lloyd Wright—tall mature bur oak trees, and Grandview Drive, which Teddy Roosevelt called "the most beautiful drive in America," for its panoramic views of the Illinois River and the valley beyond. But in the end, the Goldsteins stayed in their less grand home. Still, living there gave Betty license to think that she was "better, finer, smarter, more sensitive" than her neighbors.[13]

The Farmington Road house had a wide front porch and small lawn. Inside, there were eight rooms, including a foyer with a floor covered in black and white tiles. There was a separate dining room whose windows were framed with lush ecru-colored drapes. Miriam had had the chairs, made of dark wood, upholstered in blue velvet to match the blue-and-rose-colored rug. In one corner of the living room, she installed a Steinway baby grand on top of an Oriental carpet and in another corner, a game table for cards and jigsaw puzzles. Harry Sr. played poker with his pals at the table, and Miriam invited friends over for lunch, mah-jongg, or bridge. Upstairs, Harry Jr. had his own bedroom, but the sisters, whom their mother dressed in identical clothes until they were in junior high, shared theirs.

One idyllic aspect of Betty's childhood played a role in her lifelong interest in utopian communities: Laura Bradley Park, across the street from her house. Bequeathed to the city in 1881 by Lydia Moss Bradley, a real estate titan, bank president, and philanthropist who founded Bradley University, Bradley Park stretched over 140 acres of forest and lawn. The part near Betty's house is dotted with gazebos, tennis courts, spruce trees, a Japanese garden and bridge, and walking paths. In the summer, the Goldsteins strolled there with their German shepherd, Rex. In the winter, the children went sledding and admired the stately trees. Writing in an essay in college, Betty complained of Peoria but she saw Bradley Park as freedom. During the coldest months of the year, she "would kneel at her window late at night and look out" to see "bare branches and snow without footprints, wind in leaves."[14]

Miriam loved to cook and host parties, though she often delegated domestic tasks. At dinner, using a foot buzzer, she would summon the maid to serve the food the cook had prepared, at the dining room table, which could seat twelve. Miriam often set for six—herself, Harry, the three children, and her father. Miriam dressed beautifully, "like she stepped out of a Bergdorf Goodman window," Amy said. She succeeded at many things. For a time, she practiced eurythmics, a European style of music and dance popularized by Isadora Duncan. She played tennis well, drove competently, and she ran one civic organization after the other—the women's division of the Community Chest, the temple Sunday school. But she could be overprotective. She would not let Betty ride a bicycle (or, later, drive a car). Her daughters, who rarely agreed on anything, believed that vanity deformed their mother. Amy said: "She had a complete inability to nurture."[15]

Miriam could nurture—just not her daughters. She consoled her son, Harry Jr., during his bouts of hypochondria and when he could not throw a baseball. But she withheld that tenderness from her eldest daughter, who grew up to be clumsy at sports and a terrible driver. Years later, Betty's therapist would write that her mother "resented any and every expression of maturation in her child." But if Miriam hurt her daughters, she hurt too. She often stayed in bed, struck with colitis that left her "screaming with pain," Betty recalled.[16]

Betty escaped into her imagination and intellect. In 1927, she began to attend Whittier Grade School, a few blocks from her home. She read, wrote, and did math far ahead of the class. She skipped half of first grade. Three years later, in fourth grade, she skipped another half grade. She organized clubs, including the "Baddy Baddy" Club, which staged a series of protests against a substitute teacher by dropping books on the floor and coughing en masse. They made a clubhouse in her basement and created bylaws but disbanded as quickly as they formed.

She continued to have health troubles, including bronchitis and the flu. She wore braces on her teeth, like many other children. But illness did not ruin her childhood. She adored all sorts of fanciful games, clubs, and mysteries. And she loved reading: adventure stories such as *Swallows and Amazons* by the leftist journalist Arthur Ransome, about a group of English kids learning how to sail; E. Nesbit's Psammead Trilogy, about another such group encountering a wish-granting mythological creature; *The Secret Garden* and *The Little Colonel* series, about a bossy tomboy; *The Bobbsey Twins* and Nancy Drew, which first appeared in 1930. That book, about a bold sixteen-year-old girl sleuth and good citizen, offered Betty one role model. *Little Women*, in which Jo March, a tomboy, married after becoming a writer, may have provided another. Later she would read widely and daringly from her parents' bookshelf, writers such as Sinclair Lewis and Theodore Dreiser, both of whom scathingly critiqued Midwestern hypocrisy. Harry Sr. and Miriam soon learned that to control Betty, they had to threaten to take away her books. Harry Sr., her own beloved father, forbade her from checking out library books. "It doesn't look nice for a girl to be so bookish," he supposedly said when he saw Betty schlepping a pile of them up Main Street Hill. It was "unladylike."[17]

In early versions of this story, Betty erases her mother, but over time she gave Miriam a better role. Once she began exploring her Jewish roots in the 1970s, she focused less on her parents depriving her and more on reading as a positive attribute of her Jewish home. In her 2000 memoir, she added that her mother had enrolled her in a book club specializing in British children's literature. Indeed, the whole truth of this story reveals the Goldsteins' differing attitudes toward their daughter's gifts. In Miriam's version, she gave in to Harry's concern about Betty's reading as detrimental to her femininity; together, the parents made their daughter see a child psychologist. "He asked if we were afraid she would have a problem with boys because she was so smart. He said we couldn't change things," Miriam told a reporter in 1971.[18]

The Goldsteins abandoned their efforts to control Betty's reading. Instead, Miriam channeled her thwarted ambition into advancing her daughter's intelligence. She took both girls to Bradley University to have their IQ measured. Betty's was off the charts at 180. Yet if Miriam and Harry shared an uneasy pride about their daughter's smarts, they disagreed strongly about how to regard her writing. Harry stowed her poems and her newspaper columns in the safe at Goldstein's, where he could readily show them to customers. This irritated Miriam, who never praised her daughter's literary efforts. She would tell a reporter, "[Betty] would come by the store on Saturdays and her father would take her out for lunch with him and other prominent businessmen. I think he sort of exploited her."[19]

In her 2000 memoir, Betty described her father treating her like a smart wind-up toy. Once, Harry Sr. and his friend Charlie, a local theater owner, sent her to her room to write a play, which, after days spent staring at a blank page, she failed to do. Harry Jr. also remembered how at dinner, largely ignoring him and Amy, Harry Sr. hurled math problems at his oldest daughter: "What number can you divide into 999,919?" Harry Sr. quizzed Betty about philosophy, movies, and current events, such as the Scopes Trial, which newspapers covered prominently at the time. He considered himself a freethinker, told his clever daughter he had attended that trial, and encouraged her to emulate Robert G. Ingersoll, a dazzling orator who lived in Peoria from 1857 to 1877 and advocated for agnosticism and humanism. But Harry Sr. also continued to worry that others would perceive Betty as unfeminine and too Jewish. In 1971, she would remember him ridiculing her directness, her awkwardness: "My father, who loved me, saw in me the dreams circumstance did not let him realize himself. His armor against the pain a man can't admit he suffers doomed him to early death, but he could not bear my pain as a woman. He teased me, because I did not walk easily in high heels, because I would not use those feminine wiles on the telephone. He knew I would have to wear the mask."[20]

Although Betty's parents were friends with several Jewish families—the Ottenheimers' daughter, also named Betty, known as "Otty," was Betty's best friend—Harry Jr. remembered that his family was "very prominent until six o'clock," meaning that non-Jewish Peorians shunned them after dark. When the Peoria Country Club, located on elegant Grandview Drive, declined to admit the Goldsteins, the family joined the so-called Jewish country club—the North Shore Country Club. Housed in a former automobile club miles outside of Peoria, the North Shore Country Club would go bankrupt in 1935. But before that, Betty, Amy, Otty, and Otty's mother, Blanche, held picnics there during the hot Peoria summers.[21]

Like many Reform Jewish families at the time, the Goldsteins celebrated Christmas and Passover. They attended High Holy Day services at Anshai Emeth, where in 1937, Harry served as vice president and Miriam supervised the Sunday school. The children studied the Hebrew Bible there in English, which gave Betty headaches. At home, Miriam and Harry spoke German and Yiddish when they wanted to exclude the children. During the summers, they sent Betty, Amy, and Harry Jr. to non-Jewish sleepaway camps in Wisconsin to canoe, hike, and ride horses.

After Sandor Horwitz's wife, Bertha, died of leukemia in 1927, Sandor frequently ate dinner at the Goldsteins'. When he was at the table, the family often discussed medical topics, including communicable diseases and their cures. Sandor, whom the local press regularly quoted, recounted his travels across Illinois fighting diphtheria, smallpox, scarlet fever, encephalitis, and rabies outbreaks. He described the gruesome effects of diseases he had recently seen, driving Harry Jr. into paroxysms of anxiety. Betty loved his stories, which she had occasion to hear after her parents made her Sandor's chaperone. Years earlier, while backing out of his driveway, Sandor had crashed into another car, fracturing his nose. In 1931, after he became health superintendent for the Peoria district, which included several counties, Betty's parents instructed her to accompany him on some of his local trips. That same year, Sandor began to write erudite essays for medical journals, one titled "The Science of Medicine from Jewish Lore Gathered from Biblical and Talmudic Sources," and a biographical study of Maimonides, who was, of course, a physician. Another paragon of civic virtue was Harry's younger brother, Ben, who in 1934 would win an enormous case against Illinois Bell Telephone for overcharging customers.[22]

If the accomplishments of her male relatives buoyed Betty, the Great Depression destabilized her family life. For one, it set her parents on edge. After the Crash, Miriam and Harry Sr. fought regularly. Their battles, many over money, literally "shook our house at night," Betty remembered. Fewer people had extra cash for Goldstein's jewelry and fine china. Harry Sr. let the maid and the chauffeur go and re-mortgaged the house. But Betty recalled that Miriam continued to act as though the family was rich, spending beyond her means and starting charge accounts, then gambling to recoup but losing and confessing to Harry Sr., who had a terrible temper. Miriam made him feel inadequate. When he gave her a sapphire watch for Christmas, she "pouted and raved" that it wasn't rubies and diamonds. Although Betty makes Miriam-the-bad-mom the starting point of *The Feminine Mystique*, she acknowledged a more tender side of her mother in an autobiographical essay. Miriam "is the only person who I am always sure will understand and sympathise [*sic*] and never make me feel worse, always better," she wrote.[23]

In 1932, when Betty was eleven, a doctor determined her to be partly blind in one eye and prescribed eyeglasses with thick lenses. Her emotions became even more volatile. She pulled a chunk of hair out of the head of Otty Ottenheimer, supposedly for being dumb. She threw a book at Amy's head. (Her sister had to have stitches.) It's possible that she was reacting to her father's declining health, which made it difficult for him to run the business. Although he neither declared bankruptcy nor put his assets into his wife's name, as so many Depression-era business owners did to protect their fortunes, he did resort to bartering, trading silver trays and tureens for advertising pages in the local newspaper. He continued to provide not just for his own family but his first wife's elderly sisters, whom he visited every Sunday. But by the time Betty entered high school, he had developed heart trouble and hypertension. Although it further burdened the family's dwindling finances, Miriam arranged for at least one week-long winter trip to Miami Beach, leaving the children in Peoria.[24]

Not every moment was bleak. The family took walks in Glen Oak Park, where a Victorian fountain had a display of colored lights. During the summers, Miriam drove everyone to

Michigan's Upper Peninsula or Round Lake, near Hayward, Wisconsin, to a fishing camp. Harry Sr. came out on the weekends to fish. They also took one trip to visit Miriam's cousin in Springfield and in the summer of 1933, the family went to the Chicago World's Fair.

That fall, Betty entered Roosevelt Junior High School, where she would write for the school paper. Her mother encouraged her to become society editor, which Betty did. She also played kissing games with boys, although she felt awkward around the opposite sex. At home, every night, she said the children's bedtime prayer and the Shema, praying for "a boy that likes me best," for "work to do," and to not be discontented like her mother. At age thirteen, a few weeks before confirmation (an addition to the bar mitzvah ceremony introduced by nineteenth-century European Reform rabbis to reaffirm faith), the young freethinker informed the rabbi that she didn't believe in God. The rabbi told her to pretend she believed, and she "gave the flower offering," bringing the bouquet to the altar and "raising my eyes to the heavens."[25]

She rejected her mother's superficial interpretation of Judaism and condemned as shallow Miriam's focus on volunteerism and surface appearances. She would later describe her mother as "an anti-Semitic Jew." One battleground was her nose. Miriam advised her daughter to get a rhinoplasty, a fairly standard procedure at that time. Betty, whose nose in many high school portraits appears dainty enough, declined. Nonetheless, in her high school autobiography, she wrote that she would wind up an old maid because she lacked sex appeal.[26]

Another battleground was her lack of tidiness. Amy scoffed at her sister for ignoring "*grooming*" (her italics) and neglecting her side of the room except for occasional, middle-of-the-night cleaning spells. Harry Jr. later speculated that Betty was "sloppy" to hurt Miriam. The siblings agreed that their older sister tried to make herself look like a frump. But around this time, Betty wrote something revealing: "When I grow up, I'm going to be rich so I can hire somebody to clean my room and make my bed." It's easy to dismiss this pronouncement as privilege, but her wish to pay "somebody" to do housework lays out a feminist problem that haunts women to this day: the gender inequality of domestic labor. The tension between her mother's femininity and her growing sense of injustice may have further aggravated her temper. Harry Jr. provoked some rage, as when he attempted to see her and Amy naked through the keyhole, "Betty chased me and threw a book," he complained. "She was screaming and she scared the hell out of me!"[27]

In the fall of 1935, when Betty, age fourteen, entered Central High School, the short, pudgy bibliophile, younger than most of the other girls, wore saddle shoes with socks, and red smock dresses made of wool that her mother ordered from Best and Co, in New York. She knew more than many of her peers about Franklin D. Roosevelt's second New Deal, passed that year, with its strong protections for working people. Additionally, she may have been aware of the rising anti-Semitism since the Crash. It's possible that the family discussed the anti-Communist Father Coughlin, whose anti-Semitic radio ravings reached 40 million Americans in the mid-1930s.

But as a sophomore, Betty experienced anti-Semitism firsthand. Sororities controlled social life, organizing dances, outings, and parties and dictated who was in and who was out. Betty and her friend Otty—both Jews—were not rushed. Years later, she blamed her exclusion on anti-Semitism, which, she said, Miriam aggravated because she withheld "the comfort of knowing that I didn't get into the sorority because I was Jewish." Amy also remembered the sting. But many Peorians would dismiss the charge, saying Betty exaggerated.[28]

She had other problems. She did not have a steady boyfriend, although she did cadge a date or two with other Jewish misfits from dancing school. She often retreated to the local cemetery, where she read and wrote poetry, or to hidden spots in Bradley Park. About the classmates who rejected her, she vowed, "If they don't like me, someday they'll learn to respect me." A love affair with the theater propelled her out of her avenging isolation.[29]

As a child, she had loved enacting mysteries, always seizing the role of detective. She adored digging around in Miriam's chest and trying on her evening gowns and shoes. In junior high, she spent one summer as a drama counselor at camp. She then insisted that her mother allow her to stop dancing lessons at Miss Coleman's and take up acting lessons at Mrs. Morrill's Children's Theater, run by Mabel Nortrup Morrill, a glamorous figure whose credentials included running her own acting studio in Chicago, living in the Mojave Desert, and studying with George Bernard Shaw. Morrill, who had a turn as Shaw's Saint Joan years earlier, whetted Betty's appetite for drama.

In the summer of 1936, her parents took her to see a production of *Saint Joan* in Chicago. Shaw wrote the play in 1923, three years after the Church canonized Joan. Unlike earlier interpreters of the story, he saw the teenaged saint as a change-agent who leaps from obscurity to martyrdom, ending the Hundred Years' War by channeling holy voices before she is burned at the stake. Shaw conceived of part of Joan's power as coming from her transvestism and has his Inquisitor warn, "The woman who quarrels with her clothes and puts on the dress of a man, is like the man who throws off his fur gown and dresses like John the Baptist." Shaw pictured his Joan as a zealot. Carolyn Heilbrun writes that she is hardly mortal, as she chooses to die to become a "functioning moral being."[30]

A Broadway hit when it arrived in Chicago, *Saint Joan* starred the great Katharine Cornell. To prepare for the role, Cornell had retraced Joan's pilgrimage in France and donned a riding habit to learn to walk like a boy. In the cathedral scene, where Joan hears the voices of the saints, Cornell glanced up at the rafters to affirm that she sees their bodies too. Cornell's Joan may have knocked Betty into fighting injustice at Central High School. In her junior and senior years, Betty excelled at math and physics and dreamed of emulating Marie Curie, although her teacher warned her to aim more modestly. Betty also overcame her doubts about her writing to become an able journalist. Reviewing Sinclair Lewis's *It Can't Happen Here*, a dystopian warning about authoritarian regimes taking hold in America, for the *Peoria Opinion*, the school paper, she agreed with the author's dire outlook. Other features and reviews from that year addressed subjects such as the conflicts between workers and capitalists and the Spanish Civil War. With her classmate John "Parkie" Parkhurst, whom she had a crush on, she began a column, "Cabbages and Kings," for the *Peoria Opinion*. Some columns were proto-feminist, like one telling the fable of two types of girls, one succeeding by "the feminine touch," the other by brains.[31]

During the summer of her junior year, she volunteered at Neighborhood House, a settlement house devoted to serving Peoria's poor. Echoing the patriotism of her grandfather, then investigating tainted well water, she wrote a prizewinning essay on the Constitution and recited the Declaration of Independence at the Fourth of July fair. But theater remained a passion. Years later she would declare, "I guess I was always a ham." In addition to joining the school speech and drama club, known as Jusendra, she did something unusual for a girl of her era: she directed a stage comedy. Already, she wanted to be in charge, though few women saw directing as an option. In Jusendra, she still vied for leading lady roles but wound up with comic or stock character parts. In *Houseparty*, a 1929 Broadway hit about a college student who kills the townie accusing him of getting her pregnant, she played Mrs. Milligan, the townie's mother, a woman with a working-class conscience who screams at the young murderer, "Other people got their rights same as you!" She enjoyed that role more than any other. She also performed in a scene of a play about Emily Dickinson, possibly *Allison's House*, Susan Glaspell's 1930 drama about the poet's sacrifices, though she later wrote she would have preferred to be at the drive-in with her peers rather than skulking around in a graveyard reading poetry and "pretending I was Emily Dickinson."[32]

At the beginning of her senior year, her drama advisor in Jusendra cast her in a production of a theatrical adaptation of *Jane Eyre*. Most biographies describe her rehearsing Mrs. Rochester in front of the bathroom mirror and her scary cackle, which inspired classmates to call her "the mad woman." But she may have read passages, such as this one, from Jane's perspective:

> Women are supposed to be very calm generally: but women feel just as men feel; they need exercise for their faculties, and a field for their efforts as much as their brothers do; they suffer from too rigid a constraint, too absolute a stagnation, precisely as men would suffer; and it is narrow-minded in their more privileged fellow-creatures to say that they ought to confine themselves to making puddings and knitting stockings, to playing on the piano and embroidering bags. It is thoughtless to condemn them, or laugh at them, if they seek to do more or learn more than custom has pronounced necessary for their sex.[33]

During the 1937 Christmas holiday, she returned to Chicago with Miriam to see *Victoria Regina*, a play by Laurence Housman. Helen Hayes played the Queen, a woman people listened to despite her looks.[34] Back in Peoria, again invigorated by a strong female character, with her friend Paul Jordan and a few other students, she founded a literary magazine, *Tide*, to expose the pretensions of their town. In one planned issue, she excoriated higher education, the mass media, and the status quo. But neither her scathing essay, "Education for the Masses," nor the rest of the issue, ever appeared. In the end, she self-censored, worrying that her harsh critique would alienate her teachers, who would expel her. That decision would haunt her.

In the spring, the high school put on *The Warrior's Husband*, a 1924 screwball comedy about the war between the sexes loosely based on *Lysistrata.* Revived on Broadway in 1932, it starred young Katharine Hepburn in her first major theatrical role as Antiope, an Amazon who, having won the war, returns home with male prisoners. The play's appeal lies in the bawdy humor of the macho Greeks fighting the Amazons as romances blossom. The last line jokes about the role reversal: "women are still fighting and believe man's place is in the home." The local newspaper gave Betty a "special mention" in a character role, Pomposia, an arms dealer who makes fun of sex roles and the very institution that she would later famously write about in *The Feminine Mystique.* "These Greeks have a system they call marriage, whereby you make a contract to live for life with the father of your children" was one of her lines.[35]

Acting gave her a sense of how she could move audiences as well as craft an identity. While she never pursued show business as a career, assuming that actresses had to be beautiful, for the rest of her life, she would draw on theatrical techniques to transcend limitations—her mother's and her own. In high school, she used her dramatic flair to fight against injustice and her own insecurity. In the autobiography she wrote then, she characterized herself as ugly. "I have not been well endowed physically, neither with health nor with beauty." She declared her interest in psychology, which she traces to one rare memory before age three, when she looks in the mirror and says "how tall I am." (As an adult, she measured at most five foot three.) Yet she believed she was too clumsy to pursue medicine. She experienced sharp conflict about who she saw herself as, who she could be. She wanted to marry and have children, but she rejected conventional female roles and hungrily sought fame.[36]

Her childhood temper had not abated. A classmate wrote in her high school yearbook that she was "capable of burning jealousy and strong dislikes." Perhaps she inherited it from Harry Sr. Or perhaps the historian Joyce Antler is on to the cause of the rage when she writes that Betty "could not avoid internalizing some of Peoria's anti-Semitism." As an adult, Friedan turned that insult around, calling those who criticized her fits anti-Semitic. In the 1980s, she characterized her readiness to anger as a rejection of her mother's assimilated *politesse*. "She was so unctuous on the telephone—'my dear sweet darling'— . . . the next thing she would say is 'that bitch.' As a result, I virtually say 'you bitch' on the phone."[37]

Her adolescent loneliness generated the rage she needed to write and lead, although, like most outsiders, she desperately wanted to be inside. In a 1973 oral history, reflecting on her teenhood, she describes feeling "a little bit freakish," by which she meant feeling bad for defying conventional expectations about femininity and succeeding in a man's world. Freak is both a slippery word anti-Semites have exploited to label Jews and a word Jews have appropriated to explain their "secret selves," to borrow the writer Leslie Fiedler's expression. Friedan would use it to name how she felt growing up in Peoria and then later, in Rockland County, New York, where she wrote *The Feminine Mystique*. Throughout her life, she often acted in ways that others perceived as going too far. This would lead many who knew her later to describe her as if she were mad, meaning as far outside the norms of our culture as one can be—the ultimate outsider. Yet there was nothing mad about Betty's rage at the injustice of society toward women.[38]

# 2

## "*Split at the Root*"

Betty got into many good colleges—Smith, Vassar, Wellesley, Stanford, the University of Chicago, and Radcliffe. Yet she ended up at Smith, the school her grandfather had prevented her mother from attending. The education Miriam dreamed of would carry Betty to places she never imagined, even back to her origins. Four years at an elite women's college, plus one year of coed graduate school at Berkeley, formed Betty's intellectual preoccupations, central among them the idea of being "split at the root," to use Adrienne Rich's phrase describing the exclusion of Jewish women of this era.

In the fall of 1938, Smith was both an extraordinary college devoted to single-sex education and a holding pen for daughters of privilege while they husband-hunted. It promoted an antecedent of what would come to be called feminism, yet it reinforced strict class distinctions. The school shaped Betty's goals and gave her the scaffolding for her famous book. She roomed in Chapin House, a three-floor brick mansion built in 1903 with a gabled roof, white columns reaching up to the second floor, and a wide front porch. The residence could accommodate seventy female students, a close-knit group who ate supper on white tablecloths, attended chapel, refrained from drinking, smoked only in one room, met evening curfew, and wore white gloves. Even as a freshman, Betty had a distinctive look. Some of her classmates would later describe the short chunky young woman prone to racing madly around campus as disheveled. But her yearbook photo shows a young woman with thick, shoulder-length hair brushed back into a neat bob and a determined gaze.

In an undergraduate student body of 2,000, Betty stood out as Jewish. While Smith overall boasted a better record of admitting Jews than the Ivies, the proportion of Jews the year Betty arrived was around 11 percent. Like many other elite schools during the thirties, Smith was concerned about admitting too many Jewish students. At the same time, President William Alan Neilson, who would retire at the end of Betty's freshman year, defended Jewish students and opened the doors of the college to refugees from Germany. Still, Betty was doubly on the outside. She was not just Jewish, she was from the Midwest at a college where many young women had attended East Coast finishing schools. In later years, recalling that time, she often presented herself as oblivious to cues about Jewishness. In her 2000 memoir, she describes how, newly arrived on campus, she blithely asks her roommate, Natalie Tarlow from Brookline, Massachusetts, whether she was Jewish. The savvy Tarlow replies, "who else do you think they would give you for a roommate?" Some of Betty's accounts of trying her professors' patience also suggest genteel—or less genteel—anti-Semitism. Her medieval literature professor shouted at her, "you are too arrogant, you lack humility!" Mary Ellen Chase, a professor of English, novelist, and campus figure, wrote, in a letter of reference for Betty: "she's Jewish and a bit aggressive but always for decent things."[1]

Although she had been drawn to psychology, her love of books pulled her toward English. One early paper praised the romantic war poems of Rupert Brooke. She recognized Peoria in *Middletown, USA.* She read the economist Thorsten Veblen and *For Whom the Bell Tolls*, published that year, as well as Steinbeck, Shakespeare, and Eugene O'Neill. She wrote several plays, one titled *Before O'Neill.* Another, *Mothers of Men*, borrowed the title of a 1917 silent film starring Dorothy Davenport as a politician forced to choose between roles as mother and judge.[2]

She soon made friends and enjoyed life in Northampton. At Chapin House, she listened to her housemates play the piano in the first-floor lounge or played bridge or "took" the *New York Times.* She ventured off campus, drinking at Wiggins Tavern on Main Street and traveling to Springfield to see *Gone with the Wind*, written by Chapin House alum Margaret Mitchell. In her 1942 short story, "Saturday Night," she describes the narrator getting an erotic frisson from watching Clark Gable woo Vivien Leigh. In her memoir she describes a favorite beau, a Harvard man, James Lynch, heir to the Heinz fortune, who "had visions from Thomas Wolfe of a passionate Jewish mistress" (Wolfe's lover, the costume designer Aline Bernstein). But Betty failed to live up to this role, getting drunk on scotch but remaining a virgin. "Those were not the days that a nice Jewish girl did it," she would say in 1992.[3]

Before she learned the phrase, she encountered self-hating Jews. Not long after her freshman year started, Germany occupied the Sudetenland. Then Kristallnacht generated a shocking wave of anti-Semitic violence, vandalism, and arrests in Germany and its territories. President Neilson presented the students and faculty with a petition to increase the number of Czech Jews to whom the college could offer asylum. At Chapin House, among the students who opposed admitting the imperiled Jews were four Jewish juniors from prominent families in Cincinnati, Davenport, and Scarsdale—popular, well-dressed girls in Braemar sweaters. "They were the type that spoke in whispery voices and were utterly anemic because they did not want to be known as Jews," Betty recalled. Though she was a freshman, she declared herself in favor of the quota extension, but no one listened. The petition lay on the hall table. Every day, when Betty came back from classes, she looked at it until she and some WASP students finally signed. The Jewish girls from Cincinnati never did. Yet if she mustered the courage to speak out when the world's fate was at stake, she said nothing that year when a clique of her classmates bullied a Jewish classmate.[4]

As in high school, Betty was a brilliant student, although some of her professors found her work too fanciful. Smith split the Arthur Ellis Hamm Prize for excellent academic performance—the interest on the $5,000 (about $105,000 today)—between her and another student. She made the freshman honor list. The accolades liberated her. She wrote about the unpublished edition of *Tide*, her high school literary journal, connecting her self-censorship with that of Emily Dickinson and Virginia Woolf. She joined the school paper, *Smith College Associated News* (*SCAN*), as a reporter, as did many women who worked in journalism after the war, including Joan Cook and the sisters of William F. Buckley, Aloise (class of '41) and Priscilla (class of '43).[5]

When Betty returned to campus for her sophomore year, she continued to win both academic and journalistic success. Smith elected her to the Sophomore Push Committee, a college tradition in which, during commencement weekend, underclassmen pin the sashes of the graduating seniors' white dresses, and enact jokey, symbolic gestures, notably "pushing" them off the library steps. Smith also named Betty a Sophia Smith Scholar—an award conferred on students whose record exceeded the school's already high standards—and she became assistant editor at *SCAN*. But a last fling with the theater drove her further toward psychology and her future.

On November 2, not long after the death of Sigmund Freud, Betty performed in *The Theatre of the Soul*, an expressionist satire lampooning the thinker whose ideas she would famously critique. Written by the Russian playwright Nicholai Evreinov in 1911, *The Theatre of the Soul* starts with a comic prologue spoken by a character known as the Professor, who anticipates the new way of looking at identity as comprised of the Id, the Ego, and the Superego. "The *recherches* of Wundt, Freud . . . and others have proved . . . that the soul is composed of several selfs," he says.[6]

Costumed in a red gym suit, Betty played "the Passional Self." After the Professor's monologue, the curtain opens on a set depicting a rendering of an Everyman's heart and lungs. The action is set "within the space of thirty seconds" inside Everyman's body, as his three parts—the Rational Self, the Passional Self, and the Subconscious—present their versions of reality. The dilemma Everyman faces is: should he run away with a nightclub singer or stay with his wife? "The Passional Self" (Betty) persuades him to elope with the chanteuse, who is either beautiful or a drunk, depending on who is describing her. When Everyman discovers that she does not love him, he shoots himself. Or does he?[7]

Although she would continue to be interested in the theater, *The Theatre of the Soul* was the last play she would act in at Smith. Psychology remained a practical option for a career given the anti-Semitism in higher education during the Depression. Medical schools used quotas, but Jews could enter the "Jewish science" more easily than other areas of medicine. Also, psychology fit into her desire to understand her identity beyond what her parents taught her. At the same time, almost all of her courses advanced the "passionate journey," as she would later call it, of discovering her uniqueness. In a course on existentialism with Otto Kraushaar, she read Aristotle, Spinoza, William James, Kierkegaard, and Nietzsche, which *The Feminine Mys-*

*tique* later drew upon. She took "Survey in Experimental Psychology" taught by Marxist psychologist James J. Gibson. She learned about—and took—the Rorschach test, considered at the time to diagnose schizophrenia and identify personality types. She worried about what the ink blots would reveal, but her test came back showing that she was normal.

She continued to feel shame about her Peoria roots. She mispronounced words she had only read, never heard spoken aloud. She began to keep a list of them—"*Oh! there's another Peoria word*," she told herself. She published several wry, self-mocking poems in *Opinion*, the literary supplement of *SCAN*, where that spring, she was promoted to news editor. An unpublished poem ended with the question: "Is there something here I can make over?"[8]

In *The Feminine Mystique*, Betty would accuse her alma mater of being devoid of women who balanced careers with the happy home lives that marriage might provide. This harsh judgment is not completely incorrect. In college, she was surrounded by smart women, some of whom had, for the time, unconventional families. The psychologist Eleanor J. Gibson was one exception—she had married James J. Gibson, whose work on anti-Semitism, political action, and propaganda stirred Betty. The psychiatry professor Elsa Siipola—married to another psychiatry professor, Harold E. Israel, who would become her thesis advisor—might be counted as a role model but the couple did not have children. The radical economist Dorothy Wolff Douglas, who introduced Betty to what would become one of her key ideas in *The Feminine Mystique*—that the Nazis enforced both traditional sex roles and traditional families—was a lesbian. As was the writer and English professor Mary Ellen Chase. The companion of Eleanor Duckett, a medieval scholar, Chase sparred with Betty over politics in the pages of *SCAN*.

While observing her professors, Betty read Freud and Karen

Horney—who questioned the founder of psychoanalysis's ideas about women—and started a moral and philosophical journey that would guide her for decades. In some of her papers, she uses Freud to condemn literary figures. One about Emma Bovary demolishes the French heroine with Freud's ideas about narcissism. But her exposure to Freud may have been less thorough than she later claimed. Although in 1973 she told an interviewer that she learned about "penis envy" at Smith—a concept she would attack in *The Feminine Mystique*—her biographer, Daniel Horowitz, found "little support" for such a claim.[9]

However, in 1992, Betty recalled encountering those two words at the State University of Iowa, where she spent the summer of her sophomore year studying with Kurt Lewin, a leader in the field of Gestalt psychology. Raised as an Orthodox Jew in Germany, in 1933, Lewin emigrated to America, where he worked with the eminent anthropologists Gregory Bateson and Margaret Mead and the early behaviorist Edward C. Tolman and then wound up at the State University of Iowa's Child Welfare Research Station, a pioneering think tank devoted to studying group dynamics, especially in children. Lewin led one of the earliest studies showing that a role model can transform the behavior of his followers. The Iowa course also discussed the social consequences of ostracizing Jews. In 1976, Betty wrote that with Lewin, "I began to understand the dynamics of the anti-Semitic Jew."[10]

Though Lewin had Americanized his name, the fervent Zionist worried about saving the Jews of Germany as well as how those in exile would hold together as a people after the war. He believed that the Diaspora Jews could best fight prejudice through understanding their past. Notably, he would influence Abraham Maslow, a young Jewish psychologist then conceiving his theory of self-actualization, an upbeat anti-Freudian vision of the human psyche. Maslow's core, a "hierarchy of needs," rested on the idea that people struggle to fulfill their intangible desires after the tangible ones have been met. Betty would attack *his* ideas in *The Feminine Mystique.*

It was in Iowa, while at dinner with a graduate student from New York, that Betty heard the phrase "penis envy" for the first time. She fled to the bathroom and locked herself in, ashamed, or so she implies, to hear such an explosive phrase leveled casually, possibly at her. In a more unpleasant encounter that summer, she was "almost being raped by a professor." A German professor "took a shine to me I guess," she recalled. On the way back home after a dinner date, he stopped the car and "tried to . . . make love to me." He did not succeed, but she could not remember if she walked home or if he drove her. Another time, that professor invited her to his house and "started to advance further" and she fled again.[11]

Ordinary encounters with men went awry. After she joined Harry and Miriam in Charlevoix, a bucolic Michigan town five hundred miles north of Peoria where Midwestern Jewish families banned from resorts near Chicago headed during the war years, Betty met a suitable beau—a graduate student at Harvard. But when he drove down to Smith to see her in the fall, he gave her the creeps and she hid under a desk at the library. In another tale of college-summer-love-gone-wrong, this time set in Peoria, a crush on a young Canadian doctor named Harry imploded. Betty froze after she invited him over to her house and saw her mother "exerting all that charm I could never emulate" on him.[12]

Worse things than romantic disappointment loomed on the horizon. In the fall of 1940, Amy, the pretty sister, started at Smith over Miriam's objections. Amy's insistence on attending Smith strained the family finances as well as Betty's relationship with her father. In Betty's 2000 memoir, she writes that Harry Sr. protested that he couldn't afford tuition for two daughters. The Depression had barely ended. Betty would have to return home and attend Bradley, as Miriam had done years earlier. In Betty's telling, she turned on Harry Sr., voicing an accusation her mother would make to a reporter in 1971—he exploited her by showing news articles about her to his colleagues. Then she challenged his plan to leave the family assets to his children rather than his wife, which would humiliate Miriam. She was more her mother's daughter than she wanted to be.[13]

In the end, Betty tutored to make ends meet and Amy started at Smith. On campus, Phi Beta Kappa and Sigma Xi elected Betty, the latter for excellence in science. But the star student ignored her little sister, instead, plunging into politics and journalism, deepening her relationship with *SCAN*. Priscilla Buckley, later her roommate in Greenwich Village, would become a regular contributor, as would Priscilla's sister, Aloise, who would later try to oust Communists from Smith.

Loud, late-night discussions erupted out of Betty's dorm room. Some of these centered on the war in Europe. More avidly than many students, Betty followed the position of the Communist Party—that the U.S. should stay out rather than fight to ensure peace on a far-away continent or prevent anti-Semitism. She worried most of all about fascism coming to America.

A reading list of utopian and Marxist writers sharpened her ideology. In Economics 319, Dorothy Wolff Douglas's class about revolutionary movements, she devoured John Reed, Marx, Engels, and Adam Smith and learned about women in the Nazi regime. Gestalt psychology, an approach to understanding the self that eschewed Freud and behaviorism, centered on perception, relationships, and big philosophical questions. She first encountered Gestalt in the classroom of Kurt Koffka, another German refugee and its founder. Koffka, a Jewish émigré whose mother called herself Protestant, fled Germany in 1924. He taught Psychology 36, which promised to connect to "philosophy and discusses its relationship to such activities as literature, art, and music." Psych 36 honed Betty's ability to ask questions she would later consider central to her identity, although it's not clear that Koffka, whose mother and brother were still in Europe, revealed personal details about his losses in class.[14]

Another inspiration was Eleanor Roosevelt, who came to campus to speak. Roosevelt favored intervention in the war. Betty, still opposed to it, ran the press conference. The published piece in *SCAN* (likely by Betty, though unsigned) noted that the president's wife failed to say whether she supported student pacifists. Days later, Betty, along with thousands of young Jewish radicals of her era, attended the Washington, D.C., gathering of the American Youth Congress, an organization with a large Communist membership, to protest Lend-Lease—legislation aiming to provide aid to Britain for the war effort without selling them arms. In Betty's telling, she went as a *SCAN* reporter but became so outraged by Roosevelt's efforts to end American neutrality that she joined the protest, which she later described as pacifist.

Although Betty later identified the Lend-Lease protest as a turning point in her activism, she had been writing militant pieces for some time. The previous year, she had published a fiery review praising John Steinbeck's *Grapes of Wrath* in Smith's radical literary magazine, *Focus.* She had also been instrumental in the relaunch of the *Smith College Monthly*, where, as managing editor, she politicized the magazine. But writing news articles for *SCAN* changed her. Not long after she returned from the Lend-Lease protest, Betty tried out for editor-in-chief, though some peers judged her too outspoken for the role. Perhaps, as at other elite schools that blocked Jews from editing their literary magazines in the 1930s, this gripe was code. The pressure she felt while trying to gain the editorship generated the first of what would be a lifetime of bad asthma attacks. One biographer, Milton Meltzer, reports that, on a skiing jaunt with friends, Betty, as she put it, "burst my lung." She was rushed to the infirmary. Miriam told her over the phone that the congregation at her hometown synagogue prayed for her, then traveled to Smith to look after her daughter. Yet even before Betty recovered, she wanted her mother to leave.[15]

In the campaign for editor-in-chief of *SCAN*, Betty prevailed. On March 14, 1941, her first editorial, "We Value Freedom of Speech and Thought," signaled the commitment to liberal causes that she would champion for the rest of her life. Yet in April, well after Americans knew Hitler was murdering the Jews and long after many other radical students had adopted an interventionist perspective, Betty still supported the United States staying out of the war. It may be that, even though she had signed the petition for accepting Czech Jews on campus as a freshman, considering Jews as victims was too painful.[16]

Encouraged by her economics professor, Dorothy W. Douglas, and supported by the Smith College Service Fund, Betty spent eight weeks at the 1941 Highlander Folk School in Monteagle, Tennessee, a small town in the Cumberland Mountains. Founded during the Depression by Myles Horton, an activist Southern educator who had studied with Reinhold Niebuhr at Union Theological Seminary and James Dombrowski, a minister, Highlander attracted college students, unionists, and wealthy fellow travelers as well as Eleanor Roosevelt, who funded a scholarship there. Highlander sponsored many programs, including one on labor drama, which produced plays about issues of concern to ordinary people, and one on unions. In 1955, Rosa Parks would attend, and years later, "We Shall Overcome" would be published due to Highlander's efforts.

In June—after either the Goldsteins refused to pay for Highlander, or Betty did not ask them—she inquired about a scholarship. "Railroad fare will be about all I can swing myself," she wrote, adding that she wanted to learn more about unions. "Until I was a sophomore in college, labor as a word hardly existed in my vocabulary." She was going to the right place. That summer, numerous union groups attended weekend workshops. (Not long after she returned to Smith, the FBI would investigate Highlander.) But giving Betty a close-up view of Communism was not Highlander's only influence. Throughout her life, she would return to the idea of an "intentional" community where like-minded individuals congregated to discuss how to reform society for the greater good. Leon Wilson, the writer and union organizer running the writing workshop at the end of July, envisioned it as a forum to teach leftist journalism, playwriting, and fiction. Under the tutelage of Lealon Jones, a Missouri playwright, Mary Lapsley, an anti-fascist novelist and educator, and Charles Wright Ferguson from *Reader's Digest*, Betty read H. L. Mencken and the *American Mercury*, ground zero for American muckraking. She wrote articles and essays aimed for that magazine, the *Nation*, and the *American*, whose contributors included Upton Sinclair. She listened to a guest speaker from the Federal Writers' Project and an expert in folktales. Hearing typewriters clatter across campus thrilled her, as did her twelve fellow participants who shared leftist politics and a passion for writing. She wrote an article about Highlander that was published by *Federated Press*, where she would later work. She also wrote a story, "Learning the Score," examining the corrosive role money played in her childhood.[17] "My father came out of the Depression about as well as the next man. There were a lot of debts. They would prey on his mind because they never seemed to get paid. 'One good season and we'll be on easy street,' he would say. But then someone would have to have an expensive operation or my father would be sick and have to go south for the winter."[18]

"The Scapegoat," another story Betty wrote during that summer, is about the Jewish student—she called her Shirley—Smithies bullied out of school her freshman year. Betty has the narrator begin in denial. Unwilling to see the ugliness of anti-Semitism, she insists that Shirley's expulsion from Smith is not "about race prejudice." But she is too smart to believe that, and she worries that "the others might think I was on Shirley's side because I was Jewish too." Betty felt strongly enough about "Learning the Score" and "The Scapegoat" to approach the distinguished New York literary agency Curtis Brown, in the hope that they would represent her. But in the fall, after they had declined to do so, she complained that Curtis Brown "did not appreciate" her writing and she published "The Scapegoat" in the *Smith College Monthly*.[19]

She wanted to stay at Highlander through the start of the fall semester. But after Smith forbade it, she returned to campus, where at *SCAN*, she preached the Highlander message. The folks at Highlander tried to persuade her to return for Thanksgiving. But she was busy trying to reconcile her activism, the study of psychology, and her life at college with her family. In a paper for a class on the nineteenth-century novel, she observed that psychology could not explain literature. In English class, she wrote "And Grey with Her Pearls," a short story *à clef* in which a "Miriam" character alienates and enfeebles her husband with her conspicuous consumption. She also wrote a story about a college girl who disregarded her ailing father.

In Social Psychology, taught by James J. Gibson, she explored the phenomenon of good and bad propaganda, human appetites, and what drove people to act as they did. She sought to square the thinking of Marx and Freud, to figure out the relationship between internal and external oppression, to settle the differences between the bourgeois and working classes. Betty read more Freud, including *Civilization and Its Discontents.* She read Freudians, including Franz Alexander, who believed that much disease, especially asthma, emerged from dependence on the mother, and child analyst Anna Freud, a devotee of the art—as opposed to the science—of analysis. She read Erik Erikson, with whom she would later study. Yet she backed away from these ideas when writing her honors thesis, instead tackling a critique of Operationism, an empirical take on psychiatry, with Harold E. Israel, a professor drawn to students "who refused to accept authority blindly." Israel believed that her thesis, which critiqued B. F. Skinner and his rigid philosophy of human nature, held much promise. Shortly before her father died, she would present it at a scholarly conference.[20]

In the fall of her senior year, as editor-in-chief of *SCAN*, she used lessons from Highlander that anticipated her lifelong commitment to activism. After attending a meeting of male Ivy League newspaper editors including Kingman Brewster, at Princeton, she complained that faculty treated *them* like leaders, whereas Smith encouraged its students to volunteer or have families. She at last moved from isolationism to an anti-fascist position although even an October 1941 editorial focused on the destruction in Europe only to move to working people's rights in America: "As the Nazis rose to power in Germany they attacked and destroyed labor unions. . . . For fascism to survive all free and democratic institutions must be prohibited. . . . Union . . . members are . . . as American as the funny papers they read, the movies they see, the beer they drink, the streets they live on; their aims are basic to the protection and expansion of democracy in America."[21]

Other editorials celebrated Highlander, defended *SCAN* against Red-baiting, attacked her peers' class privilege, supported the efforts of domestic workers at Smith to form a union, and defended the college for censuring the students who ridiculed the workers in the satirical magazine *Tatler*. Did Smith deserve its reputation as a "school for the daughters of the idle rich?" she asked. While acknowledging the importance of maintaining freedom of the press, she approved of the punishment of the *Tatler* editors. She believed in an egalitarian ideal, whether writing about gender roles or arguing that Smith graduates had a special responsibility to use their education for the public good.[22]

Yet she also believed in freedom of the press when it exposed elitist traditions, even defending her friend Priscilla Buckley, known as Pritt, for a spirited prank. That fall, Buckley, then a junior, and at least two other *SCAN* reporters, snuck into the dorm room of the president of Orangemen, one of the secret societies at Smith modeled after those at Ivy League schools. Intending to reveal Orangemen as snobs, the women stole a padlocked trunk which they lugged out of the window and into a car, which they then drove to a remote field. But the trunk proved to be a disappointment, full of papers, robes, and other non-incriminating ephemera. The reporters were eventually apprehended (one had dropped her notebook on the porch), and the administration demanded they be thrown off the paper and even expelled. Betty stuck up for her team, warned she would publish the contents of the trunk (which she hoped would embarrass the snooty socialites in Orangemen), and cried censorship. In the end, Smith expelled no one.

On the heels of that battle, Betty encountered an unexpected icon: Hallie Flanagan. In December 1941, Smith announced its intention to appoint Flanagan, director of the Federal Theatre Project then teaching at Vassar, to become dean. Widowed, with one adult son from her first marriage, Flanagan had produced *Can You Hear Their Voices?*—an adaptation of a story by Whittaker Chambers about tenant farmers. A few years after that, the Dies Committee—named after Texas Representative Martin Dies and tasked with investigating Communists—had interviewed Flanagan, who famously alluded to Elizabethan playwright Christopher Marlowe, causing Congressman Joe Starnes to ask: "Is he a Communist?"

In other words, although Betty had stopped acting in the theater, she saw Flanagan as a different kind of actor, one who used the theater to change politics. "The editor of *SCAN* went to interview the new dean and the dean interviewed the editor of *SCAN*," wrote Betty. Flanagan told Betty: "there never was a time when it was more important to consider education: how it can relate to life and how it can relate to the immediate problem of the war." Flanagan's enduring influence in Betty's life is revealed in not just her theatrical approach to activism but her commitment to continual learning.[23]

Pearl Harbor sobered her. Ultimately, Betty regretted that she had not done more to fight injustice of all kinds. Her last editorial bemoaned her failure to change Smith. "We have accomplished little this year."[24]

She graduated summa cum laude and Smith awarded her an Alumnae Association Fellowship. By the time she graduated, Berkeley had accepted her into the Ph.D. program in psychology. It would grant her the James M. Goewey Fellowship for students in the social sciences. An apocryphal story has an unnamed college administrator telling Miriam that her daughter had "the most outstanding record of any student ever matriculated at Smith." Yet Harry did not travel east for his oldest daughter's commencement. He had heart trouble and maintained he was too sick, although two biographers suggest he stayed in Peoria because he worried Betty would be ashamed of his accent.[25]

Before she went off to grad school, Betty interned at the Grasslands Hospital Psychiatric Institute in Valhalla, New York, then a stomping ground for analysts interested in widening the applications of psychoanalytic theory. Her duties included administering the Rorschach test, which she had used to prove her own sanity only two years earlier. But in her spare time, she pursued radical politics. On a day off, she dressed in a sweater set and pearls, trekked into Manhattan, and went to the Communist Party at their headquarters south of Union Square, intending to join. "They didn't take me seriously," she said. The CPUSA archives contain no record of her signing up. Years later, she claimed that she aimed this move, like Highlander, to jibe at her father, whom she told of her new allegiance and who responded: "Is that what I sent my daughter to Smith for?"[26]

She also seemed eager to provoke her family—and her hometown—about Jewishness. Influenced by Kurt Lewin's ideas about scapegoats, she presented "On Affirming One's Jewishness" at Anshai Emeth, a gig that her mother, a former president of its women's club, had wrangled for her. She lectured that Jews should not turn anti-Semitism against themselves and implied that Jewish self-hatred could have devastating consequences. "I think it was strong meat for them," she told an interviewer years later.[27]

Meanwhile, Amy, who had volunteered to do farm labor in New England for a Smith College summer service program, suffered a brutal encounter. While doing good in the community, she was raped. As she put it in the yearbook of the Smith class of '44's fiftieth reunion, it was "a terrifying experience that could easily have resulted in my being murdered." Shortly after that, she met Eugene H. Adams, a twenty-eight-year-old ex-boxer finishing his B.A. at Tufts University. She fell in love. According to Harry Jr., their father threatened to disown her because Adams was not Jewish. Amy dropped out of Smith, transferred to Jackson College, the women's college at Tufts, and moved in with Adams. She received her B.A. in 1945, the same year that Adams received an M.A. in sacred theology, and the couple married.[28]

It's possible Betty did not know about her sister's trauma. In her 2000 memoir, she describes her own brush with rape in language that could be considered cavalier. She "had to fight off rape" twice, she writes, adding that she was "able to talk them out of it," making herself sound strong and clever.[29]

In the fall of 1942, when Betty arrived at Berkeley, the war had emptied men from the campus. She found the school less rigorous than Smith, but it nonetheless contributed to her growth as a thinker and activist. She took seminars with some of the great minds in psychology, including Erik Erikson, then working on his ideas about how inner and outer forces helped develop children's minds as well as his conceit of the eight stages of life, which would become central to Betty's thinking. In his class, Betty read Melanie Klein and Otto Fenichel, who tried to reconcile Freud's ideas with Marxian ideology. She read Karl Abraham's essay about the female "castration complex." She additionally studied with the behavioralist Edward C. Tolman, and R. Nevitt Sanford, a co-author of the iconic work on anti-Semitism, *The Authoritarian Personality*, and took part in a working group led by Ralph Gundlach, a radical professor, on anti-Semitism and racism. Nonetheless, according to her, graduate school—a respectable choice for a brainy young Jewish woman during the war years—stifled her. In a faculty conference about her Ph.D. thesis proposal, she announced her intention to test Freudian theories against data gathered at the Child Welfare Center in Iowa. She saw herself as a pioneer. Years later, she recalled "tossing off so blithely" the words *oral*, *anal*, and *genital*, "embarrass[ing]" both Erikson and Tolman.[30]

Anti-Semitism flourished in this suffocating atmosphere. Erikson, who would introduce America to the concept of the identity crisis, had changed his name to the Scandinavian "Erikson" when he emigrated to the United States in 1933, though his mother and stepfather were Jewish. (His real father was likely not Jewish, but this was not widely known until 1975.) Tolman, a politically engaged psychologist, advised a Jewish contemporary of Betty's with professorial ambitions to change his name. But if anti-Semitism festered behind closed doors, sexism roiled in plain sight. Even more than at Smith, her female professors had forgone domestic happiness with men and were slighted in their professional lives. Olga Bridgeman, the first female faculty member in psychology at Berkeley, was single. Although she pioneered ideas in clinical and abnormal psychology, her colleagues dismissed her as a researcher. Recently divorced, Jean Macfarlane, the second female faculty member in psychology at Berkeley, lived with her mother. Else Frenkel-Brunswik, a co-author with R. Nevitt Sanford and Theodor Adorno of *The Authoritarian Personality*, was married, but languished in obscurity compared to her male colleagues. In *The Feminine Mystique*, Betty describes her perception—and that of society—of these women: "the few college presidents and professors who were women either fell into line or had their authority—as teachers and as women—questioned. If they were spinsters, if they had no babies, they were forbidden by the mystique to speak as women . . . the woman scholar was suspect, simply by virtue of being one."[31]

Off campus, Betty, who had no intention of joining this sorority, continued her leftist activities. She lived in the same building as members of the Communist Party, and she joined a radical study group. The major primary source for this period, her FBI file, reveals a young woman flirting with Communism. However, the file, written in 1944, a year after she left Berkeley, includes redacted information and half-facts and assumptions that hardly deserve the term "classified." It digs up her high school essay "Education for the Masses" and takes swipes at her character. The file's biggest revelation, if you can call it that, is that after Betty decided she would leave Berkeley, she appeared at the gritty East Bay offices of the Communist Party, said she was a member of the Young Communist League, and volunteered to write for their paper, *The People's World.* But Steve Nelson, the chairman of the San Francisco Communist Party, turned her away, telling her that the party had too many intellectuals and that she would have more influence if she stayed in her own field. She disliked the prose style of *The People's World* anyway, she replied.[32]

She struggled to figure out who she was against shifting cultural norms about what women could be. She read Philip

Wylie's 1942 best-selling screed, *Generation of Vipers*, which introduced her to "Momism," the idea that women getting the vote and overprotective matriarchs led to the nation's disintegration and moral failure. "I give you the destroying mother," Wylie wrote. Initially, his argument appealed to Betty, who did everything she could to shed the influence of her mother. She kiddingly described herself as "fresh and naïve" and as "the lady from Smith" while hanging out with a group of radical Jewish physicists—David Bohm, Giovanni Rossi Lomanitz, Joe Weinberg, Max Friedman, and Bob Loevinger, the brother of Betty's friend Jane—all students of Robert Oppenheimer, the so-called "father of the atomic bomb." She dated at least three of them. Loevinger squired her to restaurants in Chinatown and to a protest against Earl Warren after Harry Bridges, the union organizer threatened with deportation for his labor activism, led a longshoremen's strike. According to the historian Shawn Mullet, Lomanitz recalled dating Betty "at least once" and discussing sexism with her. Betty and David Bohm became lovers, although the egalitarian romance that she longed for eluded her. He was "more inhibited than I was," she said about the beau the FBI was tracking due to his involvement with the Manhattan Project. But some pieces of her personal life remain a mystery. Fifty years later, she told an interviewer that she "still had great guilt about the sex," and that when she lost her virginity in Berkeley, the man was "nobody that I was very involved with."[33]

On her way to Peoria during the December holiday, she stopped in Chicago to see her high school friend Paul Jordan, then a medical student at the University of Chicago. Betty went home with Jordan, although they did not have sex. When he stopped fooling around with her and went to wash his hands, she froze, which she blamed on her "Peoria personality"—a frigid, conformist alter ego she would blame for a good part of her life. At her parents' home, she recounted to her father what had happened with Jordan. His face turned "angry, cold, mean," she told one biographer. In her 2000 memoir, she writes that he called her "a slut." Miriam recalled the moment differently: her eldest daughter, reeling from a failed relationship, "acted like it was the end of the world" and wanted to start analysis, but Harry Sr. "put his foot down."[34]

Betty returned to Berkeley. On January 11, 1943, someone pulled her "out of psych class" to inform her that her father had died. She again headed home. She was dry-eyed at the service, which she explains by writing that she had vowed, years earlier, never to cry in front of Harry Sr. Yet about the man who not long before had defamed her, she said, "without him there was no warmth."[35]

Back at Berkeley, she left the dorm. She thought about becoming an M.D. like her maternal grandfather, Sandor Horwitz. She took at least one lover. Her asthma erupted. One biographer dates her first experience with analysis to this moment, where she may have articulated that she hated her mother, then blossoming from a tormented housewife into the savvy owner of Goldstein Jewelry Company. When Berkeley awarded Betty the prestigious Abraham Rosenberg Fellowship, as she would write in *The Feminine Mystique*, she had to choose between her career and a man (in 1993, she would identify the unnamed suitor as Bob Loevinger) afraid of a woman smarter than him.[36] "No question was important to me that year but love. We walked in the Berkeley hills and a boy said: 'nothing can come of this, between us. I'll never win a fellowship like yours.' Did I think I would be choosing, irrevocably, the cold loneliness of that afternoon if I went on? I gave up the fellowship, in relief."[37]

A work of theater she saw in the late spring helped propel her out of the academy into an uncertain future. *Lady in the Dark*, an operetta by Moss Hart about Liza Elliot, a magazine editor who has to choose between career and romance, opened at the end of April in San Francisco. Inspired in part by *The Interpretation of Dreams*, *Lady in the Dark* staged a battle between different parts of the self. In her analyst's office, Elliot, caught between her career and her romantic possibilities, has three fantastical dreams. In the first, she hallucinates about her glamorous career and wakes up screaming; in the second, a wedding ring turns into a dagger; in the third she is at the circus where the ringmaster bombards her with her own neuroses. When she wakes up, she remembers her father rejecting her as a child and is liberated from her fight with herself. "The magazine editor career woman repents of her ways as a result of Freudian analysis, and she leaves her job and marries the advertising deputy," Betty wrote. In fact, Elliot returns to the office and embarks on a business and romantic partnership with the roguish advertising manager whom she had previously rejected. But Betty understood *Lady in the Dark* as an unnuanced choice between marriage and career.[38]

She returned to Peoria. There is little record of what she did there, save intern on the *Peoria Evening Star* and recuperate from another severe asthma attack. By the end of the summer, she had moved to New York, set on using labor journalism to transform herself and the world.

# 3

## *"My Roots Are in My Moving"*

In 1972, Betty wrote, "my roots are in my moving," to explain how her politics shifted from ensuring women's equal political representation to crusading against sexual politics. Moving contains a psychological dimension, cemented in her childhood and the theories she had studied in school. And it holds Betty's understanding of political fluidity: Ideas had to adapt to new challenges or risk becoming dogma. In an interview with Eleanor Roosevelt for *Federated Press,* where Betty would work for six years, the president's wife told her that to be effective, "you have to be on the move all the time," introducing the future leader to an idea that would become central. Yet Betty also gravitated to the idea of moving because if she stopped, she would have to think too deeply about limitations—hers, others'. Perhaps in some way, her restlessness helped prepare her to write her great book. Between the time she arrived in New York City and 1957, when she began *The Feminine Mys-*

*tique*, she had relocated eight times or once every other year. She lived her "passionate journey" long before she named it.[1]

In the fall of 1943, Betty, twenty-two, moved into a rental in Greenwich Village, at 17 Grove Street. She shared it with three Smith grads: Harriet Vance (from Peoria), Maggie Comstock, and Priscilla Buckley, her *Smith College Associated News* colleague, who would later work for United Press. In 1974, Betty characterized those years as inspired by Mary McCarthy's best-selling novel, *The Group*, describing shopping for black cashmere at Bendel's and dating married men. Yet she soon immersed herself in the world of radical journalism.[2]

With the help of friends from the Highlander Folk School, she applied to be a reporter at *Federated Press*, a news agency started by trade unions in 1919. Scholars describe *FP* as either Popular Front—a broad social-democratic movement of leftists opposed to fascism—or Communist. In 1992, Friedan minimized her politics, recounting how, at the job interview, although she did not know whether the AFL or CIO was more radical, *FP* hired her. While this may stretch credulity, there was a kind of truth in her diminishing of leftist politics as a motivation. The offices at 30 Irving Place, not far from her apartment, though they likely appealed to her politically, also offered a warm, hectic disarray—a kind of "chosen family," to use a phrase she liked later in life. The labor activist Robert Schrank recalled the Union Square office as "crowded with a dozen desks, piles of tabloid sized newspapers, and shelves sagging with papers."[3]

Seeking to forget the conformity and pain of her childhood, Betty largely cut ties with her mother and her sister. She felt that Miriam, who had already sold her childhood home and moved into the Jefferson Hotel, neither loved nor supported her. "I became very estranged from my mother," she said in the 1980s. "Very critical of her." Except for one thing. "In the pit of asthma, terrible shape," she needed her mother to pay for the analysis she undertook at the same time as she started working for *FP*.

This was not the contradiction that it sounds. Although the Party officially condemned analysis as bourgeois, some Communists believed the talking cure could advance the revolution.[4]

Betty devoted herself to her new life in New York. At *Federated Press*, she worked with many future notables from the left, including the historian Philip Foner, the radical journalists Harvey O'Connor and Mary Eaton Voorhees, and the Washington bureau reporter Virginia Gardner, who would cover the Rosenberg trial for the *Daily Worker*. Jean Roisman, the wife of civil rights lawyer Leonard Boudin, was the photo editor. But when Betty described the office in 1974, she did not mention these names. She recalled learning to write "a jazzy lead after three martinis at lunch" to keep up with the "*Front Page* types," as she called her older male co-workers.[5]

The young, single journalist went on dates at Pete's Tavern on 18th Street, where you could order gigantic steaks. She listened to jazz at Nick's, at Bedford and the Bowery, with its moose head wall fixture. She saw French movies at the Thalia. In October, when the first Newspaper Guild Canteen opened at 40 East 40th Street, she hung out there with her colleagues, enjoying free liquor and sandwiches, dancing with soldiers, and even, she claims, volunteering as a hostess. The Canteen, a lively joint often emceed by the handsome Perry Como and Ed Sullivan, then best known as a radio announcer, featured a slate of entertainers including "the Queen of Swing" Mildred Bailey, the Barry Sisters (jazz chanteuses who sang the standards in Yiddish), and the corny song-and-dance man Jerry Lester.

Betty showed a practical mettle regarding the consequences of sex, accompanying pregnant friends to abortion doctors in dirty rooms and back alleys. She displayed courage in romance too, although that did not protect her from hurt. She fell in love with Aron "Mike" Krich, a poet (later a collaborator of Margaret Mead) and the brother of her friend Helen Krich, then getting her M.A. in English at NYU. According to Betty, Mike, as he was known, "looked like Humphrey Bogart" and "had a sardonic glint in his eye." She never got over him. Mike's son, John Krich, recounts that at his father's funeral in 1995 on Martha's Vineyard, Betty clutched the coffin slightly and, in front of Mike's widow, Toby, declared him "the love of her life." It was unrequited. In Mike Krich's 1983 sexually explicit *roman à clef Sweethearts*, he writes that the Betty character had "a racing intelligence" but was too eager to please. "You see? You see?" he quotes her pleading, trying to score some intellectual point after they had sex.[6]

Initially, her career at *Federated Press* (*FP*) did not go all that well either. Betty's editor, Miriam Kolkin (later, as Mim Kelber, Bella Abzug's speechwriter), had to rip the copy from her hand. "Mostly I find writing so painful I wonder what make [*sic*] me do it," she would write. Newsroom deadlines helped hide her anxiety as did teaming with colleagues to rewrite. (She also filed stories with solo bylines.) In her first months, she covered racism, sexism, labor, class inequality, and anti-Semitism. One early story criticized the government for failing to address the lack of childcare as the reason for women's absenteeism at work. "Women still have two jobs to do," she quoted Ruth Young, a leader at United Electric, as saying. In a preview of the anti–conspicuous consumption take of *The Feminine Mystique*, she panned a fashion show the mining industry sponsored. "It all made the life of a coal miner girl pretty glamorous," she wrote with sarcasm. And she raved about the designer Elizabeth Hawes, who critiqued sexism in the home in her 1943 book, *Why Women Cry: Or Wenches with Wrenches*. "Men, there's a revolution cooking in your own kitchens," Betty advised readers.[7]

Other articles targeted wealthy Americans or racism and fascism. She commended *New World A-Coming: Inside Black America*, by the Black journalist Roi Ottley: "He's supposed to be a citizen of a free country, and if he's fighting for democracy, it's about time that he got some of his democratic rights at home for a change." She praised Black parents in Hillburn, New York, for refusing to send their children to a dilapidated Jim Crow school. "On October 4, the school board will have some explaining to do." Later that fall, she returned to the subject of capitalists as the true enemy, writing that "monied interests are the real fascists."[8]

By the end of November, Betty had worked on several stories about anti-Semitism, including one lauding the AFL-CIO for encouraging the United Nations to compel Palestine to admit Jewish refugees from the Nazis. Over the next several months, she wrote about the vandalism of Jewish graves and anti-Semitic graffiti in Queens while continuing to file stories attacking racism and extolling Communism. One told of Blacks being turned away from polling booths in the South and another of labor leader William Green and the United States' attempt to brainwash Americans against Russia and shortchange workers. Reviewing *Facts and Fascism*, by the Marxist journalist George Seldes, Betty commended him for naming "the power behind the[se] small fry"—in other words, indicting the fat cats who were truly the enemies of the people. She believed Seldes's idea that only chance precluded America from "hav[ing] a Hitler yet," as she put it.[9]

In March 1944, she wrote one of the most compelling stories of her *FP* career—an exposé of wealthy Americans as the backers of native fascism and anti-laborism. With its oversized villains and conspiratorial air, "Well-Heeled 'White Collar League'" anticipated her use of the detective trope in *The Feminine Mystique*. "In an expensive office building in the heart of New York's great financial district," the story begins. In hardboiled prose, Betty describes the sinister ad that got her attention: "We do not want those who are interested in a union." She eavesdrops on the magnates scheming to disguise themselves as working men to infiltrate the union and destroy it. After "the chairman," Robert Routh, asks Betty to leave, she recalls a prospectus they sent her which, in her description, "might as well have been written by Hitler."[10]

Other stories she worked on show the roots of the critique of domesticity for which *The Feminine Mystique* became famous. One criticized businesses for only starting to hire women during wartime, when men were unavailable; another called out industries refusing to hire women despite a manpower shortage. "Wartime Living," a column anticipating her work in women's magazines in the 1950s, gave helpful hints about hemlines and recipes, information on scarcity and fat cats, and exposed gender and class inequality. "Rich Losing Monopoly on T-Bone Steak" and "You Can Save Your Old Stockings" were two 1943 column headlines. The following year, Betty used the column to disseminate information from Europe—Hitler "forced women into slave labor"—and to point out that according to *A Women's Guide to Political Action*, published by the CIO, Franklin Delano Roosevelt had done a lot for women.[11]

A story Betty filed in the spring of 1944 celebrated the Jefferson School of Social Science, or the Jeff, as disciples called it. The Communist Party–run school for adults, located in a nine-story former furniture warehouse at 575 Sixth Avenue, just north of 16th Street, had opened in 1943. The Jeff would be led by ex–CUNY faculty until 1956 when the government declared it subversive and shut it down. Communists and fellow travelers, including Dashiell Hammett, Raphael Soyer, Pete Seeger, and Marc Blitzstein taught there. Betty audited classes, as she put it years later, "with other Smith sisters," in radical economics. Although in the fifties, Eleanor Flexner, the feminist historian *avant la lettre*, would teach a course on women radicals, in the forties, the Jeff offered few courses about or for women. Betty later told her biographer Judith Hennessee that "nothing . . . even described the special exploitation of women."[12]

Betty continued analysis. Overall, postwar American culture

embraced and popularized Freud and his disciples, including Franz Alexander, who linked asthma to childhood and neurotic mothers. Alexandrian disciples saw outbreaks of asthma as cries for help. Betty, an asthma sufferer, demanded that Miriam, who had taken over Goldstein Jewelry, keep paying her therapy bills while "lying on a couch and complaining endlessly" to her analyst that she hated her for killing her father. In a 1974 *New York* magazine essay, "In France, de Beauvoir Had Just Published 'The Second Sex,'" Betty implies that she, like Liza Elliot, the heroine of the Moss Hart operetta she saw in San Francisco, spent time in therapy agonizing about being single and worrying about what she wanted to be when she grew up. Even after D-Day, she held onto the idea of going to medical school, which she had promised her father she would do before his death. But years later, she would cite "some interesting dreams" as persuading her to recommit to leftist journalism. So, instead of starting medical school, with its quotas for women and Jews, she stayed at *Federated.*[13]

In the fall of 1944, the apartment on Grove Street broke up and Betty moved to a second Greenwich Village share with two women she met at Berkeley. Statistically, she was an outlier. That year, one-third of the American workforce was female and of that 42.8 percent were single. At *FP,* many male colleagues saw her either as hypersexual or as the brainy androgyne her father had worried she would become. The labor leader Robert Schrank recalled Betty in the newsroom as a "tough but friendly Jewish mother" whose "pink panties" were "unashamedly visible" but who nonetheless gave him good advice about writing. "She told me to just close my eyes and imagine that I was in a bar, at a union meeting." Yet if Betty was aware of her co-workers' perception of her, she hardly wrote about it. In her 1974 *New York* magazine essay, she makes a rare remark about the gender dynamic of *FP.* Her male colleagues were "avuncular to my innocence, with occasional lecherous lapses," she observes, unnervingly sounding like the docile helpmeet she would criticize in *The Feminine Mystique*.[14]

Anti-Communist forces attacked *FP*, which endured pressure to rehire returning soldiers, displacing women like Betty, who had covered for them during their absence. Yet initially Betty kept her job. She wrote one "Wartime Living" column singling out Mrs. Roosevelt for praise for ending the diaper shortage. A bylined story recounted how FDR had exposed a "Nazi-like" quota system banning Jews, Catholics, and Negroes from professional schools. Two stories showed her reaction to the horrifying scenes in Germany as the Allies liberated the camps. One praised Jewish writers and scientists who heroically protested the Nazis. The second story, first reported by *Stars and Stripes* and republished on April 26 in *FP*, told how left-wing survivors of Buchenwald, liberated by the Allies earlier that month, had maintained their sanity by continuing their "secret political work" as Nazis committed "unheard of atrocities." In a "Wartime Living" column published four days later, Betty repeated a horrifying image—"a lampshade made from human flesh was found at the Buchenwald concentration camp."[15]

That same month, FDR died. Betty immediately filed one story about how workers mourned him. But shortly after that, *Federated Press* fired her, hiring James Peck, whose family had converted from Judaism to the Episcopal Church when he was a child. Peck attended Choate and Harvard for one year, then dropped out to devote himself to activism. The former *FP* journalist spent the war years in jail as a conscientious objector. According to Betty's biographer Daniel Horowitz, she quickly found another venue for her journalism—the magazine *New Masses*, associated with the Communist Party. Launched by critic and novelist Mike Gold in 1926, *New Masses* drew contributors including Bertolt Brecht, Tillie Olsen, Richard Wright, and Arthur Miller. Like Miller, who wrote for the magazine under the name Matt Wayne, Betty took a pseudonym—Lillian Stone. She wrote news pieces about labor unrest and the struggles of the working class. She was also briefly employed at Voters Research Institute, which did market research and political analysis on Congress of Industrial Organization (CIO) members. Its director, Bernard Conal, had worked for Henry Wallace, whose tolerance for Communism inspired Harry Truman to fire him.[16]

Betty left her Greenwich Village share for an apartment of her own, a daring step for a woman. She would enter the spartan basement studio in a red brick and limestone townhouse on West 86th Street near Central Park through the furnace room. The apartment lacked a kitchen and hot water but had bookcases and a garden where she could curl up and read. She wanted privacy, partly so she could have sex without roommates around. Trying to live on her own terms, she juggled Victory-mail correspondences with soldiers on the front and affairs with married men, one of whom she took a share with on Fire Island.[17]

Betty's newspaper stories were popular with readers. And so, by the end of 1945, *FP* had pushed James Peck out of the office, giving him a "roving" contract, and rehired her. At first, she continued as she had before, writing "Post War Living," a sequel to her popular ladies' wartime column. In an amusing installment from January 1946, "Mr. and Mrs. Jones" educate readers about the Price Control Act, which helped working families by keeping down the prices of necessities. Mrs. Jones tells her husband that even if workers protest, they still need help from the government: "Even when we win the strike we'll be no better off than before."[18]

But not long after this column ran, *Federated Press* hired Marc Stone, the brother of the radical journalist I. F. Stone, as eastern bureau manager. Marc seemed to favor James Peck over Betty. Her column ceased appearing. Undaunted, Betty poured her energy into features, producing a vivid one about the septuagenarian ex-strikebreaker Pearl Bergoff, recounting with gusto his nefarious exploits. "His dirty boys would spare no violence against strikers," she wrote. As she would show in *The Feminine Mystique*, she could deftly create outsized heroes and villains and had a gift for describing diverse groups of women uniting for a leftist cause. In a feature about the United Electric strike in Bloomfield, New Jersey, she writes: "More than half were women. Old women covering their hair with shawls, bobby soxers wearing slacks against the cold." Her proximity to the Manhattan Project a few years earlier led to lively articles about the politics of the bomb. The most radical one critiques General Leslie Groves's cover up of the bomb's destructive powers and the government's use of a spy scare to disseminate anti-Russian propaganda. She links General Electric's suppression of the betatron particle accelerator to stalled cancer research. "The issue is now up to the American people. . . . Will they let the atom bomb be used by the U.S. to blow up world peace or will they demand that it be used for all mankind?"[19]

In March 1946, Betty covered the founding of the Congress of American Women, the American wing of the Women's International Democratic Federation, an international, pro-Soviet, anti-fascist organization launched in Paris the previous year. Led by Elinor Gimbel, the granddaughter of the founder of Gimbel's department store by marriage, it attracted many illustrious women and focused on advancing many ideas Betty would later address, such as international rights, the status of women in the Communist Party, and the welfare of children. It also supported working-class women and sought to end racism. In April, a year after FDR's death, Betty interviewed Eleanor Roosevelt for the first time since college. The former first lady expressed dismay about the political "retreat" from her husband's goals of equality. Weeks afterward, Betty wrote her most powerful piece yet, echoing Eleanor Roosevelt's crusade against injustice against families. "Family Day on the Westinghouse Picketline," about the hundredth day of a Westinghouse strike, describes the impact of harsh capitalist policies on working families. "I don't know how children would have clothes for the winter," she quotes one mother as saying.[20]

But like other female journalists of her time, even as Betty wrote about women's rights, she endured sex discrimination in the workplace. In the months since he had arrived, Marc Stone's aversion to Betty and what he saw as her radical politics and sloppy reporting escalated. He took her off stories, shouted at her, and at one point, threw a telephone book at her. Betty fought to represent a radical perspective even after Stone attacked her betatron story. Three days after her Westinghouse strike story appeared, Betty made a formal complaint about Stone's "literalness"—her word describing what he saw as her casual attitude toward facts. He objected to her using the phrase "western Union picketline" [*sic*] as opposed to "picketline around Western Union" and to her writing that, at a memorial dinner for FDR, "100 people" stood on a dais under his picture. "It was a big poster," she wrote, digging in. "And ergo true." But at the end of May, Stone sent a freelancer to Rochester to cover the strike there even though Betty had pitched the story to him. "I would not send you to cover a dog fight," he told her, although in her complaint to the Newspaper Guild she bragged that her stories were "among the most popular that FP has sent out." Stone replied: "You had better start hunting for another job, because your days here are certainly numbered."[21]

If Betty no longer went to the office, she continued to file copy for *FP.* She wrote about Sydenham, an interracial hospital in Harlem; world hunger; and Frédéric Joliot-Curie, son-in-law of Marie Curie, discoverer of the uranium chain reaction which helped make the atom bomb possible, who brought together diverse groups of people fighting against fascism. During the war, the "handsome" genius united "Frenchmen from Communist workers to priests" and stole arms from the Nazis. Her brave hero knew that even scientists had to pick a side.[22]

In July, Betty started working at *UE News*, the organ of the United Electrical, Radio, and Machine Workers of America. She was unsure enough about the job to send her transcripts to the medical schools at University of Chicago, UCLA, and Columbia. As she put it in 1974 in *New York* magazine, *UE News*, in "the vanguard of the working-class revolution," had entered a period of increased antagonism with the corporations where members worked. But she stayed. In 1985, her *UE* colleague (and biographer) Milton Meltzer would describe her using language echoing that of *FP* male journalists: she "bubbled over with energy, talked in spurts, rarely finishing a sentence, her mind racing so fast the words couldn't keep up with it." Yet Meltzer also saw in her great empathy. Although the worker-journalists at *UE News* could see that she "was a middle-class woman," he recognized that she was nonetheless able to "feel what a worker's life was like." She would soon attempt to mold the tension between her bourgeois roots and her compassion for the rights of the proletariat into her greatest work.[23]

# 4

## *"It Was Almost as Good as Having a Baby"*

In the fall of 1946, Betty met Carl Friedan, a theater producer and World War II veteran. She allowed the relationship with him to develop rapidly. In the postwar era, the average age for a woman to marry was twenty-three. She was twenty-six. According to Carl, she was dating Jim Lerner, who was married, and Bob Loevinger, the physicist she had known in Berkeley who had subsequently moved to New York. And she was working. As for her family, her mother had reinvented herself, becoming the president of the Goldstein Jewelry Company, getting accredited as a gemologist, and traveling to Los Angeles for the store. Her younger sister, Amy, had started a family. Still, it is surprising to learn that only two months after a friend introduced them, Carl moved into Betty's tiny apartment on West 86th Street. They married ten months later. Over the next decade, her struggle balancing marriage and career would separate her from her leftist activism and plunge her into a more personal fight for women's "passionate journeys," as she would put it. Her family life impeded and sparked her groundbreaking book.[1]

Carl was attractive, with a thin face and light reddish hair. He was tall and wore Trotskyite glasses with round frames. He was less intellectually serious than other men Betty had dated—and more assimilated. He was born on September 22, 1919, outside of Boston, the middle son in a family of three boys. His parents, poor Jews who emigrated from Latvia as children, called him Casper Judah at birth but an aunt convinced them to instead use the more American Carl. At sixteen, he continued assimilating, trading Friedman for the less conspicuously Jewish "Friedan," even though both of his brothers kept their name.

Like his wife-to-be, Carl fled a volatile relationship with his mother into the theater. Teenaged Carl took the moniker Carlyn the Magician and traveled across New England doing card tricks, pulling rabbits out of hats, and performing the classic vanishing bird trick—making a cage and the fake dove in it disappear. As a student at the University of Massachusetts, Boston, he skipped classes to watch magic acts in vaudeville shows and after two years, he transferred to Emerson College, a conservatory of dramatic arts. In the summer of 1941, he managed his first comedy at a summer stock theater in Rangeley, Maine, near the Canadian border.

The following year, Carl, twenty-two, enlisted. During his training, he lived in New York. In his free time, he dabbled in the theater. He then went to Camp Shelby, Mississippi, where he prepared to fight in some of the war's goriest European battles. In the fall of 1944, with the 69th Infantry Division, he sailed for Europe. In the spring of 1945, his company liberated Leipzig-Thekla, part of the Buchenwald concentration camp. For the rest of his life, Carl rarely spoke of what he had seen there. After V-E day, he became technical director of the Soldier Show Company in Paris, along with the director Arthur Penn and the screenwriter Paddy Chayefsky. Carl returned to New York, found an apartment in East Harlem, and organized a summer season at the Rangeley Lake Playhouse. But by the end of the summer of 1946, he landed a job at the Lakeside Summer Theatre in Landing, New Jersey, about forty miles west of New York City. There, he specialized in plays ripped from the headlines or Broadway.[2]

Carl and Betty had their first date, a late-night supper at Barney Greengrass, the celebrated deli near Friedan's Upper West Side studio. Even though she ordered the sturgeon sandwich, the specialty of the house, and one of the most expensive items on the menu, the two lonely hearts hit it off. Later they would go to the movies or to bed or they would talk for hours about the theater and politics. Years after that, asked why she married Carl, Betty said she liked his physical appearance, that he brought her an apple, and that he "told me jokes which made me laugh." Also, he made her feel "not alone." Her mother would offer another explanation: "They thought if they got married, they could help each other."[3]

In hindsight, Betty remembered warning signs. Instead of making a date in advance, Carl would call in the afternoon to schedule her for that evening. She would rush home after work every day to wait for his call. Friedan's biographer Judith Hennessee writes that during their courtship, Betty found a letter Carl wrote to his parents in which he said that the woman he was seeing, though "not much to look at," was smart so he would never be broke. Furious, she considered ending the whole thing but decided not to. Instead, she had an asthma attack. The drama escalated further when Miriam voiced her opposition to the union and Carl's desire to wed increased.[4]

Nonetheless, right before Carl was to start working at the Lakeside Summer Theatre for a second season, the couple decided to get married. On June 12, 1947, they married at City Hall; three days later, to please Carl's mother, they held a "real

Jewish wedding" in Boston. Miriam, who had remarried Elmore S. Katz a year earlier, paid. The announcement used Carl's long-abandoned last name, Friedman. A rabbi officiated under a chuppah, and the guests ate kosher food.[5]

Betty had to adjust to marriage. According to her 2000 memoir, she "loved going to bed with" Carl. But the newlyweds bickered constantly though they also felt genuine affection for each other. Some photos show Betty off to the side, gazing adoringly at her husband, who takes up the center of the composition; others capture her alone at her desk, lost in thought—a pictorial representation of the tension she would famously write about. In fact, in the first two months of marriage, they spent some time apart. Carl worked long hours at the Lakeside Summer Theatre. Betty continued filing stories for *UE News*, publishing several pieces in August, including a review of *Crossfire*, a film noir about anti-Semitism starring Robert Mitchum.[6]

The Friedans postponed their honeymoon, instead renting a bungalow at the popular summer destination of Lake Hopatcong, New Jersey, twenty minutes from the Lakeside Summer Theatre. Betty invited friends and acquaintances to share housing, including her *FP* co-worker Gladys Carter and her husband, Carl's friends the Zesersons, and the families of leftist journalist James Aronson and Cedric Belfrage, an ex-Russian spy under FBI investigation. The following year Aronson and Belfrage, along with the progressive journalist John T. McManus, founded the *National Guardian*, a far-left newspaper. That summer, Belfrage, Aronson, and the Friedans hung out on her porch imagining it.[7]

Betty neglected the housekeeping, as Gladys Carter, her friend from *UE*, commented after she visited. "Dirty stove, sink counters. . . . The kitchen would be a mess when we arrived." Perhaps there was more to it than slovenliness. Earlier that year, Marynia Farnham and Ferdinand Lundberg had published *Modern Woman: The Lost Sex*, which argued that women shirking housewifely duties were neurotic. Betty likely read Margaret Mead's review of the book for the *New York Times*, which called it "a savage attack on the feminist movement."[8]

Betty also had to contend with Carl's patched-together, erratic income. He worked at the Lakeside Summer Theatre until the fall, and then briefly for *Theatre Arts*, an important theater magazine. He wrote a guide to successful summer stock. Carl also briefly managed the New Theatre, an ensemble group that produced a revival of the 1935 Clifford Odets hit, *Waiting for Lefty* (famously ending with an invocation to strike). But these jobs dried up. Like most women of her era, Betty, who had steady work at *UE*, felt the man should be the breadwinner. Her ambivalence about earning more sparked some of her early fights with Carl. She recalled that on paydays, she "used to lose her wallet" so that he would be responsible for the money. She was already raging that he "didn't love her."[9]

Carl remembered that she raged at her family too. She referred to the Goldsteins as "The Little Foxes," after Lillian Hellman's 1939 masterpiece, the story of Regina Hubbard Gibbens, a Southern matriarch living in a world that defines men as heirs and women as afterthoughts. Regina schemes to secure the money she felt her invalid husband, Horace, owed her, villainously refusing to give him his medicine while he has a heart attack. At the end of the play, Alexandra, her daughter, confronts her mother about her venality: "There were people who ate the earth and people who stand around watching them do it. . . . I am not going to stand around and watch you do it." Friedan saw Miriam in Regina, in "the way she sneered at my father." She saw herself in Alexandra, the truth-telling heroine who has to leave the family.[10]

But she could not leave completely. In the fall of 1947, when Betty returned to Peoria for her brother Harry Jr.'s marriage to Inette Cohen, the daughter of a prosperous local businessman, she got drunk and sparred with guests. "I thought you were supposed to be a Communist now," a Republican friend of the family known as Aunt Elsa challenged her. "Nothing is too good for the working class," Friedan replied, in the gray flannel "New Look" suit she bought in the junior department at Bendel's.[11]

At *UE News*, Betty continued to use her maiden name in her byline. Overall, although she still exposed labor injustices and celebrated labor triumphs, she wrote less about anti-Semitism. An exception was a review of *Gentleman's Agreement.* Directed by Elia Kazan and written by Moss Hart, the film stars Gregory Peck playing journalist Phil Green, who disguises himself as a Jew, leading to an undercover exposé, "I Was Jewish for Six Months." Friedan treats anti-Semitism as a manifestation of fascism, writing that Peck revealed "the festering sore under the surface of American democracy." And she continued to be obsessed with fascism taking over America. That same month, in a feature about the House Un-American Activities Committee (HUAC) in Hollywood, she described "a storm-trooper with a Southern accent" harassing the playwright Bertolt Brecht, whose testimony she quoted: "The American people would lose much and risk much, if they allowed anyone to restrict their freedom to think."[12]

Pregnancy hardly slowed her down. In July 1948, six months before her first child was born, Friedan went to Philadelphia to report on the founding convention of the Progressive Party for *UE News.* She praised its coalition of women, Blacks, and Jews (Coretta Scott, then in college, also attended, although they didn't meet). Back in New York, she "climbed up on a ladder" in the middle of the street to campaign for Henry Wallace, the Progressive Party candidate for president who had run in part by attacking Truman's Mideast arms embargo. She also stumped for populist Vito Marcantonio. Carl continued to earn extra money editing *The Summer Theatre Handbook* and producing summer stock in New Jersey and West Newbury, Massachusetts.[13]

Daniel Harry was born on October 3, 1948. Despite a prolonged labor and cesarean birth, a method of delivery experts then considered unfeminine, Friedan barely stopped writing. Published in January 1949, her first article as a mother championed Annette Rubinstein, a Communist then the Labor Party candidate for state assembly in New York. It appeared in the *National Guardian*, the radical weekly co-founded by her friend British journalist Cedric Belfrage. Friedan praised Rubinstein's work against quotas of Blacks and Jews, writing: "She has been in every fight against anti-Semitism in schools, for the rights of Negroes and Puerto Ricans, and for a fairer deal for all children."[14]

While Betty was in the hospital, Carl had fixed up their tiny studio, building a kitchen, painting the ceiling pipes, transforming the bedroom into the nursery. They slept in a new room that Carl created. But it soon became clear that the apartment was too small for three people. The family would move to an apartment on Riverside Drive at 148th Street, a racially mixed neighborhood. The apartment, besides being too far uptown for their friends to visit, was infested with roaches. The marriage became strained. According to Betty, Carl stopped sleeping with her. Her solution was to return to work, which she thought she was better at anyway. By the summer, not a year after Danny's birth, she had hired a nurse. She took her son to visit Carl in West Newbury, where he was producing *Deep Are the Roots*, a Broadway hit about a Black soldier who returns from the war, but she was back at *UE* by September.[15]

Motherhood made her more vocal in her criticism of how little money Carl earned. She urged her husband to enter the lucrative new field of television advertising instead of wasting his time in the theater. But when she discovered that he ignored her advice and merely pretended to look for work, she insisted that he enter analysis. Carl began to see Martin Bergmann, a psychoanalyst whose office was at Fifth Avenue and 96th Street. As he recalled, it contained only a couch, an orchid, and, as he put it, "a view." With his hands-on approach to Freud, Bergmann told Carl that he had married his mother and he should divorce Betty. Instead, Carl would begin an affair with a woman he had dated years earlier. But he did give up his dream of being a theatrical producer to go into business with a friend in advertising and publicity, as his wife had implored him to do. From that point until their divorce, he supported her financially.

Marital troubles were not the only shadow over Friedan's world. McCarthyism, then on the rise, threatened many friends and colleagues. In 1949, two of her grad school boyfriends, David Bohm and Giovanni Rossi Lomanitz, refused to name names in front of HUAC. Bohm would lose his job at Princeton, be arrested, and flee the country. Lomanitz lost his job too. Cedric Belfrage, publisher of the *National Guardian*, would also refuse to name names and was deported to Britain.

The Friedans decided to leave Manhattan. If the specter of McCarthyism played a role, the family of three also wanted more space and Danny, then three, needed other kids to play with. In addition, perhaps Betty was restless. She had already severed ties with her mother and sister, but now she broke the last links to her childhood. In 1950, she did not attend Miriam's wedding to her third husband, Jay Oberndorf, a liquor distributor, in Chicago. (Miriam's second husband, Elmore S. Katz, had died in 1948.) All that remained was her relationship with her brother, Harry Jr.—the only Goldstein still in Peoria. But on a trip back home, she and Harry Jr. fought viciously over money. Miriam, then shuttling between Chicago and Los Angeles with her new husband, wanted to close the Goldstein Jewelry Company and leave the Midwest for good. Harry Jr. and Betty both had stock in Goldstein's, and if their mother went west, the shares would be worthless. When Carl tried to persuade his mother-in-law to give her daughter her part of the remaining funds, it infuriated Harry Jr. In the course of an argument, Friedan called her brother "a Jew who denied his identity," as if by not letting her have what she considered her inheritance he was wiping out their legacy in Peoria. The siblings would not speak for a quarter century, even though she would write Harry and his wife, Inette, an abject letter of apology. Goldstein Jewelry Company closed in 1953.[16]

At this time, Betty likely was reading *Communitas: Means of Livelihood and Ways of Life*, first published in 1947. Written by Paul Goodman, author of the 1960 anti-establishment classic *Growing Up Absurd*, and his brother, Percival, an architect, *Communitas* decried conspicuous consumption. The book's title came from a Latin word meaning an unstructured community in which people are equal. The Goodman brothers attacked Robert Moses's idea of Manhattan connected by cars, rejected the skyscraper as the ideal urban building, and gave mixed reviews to "garden communities," areas combining low-rise buildings and parks, which sought to lift urban residents from city squalor. *Communitas* approved of green space in these communities but preferred that urbanites live closer to their jobs in the city centers.

Betty was also drawn to Parkway Village, in Kew Gardens, Queens, because of its coop nursery school. Additionally, the community's idealism appealed to her. Designed as integrated housing for United Nations workers from all over the world, as well as GIs and their families and journalists, Parkway Village would attract many illustrious cosmopolitans. Located near the original site of the UN in North Hempstead, Long Island, the 685-unit housing project was comprised of brick garden apartments and single-family homes, and large communal parks designed by Clarence Combs, an associate of Robert Moses. The Argentinian playwright Ariel Dorfman and his family moved there in 1947—his father was a UN official. Ralph Bunche, a founder of the UN and the first Black man to win the Nobel Peace Prize in 1950 for his role negotiating the armistice agreement in the Middle East, lived there, as did Roy Wilkins, then executive secretary of the NAACP. With some optimism, the

Friedans moved into a four-and-a-half room garden apartment in the planned community. She would be happy there.[17]

Then, in the winter of 1952, *UE News* fired Betty. Later, she would yet again blame sexism. Pregnant with her second son, Jonathan, and fighting asthma again, she had asked for maternity leave; the newspaper denied her. Some *UE* colleagues dispute her version of events, pointing out that the paper fired her, along with half of the staff, because during the Cold War, as demand for a Communist newspaper shrank, *UE News* withered from weekly to biweekly. Yet whatever the reason for Friedan's departure, losing her job galvanized her. She tried to get a writing gig at *Time*, but such positions were closed to women. Instead, she began editing the *Parkway Villager*, the community newsletter, where she published a profile of Roy Wilkins and features about her international neighbors. In June, she brought attention to rent gouging at Parkway Village, which the *New York Times* covered the following month.

At her Smith ten-year reunion, she read a questionnaire her colleagues filled out about the value of their education. Their answers inspired her to write her first piece defending women's colleges, "Was their Education UnAmerican?" But no magazine would publish it. At the peak of McCarthyism, Betty made the controversial argument that women who had attended college benefitted from it, besides posing no "threat" to America. A less overtly political feature she began in 1952, "More Than a Nosewiper: Housing Project Mothers Make a Backyard Camp for Their Kids," about working-class moms producing an all-female musical, she placed five years later in a parenting magazine, minus the class and gender analysis. But writing these pieces made her realize that something was missing from her life and from the lives of many women of her generation.[18]

The same month, Betty would publish the first of two pamphlets on sexism and capitalist injustices she pseudonymously wrote for *UE*—*UE Fights for Women Workers* and *Women Fight for a Better Life! UE Picture Story in Women's Role in American History*. "The purpose of this pamphlet . . . is to expose the trickery used by corporations to conceal and explain the double exploitation of women workers and set forth how UE locals have been able to win the elimination of rate discrimination against women," *UE Fights for Women Workers* begins. It traces how gender inequality benefits employers, quotes government studies, and offers solutions. One section details how the Black woman is doubly cursed for her race and her gender. Friedan's polemic would inspire the leftist feminist Eleanor Flexner, whose 1959 book, *Century of Struggle: The Women's Rights Movement in the United States*, shaped women's history between suffrage and the second wave.[19]

Jonathan Friedan was born on November 27, 1952. Like the birth of Betty's first son, Daniel, his was by cesarean. But whatever feelings of inferiority the delivery stirred up, they paled when compared to Betty's conflicted emotions about work and motherhood. Years later, she wrote that she was "relieved" to be staying home. But she also was driven to be happier than her mother, who had abandoned work when she married. So, with two young children and a husband who was earning too little to adequately support a family of four, Betty initially tried to balance familial responsibilities and writing. However, by Jonathan's first birthday, she had hired domestic help and, using her married name, she launched her freelance writing career for general interest women's magazines.

She continued writing for leftist newspapers under yet another pseudonym. In the spring of 1953, she began contributing to *Jewish Life: A Progressive Monthly* as "Rachel Roth." Founded in 1946, *Jewish Life* published Paul Robeson and Ilya Ehrenberg, agitated for the pardon of the Rosenbergs, and followed the Communist Party position on the Jews—advocating for total assimilation and covering up the Soviet purges. Friedan's pieces sharply critique capitalism and conspicuous consumption. The first starkly compares the wealthy women in American-made clothes and the bedraggled workers sewing them. "We're worse off every year," one says. In May, the second piece in the series, "A Sick Industry: But the Bosses Don't Suffer," reports on how capitalists flourish, regardless of the fate of working women. In June, "The Price of Collaboration" criticizes the International Ladies' Garment Workers Union for its conciliatory practices with employers and demands strong wage increases, something UE would back—such an ask was too radical for the ILGWU. A fourth article planned for the series did not run because the Rosenbergs were executed on June 19, 1953. While *Jewish Life* spent several issues decrying that injustice, "Rachel Roth" never wrote for them again. According to one biographer, Friedan's papers only contain a single piece of writing about the execution—an unpublished sketch, reminiscent of the agit-prop theater she saw at Highlander a decade earlier. Friedan speculates about what would change people's minds about the spies but eschews specifics. Perhaps chastened by the killing of Ethel, whom the media portrayed as a bad mother, she would cover few Jewish subjects in general interest magazines.[20]

Published pseudonymously that summer, Friedan's second—and last—pamphlet for *UE*, *Women Fight for a Better Life! UE Picture Story in Women's Role in American History*, expands the feminist arguments from *UE Fights for Women Workers* to document wage inequality in the careers of Black and white women. It also raises the issue of what the sociologist Arlie Hochschild later called the "second shift"—the extra burden that fell on women, forced to do housework after their day jobs. At the same time, continuing to edit the *Parkway Villager*, Friedan addressed women's issues in less Popular Front ways, such as extolling the feminist virtues of the integrated, global, communal living arrangement the community supported. One article published there negatively contrasted American women "chained to the house and babies" with liberated Scandinavians who had government childcare.[21]

Aside from McCarthyism, the early 1950s were a hard time for American women. Many of the promises of the prewar era had been foreclosed. Popular culture and science promoted unrealistic female ideals. The Harvard sociologist Talcott Parsons, whom *The Feminine Mystique* would attack, argued that men should be breadwinners, women homemakers. Few magazines would hire women for writing jobs. Friedan was under considerable strain. She returned to therapy for the first time since she began at *Federated Press*, seeing Dr. William Menaker, who had studied with Helene Deutsch, an early feminist Freudian. In his Upper West Side office, Menaker found Friedan sympathetic, later describing her as someone who fervently seeks change, the ability to create and love despite a tormented marriage and painful childhood. He challenged her to play a role besides suburban housewife. When she told him of a dream she had about John Hersey, who quit writing articles to focus on books, Menaker encouraged her: "You need to be a more serious writer." As she wrote in *The Feminine Mystique*, he also told her, "If the patient doesn't fit the book, throw away the book, and listen to the patient."[22]

Hersey's most famous magazine article for *Life*, "A Short Talk with Erlanger," in 1945, used several different people to tell the story of one soldier's paralysis and recovery through analysis. Initially filling an entire issue of the *New Yorker* the following year, his best-selling book *Hiroshima* powerfully documented the experience of six survivors of the nuclear catastrophe from their perspectives. Hersey's deep empathy for his subjects can be seen as one model for Friedan's articles and, ultimately, *The Feminine Mystique*. She wanted readers to care as much about housewives as they did about survivors of the bomb.

* * *

Several scholars have observed that Friedan's magazine writing in the 1950s exaggerates her role as suburban housewife, suppresses her past in labor journalism, and ignores other Popular Front writers of her era focusing on women. But these sins can't all be completely pinned on Friedan. Sure, in draft, her features are more radical, whereas in print, they often extolled the civic contributions of middle- or upper-class working mothers. A few stories survived relatively intact, such as "I Went Back to Work," detailing how, despite her guilt, she managed as a working mom by hiring domestic help. But editors played a role in censoring her. *Redbook* editor Robert Stein killed her profile of Beverly Pepper, a mother and housewife who, after analysis, became a respected sculptor. And Friedan did fight to publish versions of the stories she wanted to tell. It took a while but by the end of the decade, she had found a new voice to continue the conversations that energized her at *FP* and *UE News*. In 1962, looking back on this period, she links her success to identifying what she called her "ping"—a feeling that her interests coincided with something larger. She first felt it soon after she decided the family of four again needed more space and she and Carl began to look for a new apartment outside of New York City. She was reading *The Exurbanites*, a bestseller published that year by *Playboy* associate publisher A. C. Spectorsky, which celebrated the nonconformity embraced by ex–New Yorkers fleeing the city.[23]

Then Friedan learned about two communities whose spirit echoed those of Highlander Folk School and Parkway Village. On a peninsula off of Long Island Sound near South Norwalk, Connecticut, Village Creek was an integrated planned community started by families who wanted to live on the waterfront and be part of something bigger than themselves. When she took the train out to Village Creek, she heard her "ping." Village Creek was, she wrote in *Redbook*, "a model of democracy . . . —no discrimination because of race, color, creed or politics." Developed for GIs in Tappan, New York, Hickory Hill, as Friedan wrote in her piece "The Happy Families of Hickory Hill," was another idyllic, racially mixed American development where families supported each other. These articles, which in draft mentioned Erich Fromm and Rollo May, were whitewashed in the editorial process. In print, they omitted not only the social scientists but bigots calling the residents "Communists" and real estate agents refusing to show the properties because the community housed Blacks and whites. Nor did any mention of these utopias' resemblance to the earlier ones Friedan admired make it into *Redbook*. Yet in her interest in these communities, she followed Jewish modernist architects and urban planners who had fled Europe during the war and wound up in America creating new open spaces.[24]

Another "ping" sounded as Betty thought about Peoria. To earn enough to hire a maid, she commuted with Carl into Manhattan and holed up in a corner of his office in the theater district to work on her stories without the kids interrupting her. To take a break, she walked around midtown looking at the faces of the young hopefuls from the hinterlands. "I was part of a whole crowd of young people who used to talk about writing and acting," she mused. Out of that came her 1955 story about returning to Peoria, "We Drove the Rackets Out of Our Town," which strikingly reported on how in her hometown, men and women collaborated to extinguish corruption. She longed to feel less cynical to connect, like these idealists. "I envied the way they can feel their identity shaping the city's future."[25]

In the spring of 1956, the Friedans moved again, to a large refurbished stone barn in Snedens Landing, a tiny bedroom community twelve miles north of the George Washington Bridge with dramatic views overlooking the Hudson River. On the less populated New York side of the river, the town of a hundred houses housed artists and writers, such as Roger Angell, Katharine Cornell (Friedan's idol from *Saint Joan*), Lotte Lenya, and

Jerome Robbins. As Daniel Friedan put it, Snedens was "nonconformist." And according to his mother, anti-Semitic. While living there, she wrote a treatment for television based on a real incident of anti-Semitism that she had seen. In "The Swimming Pool," set in the fictional suburb of Brindle Hill, one couple, the Jonases, worry about being banned from the municipal swimming pool because they are Jewish. At a pool committee meeting, someone says, "I have nothing against Jews as a whole so long as we don't have to swim with them." "The Swimming Pool" was never made.[26]

Daniel was eight and Jonathan was three. Emily would be born on May 23, 1956, like her brothers by cesarean. From this moment until the end of her marriage, Betty would spend profligately. She also began drinking heavily. She later said that the suburbs returned her to feeling, as she had in high school, like a freak. Neighbors recalled marital brawling, crockery and salt shakers flying, she bopping Carl over the head with her pocketbook, cruel words shouted. At a party, Carl echoed Henny Youngman's famous one-liner "Take my wife, please," telling someone leaving on a South Seas expedition, "If you won't take me, take her!"

Not long after Emily's birth, Betty began work on "I Was Afraid to Have a Baby," about Julie Harris, who had recently starred in *The Lark*, Jean Anouilh's version of the Joan of Arc story, adapted by Lillian Hellman for Broadway. Joan had shrunk since George Bernard Shaw's *Saint Joan* transformed Betty's life in high school. As the scholar Robin Blaetz puts it, in the 1950s, Joan became "girlish"—even a victim of the feminine mystique. But Friedan wanted to use Harris to tell the story of how natural childbirth enriched her performance. In the graphic, "as told to" story, Harris relates that she had trouble preparing for her role until she gave birth naturally, shunning painkillers. And then, one morning in rehearsal, comforting her crying child, she had an epiphany. "I felt as if I could play Joan of Arc."

Although editors deemed the story too gory, in December *McCall's* published an edited version. When *Reader's Digest* republished the story the next year, the editors cut more details about natural childbirth and softened the ending to focus on the sentimental feelings of motherhood. But making motherhood and art coexist remained central to Friedan's thinking.[27]

As did homes. She stumbled across Ivies, a mansion at 205 River Road in Grand View-on-Hudson, three miles north of Snedens Landing, and fell in love. With Carl's advertising salary, a loan for World War II veterans, plus the last $2,500 of Betty's father's inheritance, they bought it for $25,000. They moved in in the spring of 1957. In her memoir, it sounds like paradise:

> On a little hill across the street from the Hudson River, on River Road in Grandview, a mile below the Tappan Zee Bridge, looked gloomy on the outside . . . it was a big old Victorian house with French doors opening out onto a front porch the length of the house, overlooking the river, with a boxwood maze in the front yard. An area of mostly ivy and woods went behind the house and up the hill to an old railroad tracks. It had a beautiful living room, an octagonal dining room, four fireplaces, a graceful stairway, all covered with coats and coats of hideous paint.[28]

Quite quickly, the three-story, eleven-room house with marble fireplaces, a mansard roof, a huge wraparound porch, and a view of the Hudson River and the new Tappan Zee Bridge became a burden to maintain. Friedan would eventually sell the boxwood maze. It was hard to keep up the oak and chestnut trees around the house on the steeply sloped lawn, not to mention the creek and small waterfall. But she dove into renovating, stripping six layers of paint off the marble fireplace and the wooden banister, repapering the walls in one room three times. She purchased a Victorian love seat at auction for $35, the twin of which, she often bragged, was in the Museum of the City of New York.

She painted the dining room bright yellow and the living room purple and hung extravagant curtains designed by the maverick designer Jack Lenor Larson. A bust of Lincoln occupied the place of pride in the living room. On one wall hung a tapestry with heraldic imagery. A large velvet couch she adorned with garishly colored satin and velvet throw pillows. Carl was working for himself and she was only earning around $2,000 a year from freelance work, so he installed a pay phone for guests.

The rest of the house included a roomy, white kitchen and a second-floor master bedroom, overlooking the river, papered with a flocked red Venetian print. A brightly colored Spanish rug covered the floor. The third floor had four rooms. Betty sometimes wrote in a back room up there facing the forest. By the window were long wooden shelves on which she placed each chapter when she had finished it, penciling the title on the shelf. In the front room, she left the old wood flooring planks intact. "Sometimes she would let the dog poop up there," said Anne Bell, who with her husband bought the house from Friedan in 1965.[29]

Betty additionally set herself apart from her neighbors with dramatic clothes, like a cape. Carl did magic shows for children. The couple hosted adult parties where the guest list was less important than the sick humor popularized by Lenny Bruce. For Jessica Mitford's book party for *The American Way of Death*, published the same year as *The Feminine Mystique*, the Friedans parked a hearse in the driveway. Friedan also liked musicals, and in her spare time she listened to well-worn cast albums of *West Side Story* and *My Fair Lady* as well as Pablo Casals and the folk group the Kingston Trio. She continued to delegate domestic tasks, hiring maids—mostly live-in—to clean up. When they quit or she fired them, her writing came before household chores. Jonathan recalled that "in our house breakfast was not a regular meal" and that the family ate a lot of TV dinners, though in fairness, that could be said of the culture generally.

Friedan often put the children in taxis to go to school, since she still did not drive. She sometimes forgot to wash their faces.[30]

Still, she and Carl were devoted parents. When Sputnik shot into space, they stayed up all night to watch it with the kids from the front lawn. They loved books and encouraged the kids to read. She was especially delighted when they liked books that she had liked, but she did not see her children as her own creation. Or not exactly. At age six, when Emily wanted to write, Betty bought her a notebook. On the front someone wrote: "Emily Friedan—I want to be a book writer. A book writer has to have a [*sic*] imaginative mind. If you want to be one you should write a page and see if you like it. If you don't like it take out the part you don't like and put another part in. If you do like it then you keep it." Betty believed in teaching her children the power of creativity and individuality, in science, and in the secular Jewish emphasis on questioning and of speaking truth to power. Carl would put the children to bed and tell them that of the five greatest men in the world, four were Jewish—Einstein, Jesus, Freud, and Marx. Daniel remembered that while there was no "connection to religious Judaism" his mother taught him to "think for myself and not swallow someone else's line," qualities he considered intrinsically Jewish. When the Friedans celebrated Jewish holidays, they did so with a secular twist. At Passover, Carl would go through the Haggadah and remove any mention of God, although the family discussed the suffering of all marginalized peoples.[31]

In June 1957, at her fifteen-year reunion at Smith, Betty began the project that would become *The Feminine Mystique*. It started when, recalling how few of her classmates had made anything of themselves outside of the home at the ten-year mark, she put together a new questionnaire. Ely Chinoy, a Smith sociologist, and the husband of her friend Helen Chinoy, helped. As she considered the completed questionnaires, she knew she had something big. The questions were, for the time, startlingly frank, the answers even more so. Some women revealed satisfaction with their accomplishments, but many others felt crimped into the roles of wives and mothers. Friedan herself took the questionnaire; her answers revealed no small amount of dismay. Her response to the question "To what extent do you talk to your husband about your deepest feelings?": "Only after an emotional crisis or rift." Another answer indicated the old worry that living up to her professors' expectations, having a career, doomed her to wind up like Joan of Arc—martyred.[32]

The Smith coeds Friedan met were more interested in getting their Mrs. degree than facing big questions. In Grand View, she began to shape the answers to the questionnaire into an article about women's education. She pitched an article to *McCall's* based on the survey, "Are Women Wasting Their Time in College?" The rhetorical title belied her strong argument—driven by her belief that Smith saved her from Peorian conformity—that women benefitted from college, and that a society that thought otherwise needed reform. When *McCall's* declined, she submitted the article to *Ladies' Home Journal*, where an editor rewrote the conclusion so that it said the opposite of what she wanted. Dismayed, she attended a lecture at the Society of Magazine Writers, where critic Vance Packard confessed that he wrote his bestselling exposé of advertising, *The Hidden Persuaders*, because magazine editors rejected his ideas.

In 1956, determined to keep writing while breastfeeding Emily, she had learned about the geophysicist W. Maurice Ewing and the geologist William Donn from a female scientist whose son was in Jonathan's playgroup. Excited by the tip, Friedan tracked down Ewing and Donn at nearby Lamont Observatory, where both were predicting that glaciers would melt and submerge North America. She read a textbook every morning to prepare to write. In September 1958, *Harper's* published her feature "The Coming Ice Age: A True Scientific Detective Story." A "best of" *Harper's* anthology, which also included William Faulkner and Mark Twain, reprinted the story. It was translated into many languages, although Ewing and Donn complained about its inaccuracies and sensationalism and considered suing. But George P. Brockway, president of W. W. Norton, the most white-shoe publishing house of its era, admired "The Coming Ice Age" and asked Friedan to contribute to his series "Primers for Our Time." Friedan declined. First, it wasn't her own work. Second, she had already begun to think about writing a book about women. Upon hearing this, Brockway, who had edited several of Erik Erikson's bestsellers, labeled her one of the worst things you could call a woman in that period—"incredibly ambitious." But he acquired a book she pitched about sex roles and housewives titled "The Togetherness Woman."[33]

Friedan's old insecurities shaped early drafts. After signing the contract with Norton, she looked for a co-writer, considering William Menaker, her shrink, and Mary I. Bunting, the president of Radcliffe. Neither panned out. Having abhorred solitude since childhood, she now went about the deeply solitary task of writing the book on her own. She tried to work at home but found Grandview-on-Hudson too isolated. Then, the main branch of the New York Public Library opened the Frederick Allen Room, with eleven carrels where writers could leave books overnight. Friedan wrangled an invitation. Her cohort included children's book author Sidney Offit, biographer James Thomas Flexner, and Lawrence Lader, a journalist and radical with whom she later started the National Association for the Repeal of Abortion Laws (NARAL).

She wrote the first two chapters of *The Feminine Mystique* in the Allen Room, taking the bus into the city three times a week and coming back with Carl, sometimes late at night. Other times, she wrote at the desk in their dining room, facing the river or spreading out on the dining room table itself. Her neighbor, William "Si" Goode, a Columbia University sociologist, checked in on her to see how she was doing and helped her with research. More and more, Carl stayed late in the city, getting home well after dinner, and Betty began to work on the book on the third floor. Years later, she remembered Emily knocking on the door to give her a May Day basket, but she, mid-paragraph, never answered. Writing *The Feminine Mystique* made her think of "secret drinking in the morning," she said.[34]

In 1958, she had launched the Intellectual Resources Pool (IRP), a program for gifted children from all economic brackets. The idea came to her a year earlier when she discovered that Daniel, her oldest, then nine, was a math prodigy. Like his mother, he skipped several grades. On weekends, Carl brought him to Columbia where he worked on the IBM 7090, an early mainframe computer. (Daniel would win a MacArthur "genius" grant years later.) "It worried me when his teacher punished him for doing math problems in unconventional ways," Friedan wrote. IRP combined her ideas about education, as shaped by Kurt Lewin and other psychologists she studied, with her conviction that teenagers needed more intellectual enrichment than they were getting from school. She wrangled famous artists, scientists, and intellectuals, such as Harvey Swados, the architectural historian James Fitch, and C. Wright Mills, to teach gifted junior high and high schoolers in Rockland County on Saturdays. The novelist William Owen, who taught at Columbia University, led a writing seminar, while Dr. Robert Menzies, the director of marine biology at the Lamont Observatory, conducted classes on the scientific method. IRP also gave classes on microbiology and led a field trip where students could examine fossils.[35]

Friedan tried to interest the press in her project without success, until 1960, when the *New York Times* covered it twice.

But then, disturbed by a power grab over the direction of the organization, she pulled away. IRP would become CRP, changing the word "intellectual" for "community." In the charged climate of the McCarthy era, some Grandviewites considered it too Communist—by which some of them meant too Jewish.[36]

She missed the money, but work on the book heated up. In 1964, she would tell a reporter: "I was at it all the time, even at night. . . . I would stew and gloom for weeks on end and Carl said, 'my God . . . other people write books without making the whole family suffer.'" He did not suffer silently. He confided to friends that "that bitch" worked on her book as opposed to his meal. He threw a sugar bowl at her. Trying to stop a mirror that she threw at him left a scar on the knuckle of his ring finger. This is not just a story about Carl-as-domestic abuser. Like many in their generation, Carl and Betty saw storminess as honesty and believed that if you didn't shout, you were a phony. Betty never flinched from a fight. Yet the intellectual backdrop of the era has left a gendered dimension to the way the couple's fighting has been perceived.

While many Jewish male intellectuals of this era wrote important books about their concerns with the passivity of their people during the Shoah and emasculation in the Jewish family, there was no comparable theorizing about women. Thus, when women shouted, it looked like bad behavior. Betty turned that into a political act. Her September 1960 *Good Housekeeping* article, "I Say: Women Are *People* Too," addressed how the unhappiness women felt due to the tension between motherhood and work was worth shouting about. Reporting *The Feminine Mystique*—meeting women who defied gender norms to shout—helped her see shouting as a collective act. As did her bouts of solitary writing. She recalled in 1973, "I have never experienced anything as powerful, truly mystical, as the forces that seemed to take me over when I was writing." But she also wanted readers to know that writing did not supplant motherhood. "It was almost as good as having a baby," she said. She renamed her shorthand for intuition—the "ping" from the 1950s became "Geiger counter," a device that "clicks when the image shows too sharp a discrepancy from reality," she wrote. The Geiger counter told her when to shout, when to create a storm.[37]

# 5

## *"The Problem That Had No Name"*

Cathartic for readers and invigorating for Friedan to work on, *The Feminine Mystique* famously begins with a portrait of housewives who, believing they were alone, were scared to change:

> The problem lay buried, unspoken for many years in the minds of American women. It was a strange stirring, a sense of dissatisfaction, a yearning that women suffered in the middle of the twentieth century in the United States. Each suburban wife struggled with it alone. As she made the beds, shopped for groceries, matched slipcover material, ate peanut butter sandwiches with her children, chauffeured Cub Scouts and Brownies, lay beside her husband at night—she was afraid to ask even of herself the silent question—"Is this All?"[1]

This passage describes perfectly the numbing gendered division of labor at home, which is one reason why so many women find their way to *The Feminine Mystique* even today.

Friedan elevates what had been a pedestrian problem—less than a problem, really—to the level of important liberal issues such as affordable housing and the environment. The housewives hum with desperation. And desperation also lurks on the page when Friedan writes about herself as a new species—one of a generation of girls who wanted to kill their mothers. Although she never says so, this impulse toward matricide might have been more acute among Jewish women. While *The Feminine Mystique* does not mention Mrs. Ben Patimkin—Brenda's mother in Philip Roth's 1959 novella, *Goodbye Columbus*—Friedan's book anticipates the mother-hatred that, twelve years later, Grace Paley would describe flooding America. With *The Feminine Mystique*, the mom entered "the villain room of . . . psychological causation," Paley writes.[2]

The themes of the desperate housewife and matricide are compelling, but the book might have faded without its shape. Friedan wrote *The Feminine Mystique* like a detective novel. It inhabits this form so well that for the first several chapters we almost do not notice that, unlike many thrillers, it lacks a clear villain. But the book did many other things: it universalized female unhappiness, introduced much of what we now take for granted about women's roles in the private and public spheres, and made many enduring contributions to feminism as we know it. *The Feminine Mystique* allowed that women have as much right to rage against powerful forces conspiring to oppress them as Black people or Jews and dictated that no woman should be coerced into having to choose between family and work. It laid the groundwork for women's rights to be regarded as a civil right and led to generations of feminists attacking Freud. The British Marxist historian Sheila Rowbotham would praise the "dauntless way in which she . . . tracks down the origins of the mystique before any political implications were apparent."[3]

Friedan sets some of the most moving parts of the book in the constricted world of magazines in the 1950s, where she assaults a myth ingrained in the culture, one necessary to overthrow. She cites many dumbed down magazine articles that appeared in *McCall's* in the 1950s and then deftly maneuvers from indicting the brainwashers to pronouncing herself guilty of participating in the brainwashing. She wrote for these magazines, and when the editors told her to make an actress look like a housewife, she did. She witnessed magazine editors rejecting Thurgood Marshall's account of the "inside story of the desegregation battle" because it would not appeal to housewives. Her shame gathers power because of her conviction that the absence of a culture supporting the life of the mind is more damaging than sexual repression, and the celebration of writers like Shirley Jackson for rhapsodizing about domesticity is more toxic than marriage. Using the Nazi phrase "Kinder, Kuche, Kirche" she links fascism and sexism, anti-Semitism and the feminine mystique. "But this was not Nazi Germany," she writes dramatically. "This was America."[4]

She had to explain the feminine mystique's appeal for herself and for women graduating from Smith. In her account of creating the book, she writes about how she turned to, among others, Erik Erikson, whom she felt could enrich the conversation by studying the identity crises of women with the same avidity that he studied those of men. Or could have, since he never bothered to do so. But while she is exploring Erikson's shortcomings, she is also using her own identity crisis to tell a story. She makes a big deal of switching from typewriter to pencil and a yellow legal pad. It is a small, homely moment and a large empowering one. The point is to show her readers that it only takes a small change to start a big one. From there emerges a journey going back farther than her own life—or even her mother's life—to give the reader perspective about the backlash against women. It says something, she writes, that at Smith she had never read—or read about—the suffragists. She read Nora in Henrik Ibsen's *A Doll's House*—Nora who famously left her family, slamming the door on the way. But Friedan did not want to leave her family. The project she takes on as she gets deeper into this chapter is to frame the roots of "the feminine mystique" as something that women have faced and could overcome without being alone. Thus, she casts Mary Wollstonecraft, Lucy Stone, and other suffragists as bourgeois, passionate, happily married yet revolutionary working wives and mothers. In passing, she makes the argument that the founding of America led to abolition, which led to suffrage. And that Elizabeth Cady Stanton's early abolitionism taught her feminism. "In organizing, petitioning, and speaking out to free the slaves, American women learned how to free themselves."[5]

But Friedan is always clear that suffrage flourishes in the middle class. Female mill workers, after twelve-hour shifts, were too tired to protest. The problem for her lies elsewhere. She notably sprinkles this chapter with 1950s sexist slurs like "man-eaters," to make readers understand that suffragists were not those things but respectable married women. Susan B. Anthony was no "bitter spinster with a cat" but rather peripatetic and noble. "Traveling alone from town to town . . . using her abilities to the fullest as an organizer and lobbyist and lecturer, she made her own way in the larger and larger world," Friedan writes, foretelling her own future. For these portraits, she draws heavily on Eleanor Flexner's book *Century of Struggle: The Women's Rights Movement in the United States*, published a few years earlier. Labor historians fixate on Friedan's replacing Flexner's stories of working women, single women, and women whose parents had been slaves with her own highly edited life story and the chronicles of middle-class suffragists. In today's context, this swap is easy to condemn, yet Friedan never aimed for diversity.[6]

The book shifts to rage at the Freudians responsible for "the feminine mystique." Not Freud, exactly, whom she defends at the beginning of "The Sexual Solipsism of Sigmund Freud" as a genius. "But I do question, from my own experience as a woman and my reporter's experience of other women, the application of Freudian theory to women today." The chapter trashes "penis envy" and "the castration complex" in the hands of "lesser thinkers." As for Freud, she blames nineteenth-century Judaism for his shortcomings. Freud, she writes, coming from a "Jewish culture in which men said their daily prayer," could only create a biased philosophy. Jewish men reciting "I thank Thee, Lord, that thou hast not created me a woman," while women recited thanks for existing was not a recipe for liberating women.[7]

Friedan indicts Freud's parents, especially his weak-willed mother. His father married a bride half his age and "ruled the family with autocratic authority traditional in Jewish families." Also, Freud's wife Martha "was as devoted to his physical needs as the most doting Jewish mother." She quotes Freud's letters to Martha, noting how he focused on her completion of the housework. Of course, Friedan's marriage, and that of her parents, were polar opposites of this.[8]

But Friedan also rails against Freud's followers, such as the feminist analyst Helene Deutsch, whom she denounces for rejecting and dismissing her own creativity. She also goes after the American psychologist and writer Marynia Farnham, who with Ferdinand Lundberg in 1947 published *Modern Woman: The Lost Sex*, an indictment of women's attempts to have lives outside of the home. The chapter on Margaret Mead disdains her as a functionalist, a school of sociology then led by Harvard's Talcott Parsons which relegated women to sex roles, thereby perpetuating the feminine mystique. Although Friedan praises the early career of the groundbreaking anthropologist and famous professional woman, she damns her for shoehorning her scientific discoveries into Freud's in Mead's 1949 classic, *Male and Female*. Mead should have followed her own passionate journey, she writes, before ripping Parsons and sociologist Mirra Komarovsky, whose work about the contradictions women faced Friedan perceived as not radical enough.

She moves on to explain how the feminine mystique has contaminated higher education. "American women have been successfully reduced to sex creatures," she writes, blaming college educators at ease with their graduates getting their Mrs. degree and elite schools she claims believe education masculinizes women. But although the scope of the attacks is one thing that makes *The Feminine Mystique* of such continuing interest, you have to pause, or you will miss the fact that the book avoids pinning the mystique directly on capitalism. If this is a detective story, here it is least clear who the villain is. Friedan withholds the name of one system that might lurk behind the feminine mystique. "Powerful forces in this nation must be served by those pretty domestic pictures that stare at us everywhere," she writes, suggesting that Freudolatry prevented everyone from seeing the social inequities crippling the nation. However, ultimately, she delivers fewer *j'accuse*s than scenes of redemption evoking an alternate childhood. She supports the findings of sociologist Arnold Green, that working-class Polish immigrants who eschewed Dr. Spock did not raise neurotic children. "In these families," Friedan writes, "stress was placed upon work," not motherlove. "Respect, not love is the tie that binds."[9]

"The Sexual Sell" and "Housewifery Expands to Fill the Time Available"—chapters exposing how big business furthers the feminine mystique—have the most currency today. "The Sexual Sell" focuses Vance Packard's critique of capitalism turning menial labor into tasks requiring expertise on housewifery. Here, as earlier in the book, Friedan plays gumshoe. Out she sets in search of a happy housewife. Wherever experts claim there is one, the woman is already occupied outside of her home, she finds. Also in this chapter, she puts to clever effect the lessons she had learned at Smith about "good" propaganda. Indeed, some things the men she interviewed for her book said demand a propagandistic response, such as the comment attributed to an anonymous executive: "Properly manipulated ('if you are not afraid of that word,' he said), American housewives can be given the sense of identity, purpose, creativity, the self-realization, even the sexual joy they lack—by the buying of things."[10]

Some interesting parts of "Housewifery . . ." accuse the International style of architecture, mostly designed by Jewish émigrés from Europe, of furthering the feminine mystique. "In this expensive modern house, like many of the open plan houses in this era, there was no door at all between the kitchen and the living room," Friedan writes. "The woman in the beautiful electronic kitchen is never separated from her children. She can forget her identity. . . . The open plan also helps expand the housework to fill the time available." When Friedan wrote these words, though, she lived in Ivies, the opposite of an open plan house.[11]

Critiquing Alfred Kinsey and the exploitation of female sexuality in the media and culture, *The Feminine Mystique* responds squarely to 1950s repression by arguing that for women to only focus on sexual freedom in the search for identity is a mistake. Friedan is no prude, as she would later claim, but a utopian who believed that women would be sexually fulfilled after they embarked on their "passionate journey" outside of the home. But this chapter swerves into "Momism"—Philip Wylie's 1942 theory—and its now-debunked connection between homosexuals and overmothering. Homosexuality, which can be a result of mothers brainwashed by the feminine mystique, Friedan writes, is spreading, "like a murky smog over the American scene." Although such passages earned Friedan the label of homophobe, they were in synch with her era: *The Diagnostic and Statistical Manual of Mental Disorders* (*DSM*) labeled homosexuality a disease until 1973.[12]

"Progressive Dehumanization: The Comfortable Concentration Camp" is the most controversial chapter in the book due to Friedan's bold—some would say brazen—comparison of the misery of the frustrated housewife to the unspeakable suffering of the Holocaust victim. Women "are in as much danger as the millions who walked to their death in the concentration camps," she writes. Having used overstatement for years in service of leftist causes, she now martialed it to convince readers of the dangers housewives faced without dignity or will, predicting their transformation into mindless victims of conspicuous consumption—anticipating Ira Levin's dystopian 1972 novel *The Stepford Wives*—as opposed to the politically engaged, fulfilled creatures she knew they could be. The historian Kirsten Fermaglich has pointed out that other postwar intellectuals also used the concentration camp as a metaphor to express various horrors, especially slavery. But borrowing language from the 1960 Holocaust memoir by Bruno Bettelheim, *The Informed Heart*, Friedan likened the camps to a sin less acknowledged. Her analogy compares Bettelheim's lone dancer, who, upon being ordered by an SS officer to perform, killed him with his own gun, and the housewife victims of the feminine mystique, who "to escape, [they] must, like the dancer, finally exercise their human freedom, and recapture their sense of self." According to Fermaglich, in Friedan's drafts, the "comfortable concentration camp" chapter connects Gestalt ideas about scapegoated Jews with monstrous mother-housewives. But the published book omits the Jewish mom–scapegoat. Well before Bettelheim was discredited in 1990, Friedan regretted this chapter, which would alienate many readers, for its excesses.[13]

*The Feminine Mystique* ends by touching on conflicts Friedan would return to in the following decades, such as the problem with female exceptionalism and the love/hate relationship of Jewish women to the feminine mystique. Jewish women are, she notes, polarized in their responses to housework. Either they are persuaded by religion and therapy to yield to it more than non-Jews, or they have a better chance at breaking free of the feminine mystique. It would take two decades for her to synthesize these opposing ideas into her family-friendly Jewishness. She came to realize—perhaps she always knew—that the attachment to family came out of a need to survive. But in *The Feminine Mystique*, she is less interested in reconciling these points of view than attacking a long list of mostly Jewish male social scientists for excluding women from their studies. The 1950 bestseller *The Lonely Crowd*, by David Riesman, Nathan Glazer, and Reuel Denney, only mentioned women to note that they were better off helping their husbands, she writes. Friedan singles out for admiration the humanist psychologist Abraham Maslow, who, despite his sins in this area, also advanced anti-Freudian theories of self-actualization recommending dropping conventional male and female roles. She believed that neo-Freudians should have adopted Maslow's 1939 study of college-educated women, "Dominance, Personality, and Social Behavior in Women," as a central text as it introduced the idea of the "high dominance woman," who preferred to be treated like a human being. Nonetheless, she observed that Maslow identified only two women—Jane Addams and Eleanor Roosevelt—for this distinction.[14]

As she moves toward her powerful closing paragraphs, Friedan pauses to scold any woman yielding to the feminine mystique. She criticizes Dagmar Wilson, the founder, with Bella Abzug, of Women Strike for Peace, for defining herself as a housewife first, citizen second. Friedan is so harsh because the stakes are high: "It is frightening when a woman finally realizes that there is no answer to the question 'who am I' except the voice inside herself," she writes. Her answers encouraged studying the humanities and working and a "passionate search for individual identity." She does add that the government should fund maternity leave and childcare. After nearly four-hundred-plus pages, she presents her magnificent ending, a pile of questions pointing to an egalitarian utopia:

> Who knows what women can be when they are finally free to become themselves? Who knows what women's intelligence will contribute when it can be nourished without denying love? Who knows of the possibilities of love when men and women share not only children, home and garden, not only the fulfillment of their biological roles, but the responsibilities and passion of the work that creates the human future and the full human knowledge of who we are? It has barely begun, the search of women for themselves. But the time is at hand when the voices of the feminine mystique can no longer drown out the inner voice that is driving women on to become complete.[15]

In the fall of 1962, Friedan's editor, Burton Beals, had approached some New York intellectuals to blurb *The Feminine Mystique*. But few writers to whom he sent a galley (Alfred Kazin and Lillian Hellman among them) responded. Eric Swenson, vice president at Norton, begged Pearl S. Buck, then seventy, to recommend it. In the end, Buck did write a blurb, "Betty Friedan has, in my opinion, gone straight to the heart of the problems of the American woman," and the book became a main selection of Book Find, a smaller analogue to Book-of-the-Month Club. But the Southern novelist and activist Lillian Smith saw more in Friedan's books than most of the people at Norton. In a letter to George Brockway, Friedan's publisher, Smith, who would review the book for the *Saturday Review*, scolded him. "Sorry you didn't get a man to praise the book too . . . but Mrs. Buck is not good on the subject of women or race relations. She is sentimental." One month before publication, Beals sent the manuscript to Abraham Maslow, whose theory of self-actualization Friedan made a centerpiece of her final chapter. Maslow agreed to blurb *The Feminine Mystique*, calling it a "blockbuster."[16]

Norton published *The Feminine Mystique* on February 19,

1963, almost two weeks after Friedan's forty-second birthday. She worried that it would not sell, that at 3,000 copies the first printing was small, and that the newspaper strike that had started in December further dimmed the book's chances. The strain aggravated Friedan's already difficult marriage although outwardly, Carl, who ran his own advertising agency, was proud of his wife. He printed press releases on his business letterhead, sent copies to readers, and hosted a launch party. "You are cordially invited as a friend survivor or both to the feminine mystique to an informal party to celebrate the book's launching on Tuesday February 19, 5 pm to 7:30 pm penthouse at 120 East 36th St," his entreaty read. Nor was Carl shy about creating a to-do list for Norton. He told Betty, "Norton fucks things up as usual." Yet the couple still fought, often violently. Tania Grossinger, Friedan's press agent, remembers her client in dark glasses to cover "her swollen eyes, black, purple, and blue."[17]

Even before the newspaper strike ended in March, some intellectuals registered Friedan's book as an important cultural event. John Kenneth Galbraith said that *The Feminine Mystique* "made the conventional wisdom [about women] totter." Alvin Toffler announced that "it pulled the trigger on history." In January, *Ladies' Home Journal* published one excerpt, "Have Housewives Traded Brains for Brooms?" In March, *McCall's* published a second, "The Fraud of Femininity." Stephanie Coontz quotes some responses in her 2011 study, *A Strange Stirring*. "Everything just clicked," said Sally A. According to psychologist Lillian Rubin, "Friedan called it perfectly." Stella J said, "I never even realized what I was feeling until I read that first chapter." In an eight-page letter, the daughter of Talcott Parsons, the Harvard functionalist sociologist Friedan attacked in her book, wrote that being an unmarried career woman "is like being a negro or a Jew." Some readers saw themselves in the "comfortable concentration camp" analogy while others derided it.[18]

Not every woman embraced *The Feminine Mystique*. By 1963,

many white women had already poured into the workplace. Now toiling away in menial jobs as opposed to enjoying a "passionate journey," many of these women dismissed the book. And although it moved some Black women, others, especially those who had been in the workforce for decades, sometimes helping the white women Friedan writes about—by 1960, 60 percent of Black middle-class families were two-earner households—did not recognize themselves in Friedan's pages. Nor did the book appeal to all college students, many of whom had already radicalized. And scholars celebrated *The Feminist Mystique*, with reservations. In a letter to Friedan, dated on the day of its publication, the historian Gerda Lerner praised the "splendid book" and compared its author to Rachel Carson. But Lerner also made the enduring criticism that *The Feminine Mystique* focused on "the problems of middle class, college educated women," which she felt had "retarded the general advance of women" since suffrage and mentioned Friedan's omission of Black women. Jessie Bernard, a Jewish sociologist who had spent the 1950s researching women's roles, applauded Friedan's indictment of "the feminine mystique" but questioned her characterization of the "suddenness" of the trend and the book's originality.[19]

These objections hardly impeded the success of *The Feminine Mystique.* Indeed, one key to the book's early triumph lay in the controversy it generated. Another can be found in Friedan's success on the new medium of television. For that, she owes much to her publicist, Tania Grossinger—the cousin of Jennie, the Catskills resort's matriarch. At their first meeting, Friedan demanded guest spots on the *Today Show*, with Barbara Walters, and on the *Tonight Show*, which Johnny Carson had just started hosting. Grossinger retorted that Friedan "spoke too rapidly," monopolized the conversation, and screamed if provoked.[20]

Friedan would get the Carson spot, appearing on the same segment as Jean Seberg and Freda Payne (unfortunately lost to history). She appeared on Merv Griffin without incident. She was a hit on the Pierre Berton show in Canada, where she "came out swinging." However, a clash on *Girl Talk* would show some of the challenges of making her argument that women were people too on this new medium. Hosted by Virginia Graham (née Komiss), *Girl Talk* was one of the most raucous talk shows on television, and Friedan made sure it lived up to its reputation. Before the show, she and Grossinger had a few drinks at Sardi's, on West 44th Street, next door to where ABC taped the show. When Friedan entered the studio, done up as a sitting room filled with eighteenth-century antiques, she took an instant dislike to Graham, with her lacquered, peroxided hair and trademark flashy outfit. One guest, the actress Hermione Gingold, known for playing overbearing mothers, had at Friedan. Appealing to housewives, her target audience, Graham asked: "Girls, who really needs bylines? What better thing can we do with our lives than do the dishes for those you love?" According to Friedan, knowing that Graham's agent fought for the size of the typeface of *her* byline, she yelled: "Women, don't listen to her. She needs you out there as a captive audience for her television program." Grossinger recalled that when taping stopped, Friedan faced the studio audience and screamed, "If you don't let me have my say I'm going to say the word 'orgasm' ten times."[21]

On March 31, the newspaper strike ended, and reviews began to appear. Many were positive. The *Herald Tribune* critic Marya Mannes characterized the book as a "damning indictment of the social, educational and commercial pressures in the last 15 years." In *Saturday Review*, Lillian Smith wrote: "The gist of Betty Friedan's thesis is that Nora is back in the Doll's House. It is now an air-conditioned split-level abode with her own car in the garage, but a Doll's House nonetheless." But many other reviews, including one in the *New York Times*, criticized Friedan. Lucy Freeman, a rare female reporter for the paper, wrote that women's maternal nature caused "the feminine mystique." "The Fault, dear Mrs. Friedan, is not in our culture, but in ourselves." Another important early critical review in the socialist magazine the *New Leader*, by twenty-five-year-old Diane Ravitch, pointed out that Friedan's argument owed much to that of Simone de Beauvoir's *The Second Sex*, which Alfred A. Knopf had published in America in 1953. "Mrs. Friedan's book represents nothing more than a rehashing and watering down of the French writer's ideas," wrote Ravitch, launching a critique that would haunt *The Feminine Mystique*. However, the criticism that the book did not, in Virginia Woolf's famous line, "think back through" her mothers, including de Beauvoir, misconstrues it—and its author. Friedan had become so intent on living differently from her mother that she saw herself as motherless. She sometimes sounded arrogant except that the world celebrated the mid-twentieth-century American Jewish literary male who announced his uniqueness with similar force.[22]

Friedan did borrow her philosophical underpinning for *The Feminine Mystique* from de Beauvoir's 1949 masterpiece. But the French book is abstract and Olympian whereas the American one is cozy and pragmatic. While de Beauvoir anticipates Friedan's focus on the irrelevance of biology and housework, the sexism of Freud, the importance of culture, the mysterious "Other," and the meaning of women gaining independence through struggle, her use of caste, her excluding men and advocating the overthrow of marriage, her pronouncements—"one is not born, but rather becomes a woman"—would have flopped in 1950s America, as would de Beauvoir's quoting Karl Marx during the Cold War.[23]

In her review, Ravitch made another criticism that would stick—Friedan blamed housewives themselves for perpetuating "the feminine mystique." Housewives disliked this, and they would like it less as the 1960s became the 1970s, and Phyllis Schlafly burst onto the scene to goad them. Then too, the few men who tackled the book argued that the things that Friedan said about women could be said about anyone. About a year later, at a conference on continuing education at UCLA, Philip Rieff, who had just written *Freud: The Mind of a Moralist*, possibly with the help of his then-wife Susan Sontag, disparaged housewife-students "in tones of such contempt," Friedan recalled, and called feminists "false prophets."[24]

Tania Grossinger convinced Norton to send Friedan on a six- to nine-day book tour across three cities—a nearly unheard-of step at the time. *The Feminine Mystique*, which would sell 60,000 copies in hardcover, went into its fifth printing. Carl met Betty in Chicago in May. After he could only find three copies in the stores, he wrote to Norton:[25]

> In Connecticut this week where she talked to the Smith club the police had to be called to control traffic and non-Smith women were turned away in droves . . . in Westchester yesterday the mental health something or other had never had such enormous crowds . . . she gets mobbed after every talk. Letters are coming in from all over the country—heart pouring, frantic, frenzied, worshipping—it's incredible, almost like the coming of the messiah.[26]

Friedan felt vindicated. "The reactions to my book have been most satisfying, even the violence of the attacks," she wrote in some notes for a symposium on the nonmonetary rewards of the book. This was partly because of what she was learning. "Writing this book seems to have catapulted me into a movement of history . . . frankly, it's more interesting, exciting to move in a world that stretches from New York and Washington to Dallas and Seattle, making new friends, having new experiences, and a voice in new decisions in education, social welfare, mass communications, and coming home, happily, to my family, and cozy suburb."[27]

But the adulation emboldened her to demand more from her publisher. "I am fully aware that narcissism and paranoia are diseases endemic to authors," she began one letter to her editor, Burton Beals. "I don't give a damn how any of you at Norton feel about me personally (you all probably are beginning to hate my guts, as my former agent did when she began to see my dissatisfaction with her performance[)]." In another letter, she complained that Norton mistreated her. She felt "betrayed, lied to, etc, when you did not advertise it [*The Feminine Mystique*] with the enthusiasm and full support" of the publishing house. Yet publicly, she said that the controversy the book incited meant that her Geiger counter had been right. A 1964 *New York Times* article quotes her as saying, "I seem to have hit an open nerve ending with American women."[28]

She sent Miriam a copy with the inscription: "With all the troubles we have had, you gave me the power to break through the *Feminine Mystique* which will not, I think, be a problem any longer for Emily. I hope you accept the book for what it is, an affirmation of the values of your life and mine." It is not known how Miriam, sixty-three, received the gift, but she had shaken off the feminine mystique long ago.[29]

Friedan used her book as a wedge against her past in other ways. In June 1963, when Congress passed the Equal Pay Act, she hoped that "the problem that had no name" would finally recede. To celebrate, she returned to Peoria for her twenty-fifth high school reunion with thoughts of avenging the ostracism she experienced as a girl. Instead, she got drunk, started swearing, and insulted a classmate. She and Carl ended up sitting by themselves. "She was a cross I had to bear," Harry Jr. said years later.[30]

Random House poached Friedan from Norton, proposing a $30,000 advance for her second book ($273,681 now). Norton's WASP publisher George Brockway invited her to lunch, where he made a counteroffer. "I remember looking him right in the eye and saying . . . 'George, you made me feel Jewish for trying to sell my book. Go —— yourself!'" Still, despite months of squabbling, her editor, Burton Beals, was sorry to see her go. "I had looked forward to working with you on the second book," he wrote.[31]

The White House released the recommendations of the Kennedy Commission on the Status of Women and affirmed some of *The Feminine Mystique*'s arguments while committing to preserving the family. In many states "the wife had no legal rights to any of her husband's property and earnings during the existence of the marriage, aside from the right to be properly supported," the report found. On page forty-three of her copy of the report, Friedan scribbled stars and exclamation points next to the suggestion that "paid maternity leave or comparable insurance benefits should be provided for women workers; employers, unions, and governments should explore the best means of accomplishing this." The commission ignored her exhortations.[32]

Demand for Friedan as a speaker surged. A reported 175 leaders of Methodist women read *The Feminine Mystique*. *Commonweal* gave the book a mixed review, criticizing its derogatory attitude toward housewives, but the theologian Mary Daly spoke approvingly of it. *The Feminine Mystique* became a talking point at synagogues. A flyer promoting one of Friedan's talks at the Sisterhood of Temple Emanu-El, a Reform synagogue in Dallas, asked, "What kind of woman are you? Frantic cook? Smothered mother? Satisfied?" The flyer promised: "Betty Friedan will help you decide." Yet although many Jewish readers, even some Holocaust survivors, celebrated her message, others resisted. In October, even before Friedan arrived for her lecture at the Jewish Federation of St. Louis, one complained to the *St. Louis Jewish Light:* "Whoever it was that voted to bring Betty Friedan to town . . . should be investigated."[33]

Television and magazines tended to present Friedan as a harridan or as a Jewish Communist. Broadcast the same month as her St. Louis trip, *Philco Presents the World Over: The World's Girls* sandwiches the attractive suburban mom quoting Ibsen's *A Doll's House* between a misogynistic segment about girl-watching across the globe and French actress Simone Signoret shunning feminism as too complicated for her. A *Life* magazine story, "Angry Battler for Her Sex," included photos of Friedan at home in Rockland County, and one of her dusting the Lincoln bust in her living room. But it also showed her for the first time transforming the 1950s cliché of the shrew into the passionate actor she had dreamed of being as a girl: "I'm nasty. I'm bitchy. I get mad, but by God, I'm absorbed in what I'm doing," she said.[34]

Friedan ditched her longtime agent Marie Rodell for Martha Winston at Curtis Brown (the agency to which she, as an undergraduate, had sent her stories). Rodell, also the agent of Martin Luther King Jr., Rachel Carson, and Pauli Murray, had not seemed wowed by *The Feminine Mystique*, and Friedan resented her for neglecting her when, before publication, she did not help her place excerpts from *The Feminine Mystique* in magazines. For her part, Rodell thought good riddance. In December, in a letter to the president of Curtis Brown, she warned: "I will be happy to split the commission . . . provided . . . this office has no further communications from or with either Mr. or Mrs. Friedan."[35]

# 6

## *The "NAACP for Women"*

On November 14, 1963, nine months after her book's publication, Friedan spoke at the New York chapter of the American Women in Radio and Television. In her trademark gravelly voice, she mentioned for the first time a new, independent organization for women that would address life after *The Feminine Mystique.* Eight days later, John F. Kennedy was assassinated. Although Friedan did not respond publicly, she was devastated. In 1966, she would bemoan the fact that "he was struck down just as he was beginning to move into his full human powers." And later, she would recall the indifference magazine editors had for women craving "political passion," a phrase she remembered him using. She lived political passion; Kennedy's death might have accelerated the urgency that she already felt about turning her book into a movement.[1]

The paperback revolution, which allowed ordinary readers to purchase classic and new works of literature for little money, made *The Feminine Mystique* an enduring hit. In the winter of 1964, Dell—the house at the forefront of this revolution—published Friedan's book in paperback. The first edition sold 1.4 million copies. Demand for Friedan as a speaker grew and she crisscrossed the country, talking to professional women's groups. An article she wrote for *TV Guide*, "Television and The Feminine Mystique," amplified ideas about television's role in consigning women to the feminine mystique. "Television's image of the American woman, 1964, is a stupid unattractive little household drudge," she wrote, pointing out that the genre treats women as badly as any minority, including making them the butt of jokes. Decades before Susan Faludi's 1992 exposé, *Backlash*, she asks network execs why there are so few female roles. "Television badly needs some heroines."[2]

The Civil Rights Act made its way through Congress. Its most divisive section, Title VII, banned racial discrimination in employment. On February 8, 1964, in part as a joke, Howard W. Smith, a segregationist representative from Virginia, offered to add the word "sex" to Title VII's racial discrimination. But Martha W. Griffiths, a Democratic representative from Michigan and the first woman to serve on the House Ways and Means Committee, picked up the idea in earnest. Although male representatives ridiculed Griffiths, she fought to include the word "sex" in the act and, two days later, it passed the House. The lawyer Marguerite Rawalt and Senator Margaret Chase Smith furiously lobbied for it in the Senate.

Friedan, who had been commuting to Washington to interview people for her second book, about women after the feminine mystique, pitched in. She told John G. Stewart, top legislative aide for the liberal Minnesota senator, Hubert Humphrey: "We've heard that some senators want to remove that amendment. I'm here to tell you, and to tell Senator Humphrey, that would be a very grave mistake. . . . The amendment . . . is one of the most important steps forward in support of American women that has ever happened. It must not be lost." Humphrey, an architect of the Civil Rights Act in the Senate, helped it pass on June 19, 1964.[3]

The success of *The Feminine Mystique* gave Friedan permission to experiment with her identity, sometimes disastrously. She went on diet pills, which made her mood swings more erratic. When she tried going blonde, the dye turned her hair green, and she soon retreated to brunette. After she threw away her girdle, she sometimes bought clothes several sizes too small—tight, low-cut blouses, hippie dresses, even a fur coat—some of the garments she had railed against in *The Feminine Mystique*. She knew what she liked, although the effect was not always flattering. One item in particular doubled as a disguise and a status buy—a reversible tan and black Rudi Gernreich cape she bought at Bendel's on sale. Gernreich, an Austrian Jewish refugee famous for the monokini (the first topless bathing suit), took it as his mission to eliminate society's ability to shame women about their bodies. Friedan wore the cape, which Carl described as "imperial," everywhere.[4]

She read *I Never Promised You a Rose Garden*, Joanne Greenberg's best-selling novel about "Deborah," a schizophrenic woman who has seizures. The book is partly set in Illinois. Deborah has slipped into a fantasy life after a childhood full of anti-Semitism. At a "cruelly anti-Semitic" sleepaway camp, a counselor and other girls ostracize her. She erupts violently. Filled with shame, she thinks she is "ugly" and tries to take her own life. But she is cured at a private mental hospital by a kind therapist, modeled after Frieda Fromm-Reichmann, the ex-wife of Erich Fromm, one of Friedan's heroes. Betty strongly "identified" with Deborah, Carl said, especially the seizures.[5]

Other books Friedan read made her think anew about the kinship between women's rights and civil rights: James Baldwin's

*The Fire Next Time*, which appeared in the *New Yorker* in 1962; Hannah Arendt's *On Revolution*, defining the American Revolution as successful because it uniquely rejected the oppressive attributes of the tyrants overthrown; William Barrett's 1958 classic, *Existential Man: A Study in Existential Philosophy.* Some of her actions between *The Feminine Mystique* and the foundation of the National Organization for Women (NOW) can be seen as experiments in synthesizing Arendt, Baldwin, and Barrett. One such experiment, her guest editorship of the June 1964 issue of *Ladies' Home Journal*, "Women: The Fourth Dimension," rehearsed ideas for her new book.

"Fourth Dimension" sounds like one of the science fiction novels that she would later gravitate to. But in 1964 the phrase referred to women going beyond the first three "dimensions"—wives, mothers, and homemakers—to fulfill themselves in work. Traveling around the country, Friedan met women who fell into this category, some of whom were older than her. As she put it in *The Fountain of Age*, these women were not "freaks" but seemed "more vibrant, more alive" than those afflicted with the feminine mystique. The article Friedan contributed to the June *Ladies' Home Journal* enumerated how women could give their lives a fourth dimension, including volunteerism, which she had condemned in *The Feminine Mystique.* Yet the "Fourth Dimension" issue did not go as planned. The publishers vetoed her idea to publish a Gwendolyn Brooks poem, which confirmed her belief that women needed more than a magazine to achieve equality. She didn't know what to do. As she wrote in 1976, she dreamed that she "was meandering, fooling around." She stood behind a curtain, unsure of herself, looked out at the audience and saw "thousands of women." The dream ended but in real life, she had to move forward.[6]

On July 2, 1964, President Lyndon Johnson signed the Civil Rights Act into law. A year later, The Equal Employment Opportunity Commission (EEOC) would be founded to enforce it. State commissions on women were founded, then stalled. Fearing retaliation, many female employees in these commissions remained silent about the sex discrimination they continued to witness.

Using money from lecture fees and book sales, Friedan bought an apartment in the Dakota, the iconic building on the corner of 72nd Street and Central Park West in Manhattan where Lauren Bacall and Jason Robards lived. She sold Ivies and filled the seven-room Dakota apartment with her Victorian furniture. She had the living room done in red flocked wallpaper, which a *New York Times* reporter would describe as "a dim ruby and sapphire Victorian parlor." She scattered colorful silk scarves everywhere. Ignoring the co-op board, she had sleeping lofts built for her children and painted over the fireplace mantel. She acknowledged her pre–*Feminine Mystique* existence by putting a primitive portrait of herself that her sister, Amy, had done, on the living room wall. In the foyer hung a *New Yorker* cartoon that Carl had given Betty. It showed several women robbing a bank. "The caption read, 'See what happens when you liberate women.'"[7]

The Dakota apartment was the first of many lavish expenditures after *The Feminine Mystique* that recalled her mother's overspending during the Depression. A more positive quality Friedan inherited from her mother can be found in her insistence on providing her children with the best education possible. That year, Daniel, sixteen, would start at Princeton, where he majored in English. (His senior thesis was a novel, never published, called *Problems*.) Friedan sent Jonathan, twelve, and Emily, eight, to Dalton, the progressive Upper East Side private school. To help pay tuition, she took on high-profile journalistic assignments, which frequently kept her away from home and from her family. As did her research trips for her second book.

She began to make new friends. She met Natalie Gittelson

while writing a piece about working mothers for the *New York Herald Tribune.* Gittelson, who lived not far from Friedan—at the Century, on Central Park West—had three kids under five years old and a job as special features editor for *Harper's Bazaar.* She wrote a popular monthly society column, "Needles and Pins." Friedan invited Gittelson over for an interview about the joys and travails of balancing career and motherhood. They would be friends for life.

Another real estate buy, a five-bedroom, brown shingled summer home in Lonelyville, Fire Island, gave Friedan an opportunity to decorate, hanging Picasso prints of bullfighters and clowns on the walls. On the island, Jonathan and Emily loved bicycling and clamming, but Betty enjoyed the beach. The ocean invigorated her. At a memorial a year after her death, the writer Phyllis Raphael told a story about how one summer night she, Betty, and a psychotherapist from Chicago set off on a walk to the town of Ocean Beach. On the way back, as clouds gathered and it began to pour amid thunder and lightning, Friedan started laughing. "I never saw anybody so happy walking through a storm," Raphael recalled.[8]

Lyndon B. Johnson, after picking up the women's commissions that John F. Kennedy had started, invited the storm walker to the White House with a group that included Ethel Merman. "We were never asked to do anything," Friedan complained. She began working on an article for *Cosmopolitan*, the magazine Helen Gurley Brown had just taken over, about one of the other women she met that day: the modernist architect Chloethiel Woodard Smith, also from Peoria. "Working Women: The False Problems and the True," put the spotlight on women—including Black and Puerto Rican professionals—to balance motherhood and career. It ended by praising Smith, "the brilliant woman architect" who designed modern, integrated, woman-friendly housing and reshaped the southwest quadrant of Washington, D.C., bringing a rare utopian feel to urban renewal. As Friedan wrote, Smith's designs "provide a blueprint" for women by replacing the old, sterile suburban houses with open living spaces.[9]

She began planning a trip to Scandinavia, France, and Israel. Instead, in the fall of 1965, she met Pauli Murray, then fifty-five, a pioneering lawyer and activist and the first Black graduate of Yale Law School who had been making a name for herself for years. A quarter century earlier, Murray had tried to overturn the ban on women at Harvard Law School. She had worked with Martin Luther King Jr., and shortly after the publication of *The Feminine Mystique* she had criticized the civil rights movement for its sexism in a searing speech delivered to the National Council of Negro Women. The speech, "The Negro Woman and the Quest for Equality," began: "Negro women, historically, have carried the dual burden of Jim Crow and Jane Crow." On October 12, 1965, Murray elaborated on these ideas speaking to the National Council of Women of the United States, at the Biltmore Hotel in New York. Murray criticized the Equal Employment Opportunity Commission and segregated help-wanted ads. She ended her talk by urging women to march on Washington. "I hope they will not flinch at the thought." A few months later, Murray, with Mary Eastwood, a Justice Department lawyer, published a groundbreaking essay "Jane Crow and the Law: Sex Discrimination and Title VII" in *The George Washington Law Review*. The essay argued: "The rights of women and the rights of Negroes are only different phases of the fundamental indivisible issue of human rights."[10]

Friedan read a *New York Times* story about Murray's speech and the women began to correspond. She confided: "I had almost begun to despair that American women would ever get beyond talk." She started to conspire with Murray, then living in New Haven, on the phone. Once Murray moved back to New York, Friedan interviewed her for her book and the two became friends. Murray introduced her to members of the "Washington underground," as she named first-wave feminists and female government employees frustrated by the government's failure to make women's equality law. Many of these renegades were using the phrase "we need an NAACP for women." They included Sonia Pressman, the first female lawyer in the office of the general counsel at the EEOC; Mary O. Eastwood, Murray's co-author on "Jane Crow and the Law"; Catherine East, executive secretary of the Citizens Advisory Council, whom Friedan called the "midwife" of the movement; and Michigan congresswoman Martha W. Griffiths, who helped add the "sex" Amendment to Title VII; and Richard Graham, commissioner of the EEOC.[11]

Friedan retitled her second book *Jane Crow: The Unfinished Revolution.* It connected the best of *The Feminine Mystique* to her Popular Front journalism. The catalog entries in Friedan's papers dedicated to "Jane Crow" include files on Lyndon Johnson, aging, homelessness, and the situation of Black women. Beginning in 1965, she traveled across the country, interviewing women including Murray, Helen Gurley Brown, female hotel workers, union leaders, soldiers, aviators, professors, employees at the Atomic Energy Commission, and workers at NASA and the EEOC. She studied the republication of Charlotte Perkins Gilman's *Women and Economics: A Study of the Economic Relation Between Men and Women as a Factor in Social Evolution,* with an introduction by Vassar professor of history Carl Degler, who would be one of two male NOW founding members. She titled the first chapter in *Jane Crow,* about the 1964 Civil Rights Act, "The Day The Men Stopped Laughing." The second chapter dealt with LBJ's tokenism.

*Ladies' Home Journal* assigned Friedan to cover the inauguration of Indira Gandhi and she flew to India for three weeks. Enchanted by the prime minister–elect's force and charm, she began to consider Gandhi the ideal female leader. "Her power with the people is unmistakable. I also was quite intrigued by the way she handled the Congress Party bosses at the Jaipur Convention," Friedan would write to Esther Peterson, director of the Women's Bureau in the Department of Labor. Friedan recounted Gandhi telling her: "The reasons . . . Americans cannot have a woman president is no American woman . . . reaches the age of 35." Friedan's four-thousand-word article "How Mrs. Gandhi Shattered The Feminine Mystique," which would run in the May issue, portrayed a woman who had surpassed any female leader in the West.[12]

Back in the States, Friedan participated in a Harvard Law School symposium, coyly titled "Women: Dare We Not Discriminate?" with Pauli Murray and Radcliffe president Mary I. Bunting. She began her remarks by comparing unfavorably the American situation to the Indian one and urged the audience to not tolerate discrimination against women. She rephrased the questions about female fulfillment she had asked at the end of *The Feminine Mystique*. "Are women truly free and equal then, if they are forced to make a choice that no boy or man is ever forced to make, that is, somehow implicitly to choose between the desired fulfillments of marriage and family and the full development and realization of whatever potential ability is in them in some serious commitment to society?"[13]

She went on to argue that unlike India, Americans had no image of mature women or men for that matter, that the only time women were free or equal was in young, romantic imagery about wedding nights and dancing. "With the fashions of today, one might say that a woman has to fight old age after fourteen," she said. Yet predictably, the young female reporter covering the event for the *Harvard Crimson* seemed to dislike her. Ignoring the fact that Friedan had just returned from India, she described her as having "rheumy, bulldog eyes" and noted that she sat up when the subject of female aspiration arose.[14]

Also speaking to the subject of "Dare We Not Discriminate" was Pauli Murray, who—with Dorothy Kenyon, a seventy-seven-year-old suffragist judge—was one of five lawyers who had recently won *White v. Crook*, an Alabama case in which Gardenia White, a Black woman, challenged the state law excluding women and Blacks from jury service. Although Friedan probably read Murray's brief, she still hesitated to launch the organization her "underground" wanted. She worried about both the necessity for it and her temperament. She would describe herself as not "an organization woman" but "a writer, a loner" whom other women were "maneuvering" into a leadership position. Yet many of her friends saw in her a galvanizing force. "She was our engine," said Muriel Fox, NOW's first director of publicity. She was "a catalytic agent," wrote Pauli Murray.[15]

Friedan turned to the Equal Rights Amendment, which suffragist Alice Paul, eighty-one, had been trying to pass since 1923. She raged about the ERA languishing and about the fact that the Equal Employment Opportunity Commission still did not enforce the "sex" part of Title VII. Yet she still would not commit to the "NAACP for women," as she remained unsure as to whether hiring concerns rose to the level needed to form a new, oppositional movement. She had to attend the third conference of State Commissions on the Status of Women to change her mind.

Held at the Washington Hilton between June 28 and 30, this conference, titled "Targets for Action," aimed to continue the work done by the President's Commission on the Status of Women under John F. Kennedy. But the first day discouraged the female delegates and Friedan, whom Catherine East, a coauthor of the commission report, had invited as a journalist. Late in the afternoon, it started to rain so the group convened in the East Room instead of the Rose Garden. Standing next to Lady Bird, President Johnson began by addressing "the distinguished and very attractive delegates." He took credit for Title VII, recommended that the women expand their volunteerism, and joked about his wife's interest in the grass in the Rose Garden. He listed accomplishments of the commission as if women's equality had been achieved and "figuratively patted our heads," Friedan recalled.[16]

The next day, the National Woman's Party, Alice Paul's organization, tried to introduce a resolution to bring the Equal Rights Amendment under consideration. They were refused. Surely irritated, Friedan invited Pauli Murray and a group of women to her room at the Washington Hilton that night. Murray joined, as did Dorothy Haener and Caroline Davis of the Women's Department of the United Auto Workers. Friedan had met them while researching her still uncompleted second book. There was also Kathryn (Kay) Clarenbach, head of the Wisconsin Commission on the Status of Women, Mary Eastwood, and Catherine Conroy, who worked for the communications union. Conroy and Clarenbach wanted to work through existing channels by introducing a motion condemning the Equal Employment Opportunity Commission. Murray, armed with a yellow legal pad, sided with Friedan's activist approach. At around 11 p.m., Nancy Knaack, a young dean at the University of Wisconsin sitting on the floor, dared to wonder if the world needed a new women's organization. Friedan shouted: "Who invited *you*?" . . . "Get out! Get out! This is my room and my liquor."[17]

Friedan stormed into the bathroom and locked herself in. When she came out, Kay Clarenbach defended Knaack. "I invited her," she pleaded. At first Knaack refused to leave, but she soon made her own exit. As for Friedan, in her 1976 account of the evening, she used macho language to cast herself as a martyr. "They [the other women] left, in what I felt was sanctimonious disapproval of *me* for suggesting anything so radical as an independent organization. And Pauli Murray, the Black scholar who'd triggered me first, and my indefatigable friends from the Washington underground, and Dorothy Haener from UAW and I just looked at one another and shrugged, '*Women*—what can you expect?'"[18]

In the chronicles of the creation of NOW, the outburst is accorded mythic status. Friedan's temper would become not just part of the origin story of NOW but an *idée fixe* about why the women's movement failed. As Judith Hole and Ellen Levine write in their classic *Rebirth of Feminism*, she was already "in some corners, greatly feared." However, Friedan did not strike out to shame women or betray the sisterhood. She did it to lift up her cause, to prod women to move, as she had.[19]

In Washington, the women gathered in Friedan's hotel room added a resolution to the conference document to enforce Title VII. The next morning, at 6 a.m., her phone began to ring. The conference officials had told her clique that they could introduce neither that resolution nor a motion to create a new movement because they were not delegates. At lunch, disgruntled, just before they left for the airport to catch their flights, the dissidents grouped at two large round tables. Friedan, scribbling on her cocktail napkin, "dreamed up NOW"—National Organization for Women—in capital letters. She knew it had to be "for" women. Its mission statement, crafted by Friedan and edited by Pauli Murray and a drafting committee, would read:

> We, men and women who hereby constitute ourselves as the National Organization for Women, believe that the time has come for a new movement toward true equality for all women in America, and toward a fully equal partnership of the sexes, as part of the world-wide revolution of human rights now taking place within and beyond our national borders. . . .
>
> NOW is the first feminist group in the twentieth century to combat sex discrimination in all spheres of life. . . . NOW is dedicated to the proposition that women first and foremost are human beings, who, like all other people in our

> society, must have the chance to develop their fullest human potential.[20]

Catherine Conroy slid $5 across the table as a member's fee, as did twenty-eight other women. The organization's first action was to send a telegram decrying sex-segregated help-wanted ads, a practice that would linger on until a 1973 Supreme Court ruling.

Of the original NOW founders, over half were white Midwestern labor activists. However, Friedan always wanted to include Black women. Before the conference, she sent a letter to Dorothy Height, president of the National Council of Negro Women, asking to interview her for her book: "I am well aware that the situation of American women as a group is not the same as that of the American Negro for there is, after all, the white women's vicarious share of the white man's status; but for all women in this country, there are still very basic barriers—some familiar to and some different from and harder to see than the barriers confronting the Negro—which keep us from full participation."[21]

After the conference, Friedan would send letters with similar language to other civil rights leaders, including Martin Luther King Jr. and Stokely Carmichael. She believed Black female leaders like Sojourner Truth would emerge to speak to her generation. The NOW Statement of Purpose, written by Friedan and Murray, observed that of the work discrimination cases concerning the organization, many of them "were Negro women, who are the victims of double discrimination." Indeed, by the October NOW conference, Black women, including Anna Arnold Hedgeman, the coordinator of the Commission on Religion and Race at the National Council of Churches and civil rights activist, would join Anna Roosevelt Halsted, Eleanor Roosevelt's daughter, and other white women, in leadership roles.

The advocate for Puerto Rican rights, Inez Casiano, became a board member. Friedan also sought male supporters, such as Robert Seidenberg, a historian, analyst, gay rights activist, and husband of NOW executive Faith Seidenberg. Clergy, like the Franciscan nun Sister Joel Read, became part of the organization. But few working-class women signed up; in 1967, around thirty members were lawyers or judges, and many women had jobs in media.[22]

Jewish women were also overrepresented, according to one estimate, at around 14 percent. Perhaps they chafed more from being consigned to domesticity because they were more educated. Or perhaps Jewish women were drawn to NOW because of a leftist social conscience, some tilting against their parents, others against Judaism itself. Many Jewish women, like Friedan, sought to participate in mainstream American life without feeling like outsiders—freaks, in her terminology. "Jewish women have energy, ability. They've been brought up to be good in school. They have all these abilities that then they're not supposed to use," she would say years later.[23]

Friedan angled for Pauli Murray to chair the board, but Catherine East and Mary Eastwood installed Kay Clarenbach, the cool-headed, Minnesota professor-activist, instead. In October, NOW boasted three hundred charter members, although only thirty would attend the founders conference, held at the end of that month in a room at the *Washington Post.* Friedan hoped the meeting would be as important as Seneca Falls. She felt liberated by being elected president, and she made her first public remarks about the connection between the anti-Semitism of her Illinois childhood and her fight against sexism. "When you're a Jewish girl who grows up on the right side of the tracks in the Midwest, you're marginal," she told a reporter. "You're IN, but you're not, and you grow up an observer."[24]

* * *

The media did not take NOW seriously. The *New York Times* story about the founders meeting ran a month later on the women's page. Other newspapers described Friedan as though she were still a Jewish Communist embodying radical views, disparaged her extremism, or ran salacious tabloid headlines about her group. "Fiery, explosive . . . expressing the most activist views." President Johnson ignored her entreaty to meet.[25]

Friedan would complain less about bad press than about the amount of secretarial work burdening NOW. Ignoring the naysayers, she immediately guided the organization on a dizzying number of public protests and anti-discrimination legal cases designed to invalidate labor laws protecting women as the weaker sex. Acting as the EEOC's enforcer, NOW worked to "put sex into" the New York State constitution, as Friedan put it. The organization protested to LBJ that despite the Civil Rights Act, someone had omitted the word "sex" from the bill on hiring federal contractors. They insisted that LBJ acknowledge women's right to equality and demanded that he hire more women in government. They tried to end sex bias in everything from divorce and alimony law to outdated work laws protecting women (as opposed to treating them equal to men). They fought weathercasters' practice of giving hurricanes female names. NOW picketed the Equal Employment Opportunity Commission to change sexist advertising guidelines, to pressure it to hire female commissioners, and to include women in guidelines for hiring federal workers. In all this, Friedan displayed a take-charge style. A classic example unfolded on February 15, 1967, Susan B. Anthony's birthday, when, impatient with how slowly the EEOC was responding to NOW's demands, she ran into the New York NOW office and called lawyer Mary Eastwood, then advising the organization.

"What do you call it when you sue a government for not enforcing a law?"

"Writ of mandamus," Eastwood said.

Friedan hung up, went outside, and announced that NOW would go to court for a writ of mandamus against the government for not enforcing the Civil Rights Act.[26]

Although NOW had few members, no staff, and a tiny budget, it spun off a legal committee, the predecessor to the NOW Legal Defense and Education Fund (LDEF). That committee filed lawsuits against the 1,300 most sexist corporations in America and defended flight attendants' sex and age discrimination lawsuits against airlines. NOW campaigned for the reassessment of divorce and alimony laws, boycotted segregated bars and restaurants, exposed sexist ad agencies, and compelled Lyndon Johnson to sign an executive order requiring federal employers to give women equal opportunity in hiring. While in these years Friedan was agnostic about her own faith, NOW convened a task force on women and religion. And Friedan herself led the organization in efforts to amend the New York State constitution.

Yet "the NAACP for women" also recycled certain conventions from the volunteer organizations Friedan's mother belonged to and which she had derided in *The Feminine Mystique*. NOW rejected applicants Friedan considered not important enough. At gatherings, she sometimes conscripted NOW members to formally introduce newbies, as if at a garden party. At an early regional meeting of East Coast NOW, a culture clash split Friedan and younger feminists already chafing at the limitations of her ideas. The meeting, held in the large apartment of Friedan's friend, NOW Director of Operations Muriel Fox, at 83rd and Madison, bristled with up-and-comers. Twenty-nine-year-old Ti-Grace Atkinson, a Ph.D. student Friedan championed because as she later recalled, she thought her "Main Line accent and ladylike blond good looks" would help raise money, would shortly become New York NOW's first president. Florynce—Flo—Kennedy, fifty-one, was a flamboyant young

Black lawyer who would soon make a name for herself representing the Black Panthers. During the Q & A, Kennedy informed the assembled that NOW "should be for Black Power!" According to Atkinson, Friedan and Fox looked at her as though she were "demented." Friedan believed that the divisive strategies of Black Power threatened women's rights and that Black women suffered as much from sexism as racism. In her 2000 memoir, she wrote: "black women . . . were being given a special African American version of the feminine mystique, which held that black men were hurt by the excessive strength of black women."[27]

In NOW's first year, Friedan pushed civil rights leaders to make them accept women's rights. Shortly after the NOW founders meeting, she had written Arnold Aronson, the executive secretary of the Leadership Conference on Civil Rights—the important coalition of civil rights lobbying groups—to demand that they accept NOW as a member. In her memoir, she bitterly complained that when she asked men at the NAACP Legal Defense Fund for help in this effort, they told her: "women are not a Civil Rights issue." Nonetheless, in the spring of 1967, to her delight, the conference finally admitted NOW. In the months that followed, traveling constantly, combining promoting NOW with journalistic assignments, Friedan often touted women as the next mass movement for justice. At Wesleyan College, a women's school in Macon, Georgia, at a time of regional unrest, she daringly predicted that her movement would be more important than civil rights. Shortly after that, she gave a talk in Atlanta, where she started a chapter of NOW. She wanted NOW to be integrated and she paid a visit to Coretta Scott King to invite her to be on the organization's board. (Scott King agreed.) Friedan also visited Jane Bond, the sister of the activist Julian Bond, at her Atlanta home. Jane Bond had read *The Feminine Mystique* and she believed that whatever advances women made in that era, "it was all due to Mrs. Friedan." But young Black women at the Student Nonviolent Coordinating Committee (SNCC) headquarters seemed less interested in NOW. That stung Friedan. In her memoir she would attribute their indifference to sexism, quoting Stokely Carmichael's infamous pronouncement, "the only position for women in SNCC is prone" (which a number of Black women in SNCC have claimed was a joke).[28]

Unlike NAACP, NOW initially lost many of its legal cases. In *Bowe v. Colgate-Palmolive*, in which a group of female factory workers argued that the company's paying them less because they could lift less was sex discrimination, the court at first ruled in favor of Colgate-Palmolive. (In 1969, the decision was reversed on appeal.) In the flight attendant lawsuit, the attorney for the airline originally proved conflict of interest—Aileen Hernandez, who would be NOW's first executive vice president, had worked at the EEOC. (The following year, the case would be resolved in favor of the flight attendants.) NOW struggled to pay the bills even though Friedan started many new chapters, inspired many women to join, raised some money, and led many guerilla protests. On Mother's Day, 1967, she and a group of NOW members tossed aprons, flowers, and fake typewriters at the White House fence. But she also found time to take the family to Expo 67 in Montreal, where they stayed in Habitat 67, the semi-communal complex designed by the young Canadian Israeli architect Moshe Safdie, who sought to reimagine housing in a new paradigm. Habitat 67's 158 apartments, each secluded from its neighbor by gardens and offering views of the city, the St. Lawrence River, or both, Betty would later praise as providing an alternative to the houses enabling the feminine mystique.

Women's Lib, on the rise, would challenge Friedan. By the summer of 1967, female members of SNCC and Students for a

Democratic Society (SDS) had been protesting sexism in their organizations for several years. Now they appealed to the male leaders of those groups to advocate for federally funded child-care; they began to talk about a new technique to liberate themselves—consciousness raising or CR. Yet Friedan did not initially register this new movement. She was maneuvering to force the *New York Times* to end sex-segregated help-wanted ads, leading a protest, picketing on 43rd Street, passing out leaflets, and marching into the office to give the newspaper the full blast of her moral energy. (The *Times* did not heed her for another two years.) She testified in the EEOC hearings on the airline industry with equal panache. At the September 12 hearing of Dusty Roads, a flight attendant who had accused the industry of sex and age discrimination, Friedan blasted airline executives for treating flight attendants like *Playboy* "bunnies of the air."[29]

Her personal life was in disarray. She was still taking diet pills, which aggravated her volatile mood swings. The previous year she had had what she later called "a sort of affair" with Tom Wolf, a news executive whom she had known since the 1950s. It ended quickly. She and Carl were still fighting, often brutally, and living separate lives—he partied and dated other women, sometimes staying out all night. Judith Hennessee, Friedan's biographer, recounts that he gave her a choice: they could continue their marriage as an arrangement if she let him handle her money. Or he would tell the world that his financial support had given her the freedom to write her famous book, exposing the great feminist as a fraud. Though she did not divorce him, she began to call Carl her "ex-husband."[30]

Her immediate solution was to travel. At the end of September, she finally took the trip she had been planning for two years. She went to Sweden, where she met the young activist Birgitta Wistrand. She spoke at a conference in Zurich, then traveled to Prague, where she "made a special trip on the way to the airport on Sunday to see the ancient Jewish cemetery and memorial which moved me enormously," as she later wrote in a letter to the Czech psychologist Hanus Papousak. She also went to Paris, and although she had reached out to Simone de Beauvoir through her translator Yvette Roudy, she did not receive a reply. Nevertheless, the trip invigorated her. European feminists believed in a two-sex revolution. She was most envious of Sweden, where feminism was accepted. She had met the activist and politician Alva Myrdal (wife of the economist Gunnar Myrdal) a few years earlier, and as Myrdal put it on that trip, "Betty Friedan . . . was surprised that she could discuss sex roles with the elevator operator." Friedan saw coed dorms and so-called "service housing," a communitarian housing offering residents paid day care, a co-op restaurant where you could eat with other families or get takeout, and pooled cleaning and gardening services. These arrangements enabled men to help with childcare to a greater degree. She began to refer to the changes she envisioned as "the sex role revolution," as the Swedes did. She also realized she had to get divorced. "She seemed unhappy," Wistrand recalled.[31]

Friedan dove into her most important political confrontations thus far at the second national NOW conference, held November 18–20, 1967. Her strongly worded President's Report, delivered in the Chinese Room at the Mayflower Hotel in Washington, D.C., warned against bias from both women and Blacks:

> Nationally NOW has won membership on the Leadership Conference for Civil Rights despite the attempt of some negro leaders to say that civil rights do not include women. We are now engaged in a dialogue with leaders of other civil rights groups, including the black power movement out of a belief that the question of full equality for women is inextricably linked with equality for all victims of discrimination. We have and must continue to resist efforts to use women to

> put down the negroes' new militancy just as we resist efforts of some misguided negro leaders to put down women.[32]

In addition to that explosive communiqué, under the beautiful domed ceiling, she advanced a bill of rights promoting two issues that would divide NOW: decriminalizing abortion rights and passing the ERA. The meetings began placidly enough. Friedan reported on what the organization had accomplished—membership had quadrupled!—and what remained to be done, pausing to praise Sweden for its "sex role revolution." After a short break, she began sparring with the assembled women about mandated pregnancy leave, which she favored. Moreover, although Friedan was aware that her bill of rights might alienate women in the labor movement, Catholics, and social conservatives, she blew up when some women present objected. She did not understand Robert's rules of order.[33]

Friedan's temper was not the only problem. There were serious ideological battles. Although some young NOW members supported abortion, a number of older ones opposed making both it and the ERA central issues. Pauli Murray argued that the ERA would result in the organization neglecting poor Black women and provoke ongoing controversy. (Anna Arnold Hedgeman, not at the meeting, agreed.) Furious, Murray would step down from the board of directors two days after the conference. UAW official Dorothy Haener was also concerned about the ERA; because the Amendment threatened labor laws designed to protect women, the union would not support it. But Friedan pressed on, insisting on the importance of both the ERA and abortion. Haener resigned from the board the following month and would describe Friedan's use of rhetoric to keep passing the ERA in NOW's bill of rights with militaristic language. Yet after the weekend, Friedan publicly spun the conference as a victory. Privately, NOW members' resistance to decriminalizing abortion convinced her that she needed a separate forum to support her position that it was a civil right.[34]

Although she appeared fearless, Friedan suffered from such battles. Her volatility contained a sensitive impatience with any possible contradiction. When women approached her to pay homage, telling her, "You changed my life," she sometimes nodded but other times snapped, "I've heard that before." Ti-Grace Atkinson recalled her temper as "frightening" and said, "people who would support her she would just humiliate." Some friends defended her, arguing that such judgments against her, though not wrong, may contain a gender bias. Or they noted that she couldn't hear well or that the steroids she took affected her. Still others speculated that the attention admirers paid her disarmed a shy woman. In her memoir, the writer Alida Brill reports that once, after she witnessed Friedan respond kindly to an acolyte, she tried to talk to her friend about it. But Friedan cut her off: she could not perform kindness on demand. She found devotion defusing and, according to one therapist, worried that people "took advantage of her good nature." But she often apologized to those she wounded, and she could show great sympathy. In a letter to her friend the lawyer Marguerite Rawalt, she pleaded with her to "make a real effort to understand the importance to NOW for the young women and students who are so eagerly joining our ranks," even defending women's liberation as necessary to NOW's survival.[35]

With the sexual revolution in full swing, Friedan continued to invite men into her national movement. She courted Robert H. Rimmer, the author of the 1966 bestseller *The Harrad Experiment*, a Reichian manifesto about the sexual lives of college students. Warren Farrell, a political scientist, would join New York NOW, where he shared his ideas about the need for feminism to help change male sex roles. And with her army, Friedan pushed to find new ways of protesting the stalemate at the EEOC. On December 15, at 8:30 a.m., she and a group of NOW members dumped bundles of newspapers wrapped in red tape in front of the New York EEOC office to support Pauline Dziob, then suing the National Maritime Union and Moore-McCormick Lines for refusing to classify her as a yeoman—a man's classification. Friedan also intended the action to symbolize the EEOC's failure to punish the press (especially the *New York Times*) for continuing to run sex-segregated help-wanted ads. "Title Seven Has No Teeth, EEOC Has no Guts," the protesters chanted. She had originally imagined a "more risqué version" of the chant, she told the *Times*. Four years after the publication of *The Feminine Mystique*, she sped beyond its vision into new frontiers for women's equality.[36]

# 7

## *"Our Revolution Is Unique"*

After NOW's tumultuous first two years, Friedan, then forty-four, urged women anew to push for legislative action to achieve equality. But she imagined women's freedom as both existential and *realpolitik.* She was excited about *The Active Society*—a seven-hundred-page tome by Amitai Etzioni, a Columbia University sociologist and former Palmach fighter—which defined one of the most potent human needs as the creation of an aware and committed new society. And she objected ever more strongly to the legal protections unions championed for women instead of supporting the ERA. In a letter to George Meany, AFL-CIO president, she scolded him for presenting the position of white-collar women as opposing those of his blue-collar constituents. Professional women were not against the Civil Rights Act of 1964 or any state labor laws protecting women, she wrote. But NOW aimed to give women the opportunity to choose what laws benefitted them.[1]

Two days before Martin Luther King Jr. was shot, Friedan stood in front of an audience in Iowa, telling them that women were reliving the struggle that Black Americans had already encountered. By the time she returned to New York, the country was in mourning. She would mobilize NOW into a frenzy of actions, the first of which—"Public Accommodations Week"—adapted the sit-ins of the civil rights movement to the women's cause. For Friedan, whom the Oak Room in the Plaza Hotel had turned away in 1964 (as it did all women between noon and 3 p.m.), the single-sex policies "exclude[d] women from the communication network and decision-making process by denying access for women to important business contacts." In New York, even before the "week" began, she targeted the Biltmore Hotel, sweeping in wearing her black cape and a red NOW button, flanked by fifteen NOW members. But it was after hours, and the maître d' told the women the bar was closed. "Don't worry, we'll be back," she promised.[2]

She started other NOW actions, including a nationwide fast. She marched in Coretta Scott King's Mother's Day March in Washington, part of the Poor People's Campaign. She carried a banner reading "free women from poverty NOW." She stood with Scott King's protestations about restrictions in welfare. At the same time, that spring, she sent six presidential candidates a NOW questionnaire on women's issues. Initially, only two, Robert Kennedy and Senator Eugene McCarthy, even replied. (In July, a Republican candidate, Governor Nelson D. Rockefeller, would answer all of NOW's questions.) Although NOW did not endorse a particular candidate, Friedan joined McCarthy's campaign, hoping to ensure support for the Equal Rights Amendment. She worked tirelessly for him. But she noted that while some female volunteers contributed seriously to the campaign, the majority "were present as greeters, secretaries . . . wives and girlfriends." Further, McCarthy's advisors, Tom Hayden and the editors of *Ramparts*, "scolded" her for bringing up "irrelevant" issues like women's rights.[3]

The press continued to deride her. It was not just that a *New York Times* article by then style reporter Charlotte Curtis called NOW militant—NOW members themselves used that word. Curtis singled out Friedan's attire for ridicule, describing her "purple satin minidress," and used the word "badger" to suggest that NOW's efforts to make senators answer the questionnaire was akin to housewives nagging their husbands to take out the garbage.[4]

Women's Liberation, an array of radical feminist groups focusing on female separatism and sexual liberation, had now become a powerful movement of its own. The essay "The Myth of the Vaginal Orgasm," written by twenty-seven-year-old activist Anne Koedt, arguing that women did not need men for sex, was a visible early manifestation of this new phase. But to Friedan, Koedt missed the point. "I thought it was a joke at first—those strangely humorless papers about clitoral orgasms that would liberate women from sexual dependence on man's penis," she later wrote. However, if she saw Koedt as "a joke," she regarded Valerie Solanas as a menace. The playwright, actress, Factory groupie, lesbian, schizophrenic, and author of the 1967 pamphlet *SCUM* (Society for Cutting Up Men) *Manifesto*, which supported separatism and misandry, threatened Friedan's dream for women.[5]

On June 3, 1968, Solanas, then thirty-two, added attempted murderer to her list of credits, after shooting Andy Warhol in the abdomen in his Union Square office. To Friedan's horror, several NOW members rushed to her defense. Roxanne Dunbar, leader of the radical group Cell 16, visited her in jail. At Solanas's hearing at the New York State Supreme Court, Ti-Grace Atkinson and Flo Kennedy, now influential voices in the New York chapter of NOW, both showed up. In a *New York*

*Times* article whose headline was "Valeria Solanis a Heroine to Feminists," they compared Solanas to Jean Genet; Kennedy described her as a Black Power hero and as "one of the most important spokeswomen of the feminist movement." Atkinson tried to convince Friedan that Solanas's imprisonment counted as an instance of sex discrimination and was therefore worthy of NOW support, much as the ACLU had defended Sirhan Sirhan after he assassinated Bobby Kennedy. Mary Eastwood agreed, warning in a memo that "Miss S. may be being smeared as a lesbian."[6]

Friedan rejected these arguments. In a telegram, she warned Kennedy: "Desist immediately from linking NOW in any way with Valerie Solanas. Miss Solanas motives in Warhol case entirely irrelevant to NOW's goals of full equality for women in truly equal partnership with men." At a New York NOW membership meeting a few days later, she resolved that "Ti-Grace Atkinson and Flo Kennedy were speaking only for themselves and had no right to use the name of NOW."[7]

Violence swirled around her. Dr. King and Robert Kennedy had been assassinated. All across America, rioters and looters protested the Vietnam War. Friedan, who admired Gandhi's pacificism, worried that Solanas represented a breakdown of order that would lead to carnage in the women's movement. And the violence in her tumultuous marriage spiked. That summer, on Fire Island, the Friedans threw parties, drank heavily, and fought loudly. Carl sometimes called her a lesbian. "I was beginning to have black outs," she writes in her memoir. She returned to therapy while Carl brazenly continued to see other women; it is at around this time that Betty went so far as to chase him down the beach with a butcher knife.[8]

In July, she began "Violence and NOW," an essay that came as close to a confession about her marriage as anything she had written. Acknowledging the radicals' support of violence, the essay seems to link the agenda of NOW to it. "Violence and

NOW" returns to James Baldwin, this time appropriating his ideas about the certainty of violence for Blacks. "Let us face the reality of violence, as it exists under the surface, even among women, in the suburbs of America today," Friedan writes. Although she reiterates NOW's distance from the man-hating of Solanas, she acknowledges that women have thus far hurt themselves by taking pills or fighting with their husbands. And she goes on channeling Baldwin, proclaiming that there might be "a fire next time." But then, entering the realm of fancy, she writes that the "Armageddon of the sexes could make the riots of Newark and Detroit look like child's play."[9]

On July 31 at the Republican National Convention in Miami, Friedan read "A Bill of Rights for Women," which advised women to "refrain from doing traditional, menial work" and demanded that delegates give women more than "token" interest, pass the ERA, support paid maternity leave and childcare, and provide education for everyone. She also borrowed the scourge of women's rage turning inward from "Violence and NOW." Friedan was made furious by that conference, although later she wrote to Kay Clarenbach that she made some excellent contacts "with some of the younger liberal Republican women in Congress." But in a long column in *Mademoiselle*, she fumed about how "both Reagan and Nixon had official hostesses who were a cross between old-time chorus girls or high school cheerleaders and playboy bunnies."[10]

The Democratic National Convention, in August in Chicago, made her even madder. Friedan, like many other Americans, recoiled at the police's violent suppression of student protesters, including her son, Danny, then twenty. The Democratic "Bill of Rights for Women" ends with the Armageddon warning from "Violence and NOW." Then Friedan delivered an intellectual Armageddon, expressing disappointment at how Democrats and Republicans dismissed "the invisible 51 percent" and raged that "the 10 percent of population who are black seemed more visible than the 51 percent who are women." She asked her now well-worn question: "Could women power emerge, in 1968, as formidably as black power?" She saw reason for hope in the actions of individual women, but she complained that no one had taken the steps necessary to make gender equality as important as civil rights.[11]

After the conventions, Friedan remained, as Noreen Connell, president of New York NOW from 1977 to 1979, put it, "*la pasionaria*." But she began to skip women's lib actions attacking conventional ideas of femininity. In September, she missed the Miss America protest, where women threw undergarments into the "Freedom Trash Can," crowned a sheep Miss America, and hanged pageant host Bert Parks in effigy, although years later she admitted she admired that action's "verve and style." Nor did she attend, that same month, the Colgate-Palmolive "flush in" at the company's Park Avenue headquarters to protest the so-called "thirty-five" rule—companies paid female workers less or denied them consideration because they could not lift over thirty-five pounds. NOW defended Colgate employees. Another case involved Lorena Weeks, a female secretary working at Southern Bell whom the company denied consideration as a "switchman" because of the thirty-five rule. NOW got involved in 1967, after the judge ruled against Weeks. (She would win in 1969 after she proved she regularly lifted her thirty-pound typewriter.) These cases led to the formal launch of the NOW Legal Defense and Education Fund (LDEF). "Our newfound collective strength, coupled with the potency of Title VII, was overturning laws," Friedan said years later.[12]

But the Park Avenue "flush in" showcased the power of the radical feminists. Kate Millett had sculpted a woman's legs and feet in high-heeled shoes straddling a toilet bowl, which, on "flush in" day, NOW members installed in front of the Colgate-Palmolive building. Flo Kennedy and others carried signs with slogans like "Cold Power versus Women Power," and "Down the Drain with Ajax." Protesters danced around the toilet and dumped Ajax in it. As for Friedan, a few days later she, along with a few NOW members attending a NOW national board meeting in Kentucky, made a detour to walk a picket line near a Colgate-Palmolive factory. She announced a boycott of all Colgate products.[13]

Friedan could sometimes sound strangely close to women's liberationists, as when she warned the *Washington Post* about an upcoming NOW protest: "I hope we are not going to encounter bullwhips of sheriffs, but we will really have to gird our loins to take on the really massive resistance." But privately, she worried that the women's libbers were stealing media attention from her centrist movement. When Ti-Grace Atkinson ran for reelection as president of New York NOW on a radical ticket, Friedan rallied her allies to help beat her former disciple. Consequently, Atkinson lost and loudly left NOW with Flo Kennedy to found The Feminists, a radical group that supported egalitarianism in its organization, the repeal of existing abortion laws (as opposed to their reform), and destruction of the patriarchy.[14]

Once Richard M. Nixon became president, Friedan redoubled her efforts to erase radical feminists. In a letter to her friend and NOW colleague Wilma Scott Heide, she defined the threat Atkinson and Kennedy posed to women's struggle for equality as "fairly serious." In the green room, before a TV debate with Roxanne Dunbar, a supporter of Valerie Solanas and the founder of the Boston radical group Cell 16, Friedan criticized Dunbar for her "scruffy" look, a gripe that echoed Miriam's carping at Betty's disheveled clothing during her childhood. But Dunbar's appearance was not the only thing that worried Friedan. At the third annual NOW conference, held at the Biltmore Hotel in Atlanta in December 1968, Friedan's speech, "Our Revolution Is Unique," dismissed the women's liberationists' pro-violence approach as impractical and derivative: "They tried to adapt, too literally, the ideology of class and race warfare to the situation of women." She advocated fighting for legislation and for women and men liberating themselves from conventional sex roles. Yet her centrism and incrementalism sped up the mass defection of young women from NOW. More interested in anti-Vietnam protests and her journalistic career than a movement geared to the concerns of housewives, Gloria Steinem, twelve years younger than Friedan, never joined NOW, instead becoming infatuated with the radical group Redstockings, founded by Shulamith Firestone and Ellen Willis. By 1968, Kate Millett, a thirty-four-year-old Irish Catholic graduate student and artist and the first chair of NOW's Education Committee, had drifted into radical groups. Robin Morgan, then twenty-seven, founded New York Radical Women with other young activists. These feminists rejected NOW because they condemned the patriarchy. But they also rejected Friedan herself. As late as 2016, Millett complained that Friedan was hypocritical to ask for speaking fees for her lectures while she ran NOW as the kind of volunteer organization she had criticized in *The Feminine Mystique*. Although this critique is not completely unfair, Friedan would not have seen it that way. She had three children to support, and she did many NOW events for free.[15]

Friedan invited Coretta Scott King to join NOW's national board of directors and backed her initiatives for mothers on welfare. More important, in her five most powerful speeches, delivered between 1968 and 1972, Friedan drew from the work of Black writers and activists, notably James Baldwin and Martin Luther King Jr. She seems to have been especially influenced by "Letter from Birmingham Jail," where King talks about fighting injustice. Later, Friedan would liken women criticizing her for joining the campaign of Eugene McCarthy to Black activists criticizing King for protesting the Vietnam War. And it was not her alone making the comparison. In the radical journal, *National Guardian*, published by her old friend Cedric Belfrage, a journalist mused: "It is not frivolous to call her the Martin Luther King of the feminist movement." Yet Friedan was unable to fully articulate why the women's movement mattered as much as civil rights. "Our Revolution Is Unique" acknowledged this problem. "Our own revolution is unique: It must define its own ideology." But the speech did so by first applying the phrase "invisible man" from Ralph Ellison's famous eponymous novel to women and then by hoping that feminism would develop heroes as great as those of the civil rights movement. "By 1972, we will have our own 'Julian Bonds,'" she proclaimed. Ironically, the resolution she pushed forward at the Atlanta conference, so-called Public Accommodations Week, copied civil rights, equating segregation with so-called "sexgregation," and alienating some Black women in the process.[16]

At the Cornell Conference on Women, held in January 1969 in Ithaca, New York, Friedan tried yet again to convey how *her* women's movement differed from both civil rights and radical feminism. She succeeded in the sense that the conference attracted huge crowds, launched women's studies as a field, and raised consciousnesses. Friedan's remarks, some of which were later gathered into a speech titled "Tokenism and the Pseudo Radical Cop Out: Ideological Traps for New Feminists to Avoid," also for the first time directly addressed women's liberationists, including Kate Millett, who was on the same panel. Millett had already published a stinging pamphlet on sexual politics that would become chapter two of her influential book *Sexual Politics*, and had delivered her own successful talk on it at Cornell a year earlier. Indeed, some of Friedan's most conciliatory language—"All of us have been thinking about revolutions in this era—how they are in danger of being aborted by Establishments, the traps we fall into"—sounds as if she was trying to forge an alliance with Millett. And it is surprising to learn that the person she tangled with most directly was not Millett but the thirty-nine-year-old sociologist Andrew Hacker, who dismissed *The Feminine Mystique* and the women's movement, arguing that the so-called "liberal arts fallacy" applied: just because people understood new ideas did not mean they would adopt them. "Men . . . will still turn into the typical sort of husband like their grandfather," said Hacker, complaining that Friedan was "asking us to give up a lot that is real."[17]

Friedan responded forcefully, characterizing Hacker as a slave to an outdated norm: "The danger of the 'liberal arts fallacy' (or the woman question as it's so often called) especially in discussions about the sexual revolution is that it's very easy to use words and psychological concepts and very glib formulations to somehow rationalize the status quo." She then maneuvered the conversation to how radical feminists shortchanged equality between the sexes by focusing on the female orgasm. Women's rights should be about more than "just simply when and with whom you go to bed," she said, although she could not resist a half joke which also demonstrated her credo that the women's movement should not make men the enemy. If she had to choose between having sex and making a revolution, she would choose sex, she said. Not only that: she wanted to give Blacks *and* women a seat at the table: "You will change society if you give women an equal role in it," she said.[18]

From there, she again defended NOW against charges that it only served middle-class white women by roping in phrases from the civil rights movement. "I do not think for women, any more than for blacks, separate can be equal today." She audaciously borrowed from James Baldwin's 1962 "Letter to my Nephew"—"*Whitey* has always spelled *your name*. You don't *know* how to spell *your* own *name* and until you *know*, you won't *know* the truth about anything." Then she upheld her own record as a champion of everywoman while maligning Students for a Democratic Society for treating women as second-class citizens. "It's important for women to learn to open their mouths," she said, adding that she had overheard female SDSers plotting to form a single-sex chapter because they feared if they "open their mouths too aggressively" they wouldn't get dates.[19]

During all this time, she feared "opening her mouth" about the violence in her marriage. On February 12, at the first event of NOW's "Public Accommodations Week"—the sit-in at the Oak Room in the Plaza Hotel—it threatened to derail her activism. Friedan was nowhere to be found when, at around 11:30, in the middle of a snowstorm, thirty protesters, many wearing fur coats and carrying protest signs, stormed the foyer of the wood-paneled men-only bar and dining room. They wore fur, Muriel Fox said, because they wanted "to look as if they belonged in the Plaza." Sixty press people—twice the number of participants, who included two men—had showed up. One protester snuck into the dining room, sat down at a table, and waited to be served. Eventually three others joined her. But the waiters, whom management had instructed to ignore the protesters, removed the table and the women were left sitting in a circle snacking on breadsticks, looking like actors in an absurdist play.[20]

Finally, at around 12:30, Friedan, clad in mink, appeared. She had wanted to skip the protest because Carl had given her a black eye and there would be dozens of TV cameras. But her friend Jean Faust, president of New York NOW, former drama teacher and onetime Elizabeth Arden employee, made a house call to help her apply her makeup. When Friedan removed her dark glasses to deliver her lecture about the Plaza's violation of state law on gender discrimination, no one saw her shiner. "This is the only kind of discrimination that's considered moral, or, if you will, a joke," she began, in the gilded lobby near the reception desk, before admonishing the crowd about how society accepted discrimination against women that would be unthinkable elsewhere.

The sit-in made international news and elicited negative comments from younger feminists. Gloria Steinem, then a young reporter at *New York* magazine who had demurred when Jean Faust tried to recruit her for NOW at the end of 1968, felt that the Oak Room sexgregation action proved yet again that the organization was too white, too middle class. A few months later, Steinem would mention Friedan only briefly in her influential *New York* magazine article "After Black Power, Women's Liberation" to say that housewives who went into the workforce, as *The Feminine Mystique* had suggested, did not discover equality but "found a lot of home-truths instead."[21]

Friedan believed in Public Accommodations Week because sex-segregated bars and restaurants affected businesswomen. But it was only one of the battles NOW was fighting. Another, crucial to ending sex discrimination, was legalizing abortion. The day after the Oak Room event, she learned that the only woman invited to testify at a New York state legislature hearing on abortion was a nun. As she would say: "Yesterday an obscene thing happened in the city of New York. A committee of the State Legislature held hearings on the question of abortion. Women like me asked to testify. We were told that testimony was by invitation only." On Valentine's Day 1969, Friedan flew to Chicago to the organizing conference of the National Association to Repeal Abortion Laws (NARAL), which she had founded with Lawrence Lader, whom she knew from the New York Public Library, and Dr. Bernard Nathanson. At the conference, held at the swank Drake Hotel overlooking Lake Michigan, she blazed through the keynote speech. "Abortion: A Woman's Civil Right" reframed the abortion debate by arguing for legalizing it as an intrinsic part of ending sex discrimination. She attacked male activists satisfied with merely reforming current laws and spoke in support of ensuring that abortion was at "the discretion" of the mother. "There is no freedom, no equality, no full human dignity and personhood possible for women until we assert and demand control over our own bodies, over our own reproductive processes," she said. Comparing *The Feminine Mystique*–afflicted housewife-mother to a cancer cell, "living its life through another cell," she railed against the perpetuation of women's role as a "breeding receptacle." She once again likened the invisibility of women to that of Blacks. She repeated her prediction from her 1968 DNC speech about the violence erupting because women were enslaved: "Like all oppressed people, women have been taking their violence out on their own bodies. . . . Inadvertently they have been taking their violence out too on their children, and on their husbands and sometimes they're not so subtle." In Chicago, she channeled her own suppressed violence into action, moonlighting from NARAL to join a picket line of United Airlines, still flying men-only flights from New York. The following year, the company would stop running these flights.[22]

Back in New York, Friedan attended the famous Redstockings speak-out against abortion held at Washington Square Methodist Church. She sat through a long consciousness-raising segment, where women talked about their experiences. According to the historian Rosalind Rosenberg, Friedan overheard her friend Barbara Seaman, who co-wrote a column at *Bride's* magazine with her husband, a psychiatrist, sharing details of her own abortion with a Black woman who worked at the Harlem Consumers Council. Friedan persuaded them both to tell their stories. And before the evening spiraled off into squabbling and name-calling, the media, including Steinem, still writing for *New York* magazine, picked up the story of "white, serious, well-educated" women who had been forced to such measures. After that, women finally testified in front of the New York state legislature, where they urged the repeal of antiquated abortion laws. The laws were changed in 1970.[23]

In April, Betty and Carl signed a separation agreement. On May 14, en route to a lecture date in Jackson, Mississippi, she made a detour to Chihuahua, Mexico, for a quickie divorce. "I kept my divorce as quiet as possible, to 'protect' the movement," she wrote later, worried that her enemies would use her failed marriage against the women's movement. She felt relief at ending the union that had caused her such suffering but mourned the lost time. Yet she hid these feelings. Instead, she began a crusade against the law requiring men to pay alimony in most divorces. (Meanwhile, Carl would complain that she asked for too much child support.) But she did not have time for this personal fight. She rushed to Washington to participate in an anti–Mother's Day protest against Nixon's tokenism in hiring women for his cabinet. Wearing aprons, the protesters chained themselves to the White House fence. Friedan derided the president and his wife, Pat, who said she did not believe discrimination against women existed. In New York, Friedan wrangled the female vote so that Elinor Guggenheimer could secure her bid to be Democratic candidate for president of the New York City Council. The sole female candidate in a field with twenty-one men, Guggenheimer lost. But she proved that women could run for political office by appealing to women.[24]

In this period, Friedan had her own parenting style, which on the surface seemed laissez-faire. She never did her children's homework. She did not get angry when Emily had parties in the apartment when she was away. Even amid her whirlwind schedule, she pushed them forward, often without informing them she was doing so. But her daughter made her rethink her Jewishness. The occasion of Emily's bat mitzvah inspired her to consider how such events might be feminist. Her sons' bar mitzvah invitations had read, "In the tradition of our ancestors we invite you to celebrate the thirteenth birthday of our son Daniel" or "our son Jonathan." Friedan considered the phrase "improving on the tradition of our ancestors," but did not follow through because "I was in the throes of divorce, and I don't think she wanted it."[25]

With Emily and Jonathan, Friedan left the Dakota for 9G Cooperative Apartments, a row of nine newly renovated attached brownstones on 93rd Street near Central Park West. Shared by a group of families and individuals devoted to urban renewal, 9G had started in 1964, when Jackie Robinson's wife, Rachel Robinson, and the psychiatrist Mel Roman and his wife, the artist Jo Roman, saved the buildings from demolition. The group was adamant that the project be integrated. Initially, the intention was that only nine families would purchase shares, but costs soared. Inspired by Le Corbusier, the architect Judith Edelman, then working with the group, got the idea to preserve—and widen—the exteriors while breaking up the interiors into smaller apartments for modern, semi-group living. After that, there were thirty-two apartments.[26]

In the spring of 1969, Friedan, who knew two of the families—the Fleischmans and the Mehlings—from Parkway Village, rented a duplex on the ground floor. NOW staffers Dolores Alexander and Ivy Bottini also sublet in the complex. After Bottini moved out, Friedan would take over the lease for her apartment, which had a beautiful chef's kitchen. She would stand there, eating sardines straight from the can, sometimes screaming on the phone. But she was also dreaming: "A community around a common garden, in the city, not escaping from it," she would write about her new home, the site of many NOW meetings. "How can we restructure our cities and suburbs to nourish and not block off the new human roots we need?"[27]

In June, Diane Arbus did a photo shoot of NOW members to accompany an article about feminism for the *Times* of London. Arbus took Friedan's photo from below using a close-up wide-angle lens and a flash, which hollowed out her cheeks and ballooned her chin. She would later complain that Arbus turned her into a monster. And to many colleagues, her increasingly volatile conflicts with lesbians made her one. On June 27, in San Francisco at NOW's first national board meeting on the West Coast, Friedan, according to Dolores Alexander, NOW executive director, worried that the press would take Del Martin and Phyllis Lyon, two openly lesbian members, as emblematic of the movement. At a "sexgregation" protest of the men-only Squire Room at the Fairmont Hotel, Friedan whispered: "Get rid of them."[28]

After the board meeting, Friedan and Alexander drove south along the coast to the Esalen Institute, the mecca for the Human Potential Movement (HPM), the influential New Age doctrine that some social critics blamed for contaminating feminism's communitarian aims. But for Friedan, the dive into self-help may have saved her life. Created in 1962 to celebrate Aldous Huxley's idea of realizing human potential, the compound sat on the rocky cliffs of Big Sur, high above the Pacific Ocean, on a 150-acre campus full of wildflowers, hot springs, pine and eucalyptus trees, and old redwood forest. Esalen offered Gestalt therapy—though not the version that Friedan had studied years earlier with Kurt Koffka and Kurt Lewin. This Gestalt focused on emotional growth, spontaneity, LSD, encounter groups, and "body work" (including rolfing, an erotic form of massage). Supposedly faster than analysis, Gestalt stressed humanism, integrationism, individualism, and the transformation of the physique to transform the brain. As Michael Murphy, one of Esalen's founders, said, it offered "more options than our parents and rabbis told us."[29]

Hungry for those options, Friedan gravitated to Esalen, one of whose founding figures was Abraham Maslow, the therapist whom she had half praised in *The Feminine Mystique* for at least trying to figure out women. Esalen also recalled the intentional communities from Friedan's past. It sponsored lectures by luminaries like Joseph Campbell, Buckminster Fuller, Joan Baez, and Susan Sontag and held forums on environmentalism, racism, and sexism. But seekers, including Friedan, came mostly for the Gestalt icons, such as seventy-six-year-old Fritz Perls, who had trained with theater director Max Reinhardt, once spanked Natalie Wood at a Hollywood party, and "invented" the so-called "hot seat" whereby he would tear down one person in front of an audience in order to build them back up. This last technique, called "skillful irritation" or "skillful frustration"—confronted patients to force them out of habitual defenses. Another Esalenite, Will Schutz, the psychiatrist who made encounter groups famous, also supported this sort of truth-telling.

Although it bothered Friedan that the female hippies at Esalen baked bread and bore children without fulfilling their "personhood," the community's excesses—Schutz's frankness, people swaddled in wet sheets, buried in silt, having sex in public—intrigued her. The encounter groups, nude hot tub bathing, nude "sensory" massages, and redwood forests renewed her. But the highlight of her stay was a consciousness-raising session for therapists run by the legendary family therapist and psychiatrist Virginia Satir, the first director of training at the institute. According to Dolores Alexander, there were a hundred people at the session, fascinated by Satir's passion for disruption and commitment to women's equality. Described by many who knew her as a towering figure in family therapy and a brilliant clinician, Satir introduced Friedan to the phrase "New Learnings," a definition for the process of change that became central for the feminist. Satir also insisted that Friedan remember the importance of individualism, chaos, and change, and she connected the leader to buried positive parts of herself.

At first, Friedan balked in the sessions, trying "to intellectualize" while more willing disciples shared stories. Then mid-session, she bolted—she had to attend a NOW meeting in Los Angeles and a champagne reception and NOW fundraiser, as well as do some television and radio interviews. When she wanted to return, the therapists voted to ban her. It took the intervention of Alexander and Satir to change their minds. Friedan stayed on for another month while Alexander returned to New York to helm NOW. Years later, Friedan said that Satir argued for her because she was "a change agent." But Satir's description has its limitations. Friedan arrived in California on the weekend of the Stonewall Riots, and there is no evidence that she knew about the protests in New York. Gay rights was never her focus. Indeed, over the next decade, she would become increasingly preoccupied with outsiders of all sorts, shattering the fragile gains of the movement she founded.[30]

With Satir, she concentrated on reconciling her painful past with her fragile present. Satir introduced her to "family reconstruction"—a group therapy role-playing technique designed to help patients see their families without blame by having them act out situations from the point of view of their ancestors. Friedan was so moved by this experience that later that summer, she brought her son, Jonathan, seventeen, on a two-week Satir workshop for families in the Sierra Mountains. They did a family reconstruction going back several generations. Friedan thought about doing a book on the Human Potential Movement. But in the end, she turned back to rethinking the connection between fighting for equality for women and fighting for her own liberation.

# 8

## *Sexual Politics and the Women's Strike for Equality*

While Friedan was working with Virginia Satir, Kate Millett published an essay, "Sexual Politics: Miller, Mailer, Genet," in the *New American Review.* The essay—a chapter of Millett's book of the same title brought out to great acclaim the following year—celebrated Simone de Beauvoir, attacked Freud, and argued that the patriarchy, embodied in the books of male writers like D. H. Lawrence, Norman Mailer, and Henry Miller, enslaved women. Millett blamed men for being part of a larger system responsible for sexual discrimination, abuse, and even rape of women. In language rebuking Friedan's dismissal of homosexuality in *The Feminine Mystique,* Millett applauded the writer Jean Genet for novels that "constitute a painstaking exegesis of the barbarian vassalage of the sexual orders, the power structure of 'masculine' and 'feminine' as revealed by a homosexual, criminal world that mimics with brutal frankness the bourgeois heterosexual society." Millett's stress on sexual oppression eclipsed Friedan's core concerns—"the feminine mystique," equal political and social representation, and reproductive rights.[1]

"I don't agree with much in Kate's *Sexual Politics*," Friedan would write. She worried it would ruin the First Congress to Unite Women, a NOW-sponsored event intended to unite all women. In a NOW memo, she wrote: "Young women only need a little more experience to understand that the gut issues of this revolution involve employment and education not sexual fantasy." But the activists Sidney Abbott and Barbara Love saw Friedan's scoldings as a betrayal and complained that she omitted Daughters of Bilitis, the country's oldest lesbian organization, from the list of sponsors of the Congress, as well as New York NOW.[2]

Held at a high school in Manhattan, the Congress drew over five hundred people. But Friedan became dismayed as she watched one member of the extremist group Cell 16 chop off another's hair on stage. Believing challenging ideals of female beauty induced little substantive social change, she would condemn the haircutting as "a hysterical episode." Yet she continued to try to bridge radical and liberal women's groups. She began the December NOW executive committee meeting in New Orleans with an entreaty for unity, then argued that because Nixon had ignored NOW's letters and broken his campaign promise to exceed the number of women that any previous president nominated to his cabinet, NOW would fight for female Supreme Court justices and women astronauts. But then unexpectedly Friedan said (in one account muttered) that lesbians who wanted to make their identity central to NOW were the "lavender menace," a phrase evoking the McCarthyist "Red Menace." According to the activist Sidney Abbott, she outed Dolores Alexander, then married and in the closet.[3]

That incendiary phrase "lavender menace" demands explanation. Friedan's biographer Daniel Horowitz argues that her roots in Popular Front egalitarianism made it impossible for her to tolerate sexual politics. Friedan herself sometimes blamed her own Midwestern prudishness, insisting that she wanted people's sexual choices to be private. Other times she contended that the lesbians were CIA plants, embedded to destroy the movement. Her supporters offer the most palatable theory—which she would also espouse—she feared that including lesbianism in NOW would alienate mainstream American women, tank the movement, and fail to generate the vast social changes she hoped for.[4]

Friedan uttered the words "lavender menace" four years before the American Psychiatric Association removed homosexuality from its list of mental illnesses. And while it is true that she uses divisive language to accuse lesbians of divisiveness and that she overstates her case about sexual politics distracting from women's economic and political equality, she was not completely wrong. In the forty-some-odd years since that moment, women's choices, especially in terms of their private lives, have expanded whereas the social, political, and economic equality for women that Friedan imagined remains elusive. Also, NOW would be the only mainstream organization for women—the subsequent ones have been either radical or right-wing. Moreover, it's worth considering whether the extent that "lavender menace" galvanized lesbian activists against Friedan accelerated their acceptance by mainstream feminism. NOW would formally welcome lesbians in 1971, whereas Friedan's slur, plus what her enemies called a "purge" of lesbians from official NOW posts (her allies deny such a thing ever happened), would marginalize her and make her a scapegoat.

She was under pressure. According to Muriel Fox, under NOW bylaws, the woman whom historian William O'Neill called "its [feminism's] Mary Wollstonecraft" had to step down from the presidency after two terms. Her second book was overdue, and she was toying with a run for the U.S. Senate. Aileen Hernandez, the favorite to replace her, was the right person for the job; her parents were Jamaican immigrants, she had worked at the ILGWU and the EEOC, and she supported lesbian rights. Even so, Friedan was loath to exit. Complicating matters, she had begun to suspect that a CIA or FBI mole had infiltrated NOW. She first aired these suspicions early in 1970, before she testified in Washington in front of the Senate Judiciary Committee that G. Harrold Carswell should not be nominated to the Supreme Court because the segregationist Georgia politician and attorney was also a sexist. Only a year earlier, sitting on the Fifth Circuit Court of Appeals, Carswell had refused to rehear *Phillips v. Martin Marietta Corp.*, a case in which the Georgia aerospace company declined to hire Ida Phillips. The company claimed her preschool-aged children made her unreliable, whereas they routinely hired men with children. Phillips sued; the ruling against her became known as the "sex plus doctrine."[5]

Friedan sent a telegram to Nixon protesting "the nomination of a man who has so little well being for the women of this country." But as she prepared her remarks against Carswell, Dolores Alexander gave her a heads-up: some government agency had assigned two NOW members, Rita Mae Brown, an out lesbian, and Anselma Dell'Olio, a feminist and theater director in the downtown scene, to seduce her. Although this seems lurid and far-fetched, recently released FBI documents show that the organization had started surveilling NOW in March and an operative had made contact with Alexander in June. In any case, Friedan's response to Alexander was to angrily turn on the messenger. The night before the Carswell hearing, she phoned her friend to help her copy her speech, but Alexander did not reply. According to Ivy Bottini, in her living room, she started a terrible scene, stamping her feet "like a five-year-old." "Dolores just stood there and just looked at her and finally said, 'fuck you lady,' and turned around and walked out." Bottini offered to write the speech in shorthand.[6]

On January 29 in Washington, Friedan spoke directly after Patsy Takemoto Mink, the Japanese American Democratic congresswoman from Hawaii, described Carswell violating Title VII of the Civil Rights Act of 1964 and the "sex plus" doctrine. In her unmistakable theatrical style, Friedan began her five-thousand-word remarks by repeating the concern that a justice with "proven insensitivity" to women whose employers violated Title VII of the Civil Rights Act of 1964 had no place on the Supreme Court. But she then displayed her instinct for political drama. After referring to women as "invisible," she pounded the link between sexism and racism, citing Swedish sociologist and economist Gunnar Myrdal's bestselling 1944 book, *An American Dilemma: The Negro Problem and Modern Democracy*, as an influence. She also borrowed phrases and tactics from women's lib and even feminist theater, dramatically using direct address to ask the senators: "How would you feel if in the event you were not reelected . . . "[7]

Laughter from the floor. Friedan pressed on, intent on making the senators feel sexism: "You applied for a job at some company or law firm or university and were told you weren't eligible because you had a child," she began. She listed the legal cases NOW had won thus far, and continued: "I can assure you that the emerging revolution of the no-longer-quite-so-silent majority will pose many pressing new problems to our society, problems which will inevitably come before the courts and which indeed will probably preoccupy the Supreme Court of the 1970s as did questions arising from the civil rights movement in the 1960s."[8]

Friedan concluded with a plug for the Equal Rights Amendment. Thus, she helped enable Carswell's defeat, which resulted in victories for working mothers: Harry A. Blackmun, the liberal mind behind *Roe v. Wade*, would fill the empty seat on the Supreme Court; Ida Phillips would win her case against Martin Marietta. So, despite the "lavender menace," Friedan continued to draw followers. She was the story itself—not just the teller. Audiences produced deafening applause after her raspy sermons either in appreciation of her message or in celebration of the fact that she had finally stopped speaking.

Back in New York, Friedan gave leaders on the NOW board an ultimatum: she would hold a press conference saying lesbians had overrun the organization unless they fired Alexander. "She tired us out until we capitulated," Fox said. At 11 p.m. one evening, "my husband and I were going to make love" when Friedan called to make her case. She was angry and hurt. In a letter to the Los Angeles–based feminist Sylvia Hartman, Friedan called the whole thing "a sick internal mess, which seems to involve mainly disaffected New York people." She refused to back down, especially after she learned that she was not on the slate of NOW officers for the next election. "If it is not stopped soon it is going to drive me out of the movement, which is evidently its intention." Nine years later, she would suggest that the board lacked confidence in her due to her unfeminine Jewish style. "It's all very well to, say, speak in a soft tone of voice—but sometimes you have to speak loud enough to be heard," she told the *New York Times*.[9]

By the spring, the Friedans' contentious legal divorce proceedings had dragged on for almost a year. Friedan owned everything, yet, overcommitted and struggling to pay the bills, she asked Carl for $100,000. The couple fought viciously over money. Muriel Fox recalled that during a NOW meeting, "Carl was downstairs, and he phoned me . . . 'I'm gonna call a press conference, the fake feminist is asking for money in our divorce.'" Then he disappeared. Eventually, the judge hearing the settlement ruled that Carl start by paying $300 a week in child support and taper off from there. But Carl did not abide by the ruling. Betty went to court and, in the end, the Friedans sold the apartment in the Dakota for $80,000 and the Fire Island house for $45,000, both less than their worth.[10]

On March 15, Susan Brownmiller's *New York Times* piece "Sisterhood Is Powerful" treated Friedan as a relic who "had not envisioned a movement of young feminists emerging from the college campus and radical politics" and "groused" about the lavender menace. It is too simple to say that Friedan was inspired by those words alone. Yet four days later, while flying to the fourth annual NOW conference, she remembered a letter that Betty Armistead, an administrator at Osceola College in Florida, had sent her about NOW commemorating the fiftieth anniversary of the ratification of the Nineteenth Amendment with a strike. Later, she conceded that Armistead suggested "the germ of the idea" to her. Nonetheless, *she* put the ideas together in her hotel room outside of Chicago at the conference where Aileen Hernandez, the new president, was to be sworn in. Friedan's speech, "Call to Women's Strike for Equality," which she delivered on the evening of March 20, at the O'Hare Inn, would cement NOW's future. She began by acknowledging where women had been and where they were, then repeated and elaborated on her warning about Millett's sexual politics leading to fascism (although she refrained from mentioning the younger woman's name). She went on as if oblivious to her audience, time, and space. In her second hour, she waxed lyrical about a nationwide work and sex stoppage which focused on three things: childcare, free abortion on demand, and wage equality.[11] "And when it begins to get dark, instead of cooking dinner or making love, we will assemble, and we will carry candles symbolic of that flame of the passionate journey down through history—relit anew in every city—to converge the visible power of women at city hall—at the political arena where the larger options of our life are decided." The words that made her sound like Lysistrata ended by celebrating the promised land women found and hoping for a better one: "I have led you into history. I leave you now—to make new history," she said. There was a standing ovation.[12]

As Friedan later said, "the incoming officers thought I was off my rocker" by demanding a huge action in five months. And yet, with national and international press in attendance, the officers had to enact her vision. In part because there was so little time, some NOW leadership took a laissez-faire attitude toward the action. Friedan championed the idea that it should be less a strike per se than a coalition of groups doing a work stoppage and suggested that it start at 5 p.m. to accommodate women with day jobs. Because she insisted that the march appeal to women from a wide variety of political perspectives, the first organizational meeting in New York attracted women's liberationists, nuns, students, members of the YWCA, and socialists. Friedan saw herself as the protector of the marginalized, by which she meant mothers, wives, and Midwesterners. "I kept moving to figure out new ways of bringing back the women the others were alienating," she said. She enlisted Ruthann Miller, twenty-two years old, a socialist activist, to organize young radical women and Karen DeCrow to be the strike coordinator.[13]

At first, the radicals and the moderates fought bitterly. Perhaps, occupied with these battles, Friedan chose not to attend the Second Congress to Unite Women, organized by NOW and other women's groups and held on May 1, at I.S. 70 in a dingy middle school auditorium in Chelsea. This Congress—like the first one—aimed to bring together radical and moderate feminists to talk about childcare, the ERA, and abortion rights. At least three hundred women showed up. Rita Mae Brown, recently fired from her job as editor of NOW's newsletter, and a band of radicals had plotted to subvert the event. Someone turned out the lights and Brown and the others, wearing hand-dyed purple t-shirts emblazoned with the phrase "lavender menace," began the infamous "zap"—a consciousness-raising session about anti-lesbianism in the movement. Many women joined them on stage, including Millett, who began to talk about her own sexuality. Some radicals distributed a pamphlet, "The Women Identified Women," arguing that feminism needed lesbian separatism. In the audience was Bella Abzug, a happily married feminist politician then running in her first primary race for Congress, and Susan Brownmiller, who had written about Friedan's "lavender menace" gaffe for the *New York Times.* NOW organizers tried to restore order, but the radicals prevailed.[14]

Friedan was spending all her time on the strike. She mentioned it in a talk at Alfred College in Elmira, New York; on May 7, six days after the zap, testifying at a Senate subcommittee hearing in Washington for the ERA, she "warned" senators that she would track them down in their vacation homes if they did not pass the act before August 26. Yet even as she was forcefully maneuvering for women's rights, she drifted into depression as her sons reached adulthood. "The divorce didn't end family life as much as the boys leaving," she wrote. Daniel had graduated from Princeton; Jonathan was in his last year of high school at Dalton. But Friedan's hard-won reputation would shortly derail the life of the son she called "a leader of men" in ways she had never imagined. Although an excellent student, Jonathan was, like many young people of his generation, a radical, according to his friend Jonathan Slon even inviting members of SNCC and CORE to speak at school. Donald Barr (father of future attorney general William Barr), then headmaster, disapproved of Friedan's activism, and sank Jonathan's college applications by referring to him as a troublemaker in a letter of recommendation. The only school Jonathan got into was Columbia. Friedan was devastated. Then she found out what Barr had done, and she was furious.[15]

* * *

She launched a "respectable, non-hippie commune," as she would call it, in a rented house in Sagaponack, on the South Fork of Long Island. Friedan brought the daughter she referred to as "My Emily" to the "commune" during the summer and later, on weekends and holidays. She adored "her" Emily. But the commune was an adult project, a refuge for writers and scholars living together as friends, lovers, and dinner companions who shared Friedan's yearning to "form community everywhere." Core communards included the *Look* magazine writer Betty Rollin and her then-husband, the writer Arthur Herzog, also a campaign manager for Eugene McCarthy, as well as the sociologist Si Goode, whom her friend Natalie Gittelson described as "the only person close to Betty who wasn't Jewish." The group celebrated marriages, commiserated about breakups, gathered for holidays, and wrote books there.[16]

Friedan occasionally whipped up the odd clam chowder or ratatouille. But overall, she did not speak domestic labor. While grocery shopping, she often forgot key ingredients. She preferred to delegate shopping and cooking to her fellow communards so she could rebuke them. When they made hors d'oeuvres, she would shout: they were doing it wrong! She never cleaned up or took out the garbage, and she often forgot to tell guests that they had to pay for room and board. In fact, the South Fork mansions were more Catskills boardinghouse than commune. Nevertheless, the situation endured, with different players and in different houses. It would include, for example, Ross Wetzsteon, the future theater editor of the *Village Voice*, and Michael Macdonald, the son of critic Dwight Macdonald. A decade later, Friedan would reflect that living in a group taught her that "nothing could be taken for granted" in terms of "sex roles." Ultimately, structural obstacles—like the fact that three people could not be on a lease or sign a mortgage—prevented the group from continuing to live in what she called a "chosen family."

She had fallen in love with Arthur Whitman, a tall, red-headed freelance writer. The couple spent a sublime week together on Sanibel Island. Now, she began a more serious affair with David Manning White—the chair of the division of journalism at Boston University—whom she encountered at a Gestalt workshop on Cape Cod. White was attractive, with white hair and a white moustache. Friedan saw him as her soulmate. Like her, he was a Midwestern Jew. He too had studied with Kurt Lewin in Iowa and worked as a journalist. He had taught journalism at Bradley University in Peoria. In 1950, he had published his most important article, developing Lewin's idea of "gatekeepers"—individuals who carry an idea from the margins of society to the center—in the media. The only problem was he was married to Catherine Wallerstein White, a beautiful chemist from a prominent family. But if some of Friedan's friends saw her affair with a married man arising from her insecurity with the opposite sex, her feelings may have been more adventurous. If she was trying to protect herself from hurt, she may have also been defying the stereotype of the forty-something divorced Jewish mother who couldn't get a date. And she also loved him. In her 2000 memoir, she claimed the arrangement was perfect and that she found what she wanted with David, who "had great joie de vivre and was great in bed."[17]

She continued her post-divorce reinvention through clothes. She wore the sort of flowing blouses associated with Romantic poets, or sheer shirts, or slinky dresses with plunging necklines. She favored maxi skirts over minis for their practicality and she styled her hair short, tucked behind her ears or blown out in the WASPY bob perfected by Vidal Sassoon. She could be persuaded to wear ridiculously complicated or impractical items that didn't suit her or the climate; in the middle of a snowy Boston winter, she wore high-heeled sling backs with skinny heels.

Friedan's friends could be critical of her appearance as well as her character, using (never for attribution) words like "ruthless," "self-centered," and "starfucking" to describe her. The first two words are qualities that in men are often considered prerequisites for success; as for "starfucking," while it's true that, once catapulted into celebrity, Friedan preferred to be in like company, snobbery insulated her from her demons. And then there was Friedan's style of femininity, which could be confounding to her audience and her associates. "She liked to think she was sexually charming. Not a vamp. Insecure and proud about being heterosexual, so there was a flair there," said Catharine Stimpson. Indeed, Friedan pursued men in an era when radicals like Kate Millett compared women in heterosexual relationships to slaves. One friend from the movement called her flirtatiousness "grotesque," arguing that it conflated anti-Semitic stereotypes of hypersexuality and sexist stereotypes about womanly purity. In *Vanity Fair*, Germaine Greer would describe her as though she were an aging coquette. Another movement colleague analyzed her seductive behavior as "reflecting an obsolete feminine ideal that unsettlingly contrasted with her professional stridency." Yet was Friedan's "man-chasing"—the outdated phrase of several so-called friends—a precursor to Erica Jong's "zipless fuck" or a result of her characteristic impatience? Was it retrograde, the product of lack of confidence, or ahead of her time in its refusal of what she would call the either/or choices society asked women to make?[18]

By the middle of the summer, the strike was coming together. Friedan hoped female TV anchors would stop talking and ordinary women would dump sexist items in Freedom Trash Cans. But tensions surged again on the hot afternoon of August 10, when Friedan, with Gloria Vanderbilt Cooper, Edith de Rham, and Gloria Steinem, hosted a big-ticket fundraiser for the Women's Strike for Equality at the East Hampton mansion of art collectors Ethel and Robert Scull. There was reason to celebrate. Two weeks earlier, Representative Martha W. Griffiths, the Michigan Democrat who helped pass Title VII, had collected enough signatures for a discharge petition for the Equal Rights Amendment, bypassing House Judiciary Committee chair Emanuel Celler, a Democrat from New York with labor ties who had blocked hearings on it for two decades. That very day, the ERA reached the House of Representatives, where it passed by a vote of 350 to 15.

Standing by the Sculls' pool in front of some one hundred socialites, movement people, and press—many of whom had paid $25 to attend—Friedan pitched the Women's Strike for Equality as "a bigger success than the Vietnam moratoriums." She introduced the guest of honor, Patsy Mink, the Japanese American congresswoman from Hawaii who had testified with her against Carswell. Recently, Mink had forced Dr. Edgar Berman, a member of the Committee on National Priorities, to resign after he announced that women were unqualified for executive positions because of their "raging hormonal influences."[19]

The radical lesbian and dance critic Jill Johnston crashed the party. In her account, she cornered Friedan into talking about "the relationship" between the gay liberation front and the women's movement. Friedan resisted, "her eyes bulging," Johnston writes, and snapped, "there is no relationship" before walking away. Johnston took off her pants, jumped into the pool in a denim shirt and her underwear, and began doing laps. When the partygoers ignored her, she removed her shirt—she was braless—and launched into a backstroke. Robert Scull fished her out.[20]

Friedan faced her own sartorial issue. Her friend Betty Rollin had encouraged her to buy a red maxi-dress with white polka dots and a low scoop neck for the party. As the *New York Times* reporter Charlotte Curtis described it, when Friedan stepped closer to the mike, her NOW button weighed down the neckline of her dress, exposing her breast at the same moment she called Johnston "one of the biggest enemies of this movement."

Friedan began an insistent chorus of "Liberation Now," a song she had adapted from the composer and children's book author Jacquelyn Reinach.[21]

We're breaking out of our cage of ruffles and rage;
It's time to spell our own names, we're people, not "dames";
We're more than mothers and wives with second-hand lives;
It's time for woman and man to walk hand in hand: Liberation, Now![22]

If the *Times* cast her as a buffoon and her party as a joke, other papers derided the women's movement, sniping that the party made less money than those for the Black Panthers or Cesar Chavez. But Friedan would write, years later, "I will not apologize for that hilarious, glamorous event. If you are serious about anything in America, to make it fashionable helps."[23]

Less than two weeks later she was in Boston, preaching at historic Arlington Church with theologian Mary Daly. "The mood of the strike is serious, determined, confident," she said. The day before the great event, the strike committee announced it was boycotting Silva Thins cigarettes, *Cosmo*, Prestine feminine deodorant, and Ivory detergent. In New York, Friedan gave a press conference with Charles E. Goodell, a Republican promising to work for new federal legislation "for the 53 percent." And then, on August 26, women all over the country marched in the Women's Strike for Equality. The largest march, in New York, official estimates count at 10,000, though NOW claims that there were as many as 50,000 strikers. Whatever its numbers, the New York march united fifty-four separate women's groups—women of diverse ages, races, classes, ethnicities, sexual preferences, political affiliation, and fashion choices. The High School Student Alliance, Older Women's Liberation, and Third World Women's Alliance were all represented. In her memoir, Friedan called the march the "high point" of her political activism.[24]

That morning, Friedan stopped by a model childcare center—a "Baby-In"—set up on New York's City Hall lawn. Women had parked baby carriages nearby; someone hung lollipops from tree branches. She gave a short speech about women's rights while the press took notes. Next, on to the Social Security Building at Federal Plaza. About twenty-five demonstrators milled about. Friedan got the doors open. "We are Americans—even though we are women," she proclaimed, insisting they had as much right to pay taxes as men. She had lunch at the bar of the Wall Street restaurant Whyte's, drinking a whiskey sour and eavesdropping on financiers' conversations. She had wanted the final leg of the march to start in Harlem to make Black women feel central, but instead, at 5 p.m., female—and some male—marchers gathered at Fifth Avenue and Central Park South, near the Plaza Hotel. Some women were putting up a symbolic statue of Sojourner Truth and a steel band played.[25]

Making her way uptown, Friedan boarded a bus, where women kept coming up to her to hug her. Traffic was so bad that she got off to walk the last five blocks. As she approached 59th Street, she saw a sea of women. The strike finally started at around six, late because of the size of the crowd. It stretched across Fifth Avenue although Mayor Lindsay, worried about rush hour, had only issued a permit for one lane of traffic. But the women took the whole street. Despite boycotting *Cosmo*, Friedan walked alongside Helen Gurley Brown, as well as her "beloved" judge and first-wave feminist Dorothy Kenyon, now eighty-two years old, Shana Alexander, Eleanor Holmes Norton (then New York City Commissioner on Human Rights), and Steinem. They moved downtown, following the route the suffragists took fifty-five years earlier. Some women dashed into the formerly men-only bar at the Plaza. Others carried a banner, "Women of the World Unite." Marchers held placards with slogans like "Don't Iron While the Strike Is Hot" and "No Vietnamese Ever

Called Me Chick." Still others yelled "join us." A few women paused to cut up a midiskirt in front of Bonwit Teller. Horns blared and some men heckled, but onlookers mostly cheered. Finally, they came to 41st Street, where a line of horses and cops in riot gear stood. They pressed on.[26]

The Women's Strike for Equality was the first women's movement event to get front page above-the-fold treatment in major newspapers. But the press coverage was not all positive. A week beforehand, a *New York Times* advance feature had quoted Friedan distinguishing it from a strike "in the typical labor union sense" and emphasizing her goal of including all women. Yet on August 23, a second *Times* advance feature portrayed her as a radical. Friedan repeated her threat that if politicians failed to listen to women's demands, "what could happen with women might make the race riots in Detroit look like child's play." (She later said reporters pushed her to say something extreme.) Instead of interviewing marchers, the *Times* talked to anti-feminists and patronizingly described Friedan as "a gray-haired combination of Hermione Gingold and Bette Davis." On the day of the march, a sidebar noted that she was late for her first press event because she was getting her hair done at Vidal Sassoon. "You don't have to make yourself look ugly to be a woman for equality," Friedan said. A few newspapers tilted more positive. *Newsday* quoted Friedan as saying, "this is our hour of history, and we are going to take it. I am not threatening violence, merely expressing determination." But television coverage trivialized the demands of the strikers, ignoring women of color, misrepresenting feminists' concerns as focusing on beauty standards, and presenting Friedan as a virago.[27]

The rally at Bryant Park was ecstatic, a Woodstock or Stonewall for women. Thousands of people gathered behind the main branch of the New York Public Library to hear the leaders of the women's movement speak. Of Friedan's children, though, only Jonathan was there. As he would later tell his cousin Emily Bazelon, "This was the moment I realized who she was."[28]

At a podium on a stage in the middle of the park, Friedan stood among a who's who of women's liberationists and movement bigwigs. Gloria Steinem, because of her media visibility, had been asked by the strike coordinating committee to deliver introductory remarks. Bella Abzug, soon to become the second Jewish congresswoman, followed. Next Eleanor Holmes Norton, then an ACLU attorney, spoke eloquently against racism, poverty, anti-Semitism, and sexism. Wearing African dress, she concluded with the powerful remark, "black women have a stake in the fight for equality for women because they are the most exploited women." Dorothy Height, of the National Council of Negro Women, also spoke. The evening gave voice to radicals too. The socialist activist Ruthann Miller and the strike coordinator, predicted "complete and total revolution." Kate Millett inspired the crowd with uplifting words for women, lesbians, and prostitutes—"sexism oppresses homosexual people." An unnamed radical feminist from the Third World Women's Alliance, which had marched carrying a banner protesting the federal manhunt under way for Angela Davis, the assistant professor of philosophy allegedly involved in a Marin County courthouse shooting, addressed poverty and race and demanded that women smash capitalism. "HANDS OFF ANGELA DAVIS!" the banner read.[29]

When Friedan took the podium, she changed the subject—she would never support Angela Davis. Instead, she delivered an electrifying unifying message in her trademark gravelly voice. "We tonight became the greatest new force in politics. . . . We learn . . . what none of us dared to hope—the power of our solidarity." She held up men and women. She said that, if anything, the enemy was "our own lack of confidence"—and warned of the dangers of sexual politics. According to one reporter, she seemed at times on the verge of tears. Then, unexpectedly, she ended by referring to the Jewish morning blessing: "In . . . the religion of my ancestors, there was a prayer that Jewish men said every morning, 'thank Thee Lord, I was not born a woman.'" She added, "Today . . . I feel . . . I feel . . . for the first time I feel absolutely sure that all women are going to be able to say, as I say tonight, 'Thank Thee Lord, that I was born a woman.'"[30]

Applause erupted. Later, Friedan would say she was the last speaker. In fact, Martha Shelley, a twenty-seven-year-old Jewish lesbian, closed the evening. "We want your bodies on the line," she yelled. The rally ended with a song from *The Mod Donna*, a feminist musical that had played at the Public Theater in May, and a chorus of "Liberation Now."[31]

The Women's Strike for Equality accelerated the feminist incursion into American society. Historian Ruth Rosen has called it "a stunning success." New York City mayor John Lindsay, governor of New York Nelson D. Rockefeller, and President Nixon all affirmed the day's importance. (Actually Lindsay sent an aide to declare it thusly in his stead.) But the victory was not just symbolic. Bella Abzug would push through Congress a resolution to name August 26 Women's Equality Day. In 1966, Friedan had started NOW with twenty-eight women in Washington. And while before the strike, NOW had boasted at most three thousand national members, in the ensuing weeks, the number of women joining would grow by 50 percent. Soon, passage of the ERA was in sight. "It succeeded beyond our wildest dreams," Friedan would say. But *Time* magazine put Kate Millett, whose bestselling *Sexual Politics* Doubleday published a few weeks earlier, on its August 31 cover as the face of the movement. The media had anointed a younger, more telegenic leader, fulfilling Friedan's prediction.[32]

In the following months and years, many Jewish women would develop new ideas about the relationship between feminism and Judaism. Some, like Shulamith Firestone, who wrote *The Dialectic of Sex: The Case for a Feminist Revolution*, rejected Friedan, the family, motherhood, and childbearing. But many other Jewish feminists would simply ignore her and her Bryant Park remarks. Neither the mostly Jewish founders of *Ms.* magazine and *Our Bodies, Ourselves*—two successful feminist publishing experiments of the early 1970s—nor the secular Jewish female leftist magazine *Brooklyn Bridge* named Friedan as inspiration. Not long after Bryant Park, Trude Weiss-Rosmarin, the editor of the monthly magazine the *Jewish Spectator*, argued that one source of many Jewish women's silence on Friedan was her disapproval of housework: "The real challenge of women's liberation is not taking women out of the home but emancipating the homemaker as homemaker by placing dignity on her work, instead of derogating it." Years later, Orthodox Jewish feminist Blu Greenberg gave another reason for the indifference of devout Jews—Friedan's name simply did not "mean me."[33]

As for Friedan, she returned to promoting labor and economic issues that would benefit women. At the end of September, she flew to Washington to testify at a hearing of the Senate Select Committee on Nutrition and Human Needs (also called the McGovern Committee, after George McGovern, the chair) charged with studying hunger and poverty in America. She blamed the oppression of middle-class housewives on male architects and urban planners who had forced them into "sexual ghettoes." She combined her condemnation of the suburban open plan home from *The Feminine Mystique*, her commitment to helping poor women, and Paul and Percival Goodman's 1947 book *Communitas*, which proposed utopian communal spaces to end segregation and the inhumanity of modern cities. She delivered a dense, sometimes garbled testimony of more than four thousand words, arguing that suburban housing worsened the oppression of women: "I am delighted to be here to speak for the truly silent majority in this country who have no voice at all in the conditions in which they are housed, whether we are talking about city slum, inner city ghetto, or the sexual ghetto of the suburbs" she began. "I submit that an obsolete concept of women . . . I call the feminine mystique, is structured into the stones and wood and concrete block steel and girders of every suburb of private housing and public housing." She talked for ten minutes before Senator Charles Percy, an Illinois Republican, broke in. "I will be finished in a minute, Senator," she said testily, an exchange captured on national television. She returned to her monologue, recommending that Americans adapt the "service housing" she had seen in Sweden a few years earlier. When McGovern expressed skepticism that such a thing would work in America, she accused him of turning her idea into a cartoon: "The image that you portray of a day-care center sounds to me like some Sing Sing."[34]

Yet her public ferocity sometimes hid private suffering. As the journalist Lyn Tornabene reported, at Augsburg College, in Minneapolis, when she learned that her ex-lover, Arthur Whitman, who had been ill with hepatitis, had died, she broke down sobbing right before her talk. During his illness, she had organized a blood drive, collecting eighty quarts of blood for transfusions. But despite her sorrow, she recovered to give a rousing speech. From there, back to New York and on to deliver a keynote at the "Women's Teach-In" at Wayne State in Detroit, where she again expressed her support for funded day care, "service housing," and welfare alongside of Dorothy Haener of the UAW, Martha Griffiths, Frances Beale, and Beulah Sanders, vice president of the National Welfare Rights Organization. But Friedan clashed with anti-ERA labor activist Myra Wolfgang, whom she called an "Aunt Tom," a phrase dating back to the Black newspaper the *Chicago Defender* in the 1950s but which, after the rise of Black Power, white feminists appropriated as a term for a woman who acted subservient to men or betrayed her sisters. (Wolfgang called Friedan an "Aunt Tom" in return.)[35]

On November 29, the *New York Times Magazine* published a lengthy unflattering profile, "Mother Superior to Women's Lib." Written by thirty-two-year-old Paul Wilkes, the hatchet job begins with an account of how Friedan's "long" nose ostracized her in school. Wilkes describes Friedan as a slovenly shrew with a Haitian maid and quotes her spouting Freudian jargon about Miriam. "She belittled, cut down my father because she had no use for her terrific energies. It's a female disorder I call impotent rage." Wilkes also reveals, for the first time in the *New York Times*, details about the marital violence, including her throwing a mirror at Carl. The piece additionally includes condescending quotes from several of Friedan's supposed friends and allies, including Gloria Steinem, who claimed that for the "mother superior," the women's movement compensated for personal wounds: "She has undertaken the immense job of bringing up the status of women so that love can succeed. Hopefully so that her own emotional needs as a woman can eventually be fulfilled." Allowing that Friedan "held the shaky coalition of women's groups together" by becoming "some great Shakespearean performer," Wilkes ends his portrait with his subject comparing herself to Joan of Arc facing the flames—"All that I am, I will not deny."[36]

In an interview with the quarterly *Social Policy* shortly after Wilkes's article appeared, Friedan dismissed Kate Millett's theories as "highly diversionary" and repeated her argument that a women's movement grounded in sexual politics would lead to fascism. It "may even provide good soil for fascist, demagogic appeals based on hatred" and "will produce no significant changes." She did not see that sexual politics, which had contributed to her exit from the presidency of NOW, would drive her out of the organization.[37]

* * *

On December 12, she stood in the sleet in front of Gracie Mansion at a protest for childcare and abortion reform that she had organized. She had hoped it would be a sequel to the August 26 strike, attracting thousands of supporters. But only three hundred marchers showed. Bella Abzug and Shirley Chisholm did not seem to be there. Someone handed Friedan a lavender armband, a symbol of support for Kate Millett, whom *Time* magazine had dethroned as the spokeswoman for feminism after she admitted she might be bisexual. While Gloria Steinem and Flo Kennedy donned their armbands, Friedan either stomped on hers or dropped it, depending on whose story you believe. She later explained that rally organizers had ambushed her with the "purple armband caper." Privately, Friedan told Millett, whom she respected despite abhorring "sexual politics," that radicals were exploiting her.[38]

In her 1974 memoir, *Flying*, Millett describes the lookism Friedan inspired in her peers in those years: "her face, haggard, beautiful, ugly, in the center the great nose that they all hate, so grandly Jewish." Perhaps anti-Semitism explains why it would take the fight for the ERA, her struggle with her own daughter, and a visit to Israel, to concede that lesbians deserved what she had demanded for all women—equal rights.[39]

# 9

## *"I've Been More of a Jewish Mother to the Movement Than I Have to My Own Children"*

In 1971, one year into the Me Decade, Friedan, fifty, found herself alienated from the women's movement. She was a divorcée with grown children at a time when many celebrities in women's lib—Kate Millett, Andrea Dworkin, Gloria Steinem, Shulamith Firestone—were unmarried, in (for her) unconventional marriages, or childless. Of course, there were women, like Bella Abzug, who were happily married. Divorced and premenopausal, Friedan was caught between the wrath of her teenaged daughter, Emily, and that of her movement sisters and daughters. For her, the personal had become political in a particularly harsh way. And then two things happened: first, three days after her birthday, in a February 7 *Washington Post* story, Carl, himself fifty, boasted about his new bride—a thirty-six-year-old blonde model named Norene—making him chicken soup and shining his shoes. In the *Boston Globe*, Friedan snapped her retort: "I can barely shine my own shoes." Second, Germaine Greer began her U.S. book tour. Greer had published *The Female Eunuch* the previous year to much acclaim. The American media crowned another young, sexy feminist. Friedan threw Greer a book party at 9G, but the provocateur had repaid her with a cruel anecdote about her looks and by befriending her nemesis, Flo Kennedy.[1]

Betty started "Betty Friedan's Notebook" for *McCall's* to push back. In her first column, defining herself as both a "revolutionary" and an "American pragmatist," she takes a swipe at Kate Millett—the separatist daughter who had attacked D. H. Lawrence in *Sexual Politics*—by citing *Women in Love* as her inspiration and guide. In her second column, "What's the Point of Making It If You Can't Celebrate Being 50?," she complains that the women's movement burdened her more than her own family: "Sometimes I feel like a mother with a million children all crying 'help!'" Still the beleaguered mom enjoyed her new, liberated post-marriage freedom: Drinking with a movie producer in a hotel she writes, "I feel glorious." She mentions her lover, "David," and remarks upon how this birthday had allowed her to make new personal and political discoveries. "I celebrate putting it all together finally, this half century that's me, all of it, pains and roots in Peoria, Jewish ancestors . . . the net I've cast for herstory."[2]

Privately she fumed about the slow crawl of women's equality in mainstream politics. In March, the New Democratic Coalition—a group of progressive politicians started in 1968—invited her to their New York convention of judicial delegates and then ignored her. If she convinced 7.9 million *McCall's* readers that she could be a mother and the mother of the movement, she had not persuaded male progressives that women's rights deserved as much attention as civil rights. The writer Claudia Dreifus wrote that Friedan "was too old, too bourgeois, too organization-conscious" to lead. New York intellectuals—the secular, mostly Jewish clique identified with *Partisan Review* that defined postwar culture in America—mostly ignored her. But she kept trying to "shift the paradigm," as she might have said, even at unlikely forums like Town Hall, a benefit for the women's movement that Germaine Greer, one of the panelists, dubbed "Town Bloody Hall." Held on April 30, 1971, and affiliated with the powerful *New York Review of Books*, Town Hall was organized after Norman Mailer attacked Kate Millett in his article "Prisoner of Sex" in *Harper's* magazine. Millett, Steinem, and Robin Morgan declined to participate. Diana Trilling, wife of the critic Lionel Trilling, took over as moderator after Hannah Arendt begged off. Friedan was not on the panel but sat in a special invited section of the audience among the likes of Susan Sontag, Arthur Schlesinger Jr., Jules Feiffer, Norman Podhoretz, Philip Roth, and Elizabeth Hardwick.[3] The panelists were Mailer, Germaine Greer, Jacqui Ceballos of New York NOW, and the writer and anti-Friedanite Jill Johnston. Born in 1905, sixteen years before Friedan, Diana Trilling, the moderator, disliked feminism's shrill tone but believed in its principles. However, she was friends with Mailer and admired some of what he wrote, especially about D. H. Lawrence. Germaine Greer was a six-foot-tall Australian ex-actress whose book, *The Female Eunuch*, shocked American readers with its sexual politics-on-steroids argument.

The panelists' attire was part of the show. Trilling wore a skirt and blouse and had her hair up. Greer sat next to Mailer in a sleeveless maxi-dress with a deep V-neck, a long chain with a pendant of the Venus symbol, and rings on every finger. Johnston was dressed in bell-bottom jeans, a denim jacket patched with stars and the Union Jack, and dark glasses. Ceballos sported a black pants suit with a top embellished with gold braid. As for Friedan, the radical feminist journal *off our backs* noticed her in the audience in a "fur trimmed tie-dyed floor length velvet coat" and white lipstick.[4]

Ceballos began with a list of NOW's accomplishments. But

her sincere description of the organization liberating the entire spectrum of women from welfare mothers to Vassar coeds and divorced, working moms, was drowned out by the poet Gregory Corso screaming from the audience about the rights of "all humanity" before stomping out. Friedan added from her seat, "men are as much victims as women!" The panelists ignored her remark, though Mailer asked (rhetorically) if NOW "could make life less boring." Greer lectured about the sins of male writers: "The paths of masculine artists are strewn with the husks of people worn out . . . by his ego" and quoted Freud. Then Jill Johnston recited a bawdy performance poem that began "all women are lesbians." She kept reading until two women from the audience joined her onstage in a mock orgy. "Be a lady," Mailer scolded, using a word he fell back on repeatedly during the evening.[5]

When the question-and-answer period began, Friedan agreed with Mailer that the movement should also speak to the challenges men encountered. She rocked back and forth excitedly in her seat. "Be accurate, Betty!" Mailer commanded. She replied, "Norman, I will define accuracy for myself . . . !" and continued, in sing-songy tones, to address his complaint that feminism bored him:[6]

> I was wondering if it might possibly, even tonight, indicate that the world might be much less boring when instead of the monolithic, changeless eternal face of Eve who never transcends her biological self we finally reach the beginning point of self-definition which you are reacting to somewhat like uh your predecessors 100 years ago who said the dog talks! you know. That a woman should be here talking at all is something you're finding a little hard to take! But that we talk in different tones! We don't all agree! We have the right to define our own differences and quarrel over our own accuracies and find our own ideologies and even you might find that less boring in the end.

Mailer put her down. "You're talking about it [women's liberation] as if I was opposed to it which I never was." The Q & A moved on. Sontag objected to Mailer's use of the phrase "lady writer." Cynthia Ozick silenced him by ridiculing his infamous remark, "A good novelist can do without everything but the remnant of his balls."

"Mr. Mailer," she asked, "when you dip your balls in ink, what color ink is it?"

Town Hall ended with the critic Anatole Broyard trying to provoke Germaine Greer into telling an erotic story. Friedan's solid-minded plea to imagine feminism as more than men versus women could not compete.

The upcoming presidential election made urgent the fulfillment of an idea Friedan had been thinking about since 1968—ensuring women had an equal voice in the political process. She had begun to scheme about forming an organization dedicated to that goal, which she called the National Women's Political Caucus (NWPC). An early meeting happened at Elinor Guggenheimer's apartment, where the fighting also began. Somewhat later, Bella Abzug, newly elected to Congress, thinking along the same lines, drafted Gloria Steinem to form a similar group. Immediately tension arose among Steinem, Abzug, and Friedan. From Friedan's perspective, "Battling Bella" had betrayed the women's movement at the Second Congress to Unite Women, where she became an ally of lesbians protesting the phrase "lavender menace." Among her many sins, Steinem, working on a sample insert of *Ms.* magazine, which would be published in December, had not asked Friedan to write for it. So, although Friedan, Steinem, and Abzug joined forces in the spring of 1971, even before the founding meeting of NWPC on June 9 in Washington, D.C., fights erupted about who headed the organization and what direction it should take. Friedan, who claimed to have made it possible for Abzug to get elected to Congress, accused her co-founder of stealing her idea. In 1976, she would write, Abzug was "determined to blot me out of existence."[7]

For her part, Abzug believed that Friedan did not understand politics, objected to her bipartisan efforts, and found her media-centric approach distasteful, wondering if she "realizes that forming a political movement is [a] more complicated thing than . . . appearing on the *Dick Cavett Show*." At the stormy June 9 NWPC meeting in Abzug's office, Friedan shouted, "the hell with" a charter and demanded that others start task forces and conference-planning with an eye to an August 26 event. The women ragingly disagreed not only about the timetable but about what kind of organization NWPC should be. Friedan imagined it as a bipartisan, diverse engine for women's political power and as a "catalyst." She imagined "women putting humanists in power." She compiled her own list of women to invite, including Republican Jill Ruckelshaus, wife of William Ruckelshaus, the head of the Environmental Protection Agency, and Priscilla Buckley, her classmate from Smith, now editing the *National Review*, Marian Wright Edelman, and Francine Du Plessix Gray. Around one-third of the bigwigs who eventually signed on officially or unofficially were Black, including Shirley Chisholm, Fannie Lou Hamer (a founder of the Freedom Democratic Party), Myrlie Evers, Dorothy Height, and, against Friedan's wishes, radical Flo Kennedy. There were women associated with Hispanic politics. Friedan convinced LaDonna Harris, a Comanche activist and wife of Democratic Senator Fred Harris, to join.[8]

As for policy, while Abzug and Steinem talked about women as an oppressed class, Friedan opposed the strategy of portraying women as victims. She fought her colleagues as well on the idea of including other social issues, including Vietnam, protests against domestic abuse, and rape, in the NWPC platform. Her NWPC aimed at new human politics that bosses won't be able to contain nor polls predict.[9]

On July 10, Friedan, Steinem, and Abzug convened the first official NWPC conference at the Statler Hotel in Washington, where Dr. King's followers had gathered after his "I Have a Dream" speech. Here too, Friedan's keynote revealed a vision sharply diverging from those of Abzug and Steinem. Before an audience of over two hundred women, "The Next Step: Women's Liberation—Human Participation," reframed feminism as the entry point to a humanist struggle. "It is hoped that there are thousands of us now sufficiently liberated to take on the responsibility and demands of running for political office." Startlingly, Friedan declared that gender equality would reach the White House in four years. "It is not so impossible that a woman might run for president in 1976," she predicted, skipping the election at hand. She bore down on warnings that movement gains would only occur if NWPC increased political representation of women—and if she was leading the organization. Her masterful working of the crowd received many standing ovations.[10]

Yet Friedan was not the only exciting speaker. Fannie Lou Hamer announced her candidacy for U.S. Senate. Attendees wrestled with the question of whether NWPC should support women because of their gender or whether they should support specific positions on specific issues. But tension among Friedan, Abzug, and Steinem limited the actions NWPC could take, besides condemning racism (after Black women insisted). Finally, NWPC only elected to uphold guidelines of certain positions and bills including the ERA and reproductive rights. All three founders were elected to the NWPC steering committee.

The formation of NWPC revealed both how far women had come since 1963 and how entrenched misogyny remained in politics. The Republican Party recommended that half the delegates at their convention the following year be women and the Democrats went farther, pledging that 50 percent of delegates would be women. Yet three days after the conference ended, a scandalous conversation among Secretary of State William P. Rogers, Henry Kissinger, and Richard Nixon leaked to the press, including the *New York Times*. The men were discussing a photograph of Steinem, Friedan, Abzug, and Chisholm. "'What did it look like?' Mr. Nixon asked. 'Like a burlesque,' Mr. Rogers replied."[11]

Cruel media coverage of Friedan surged. Photographers shot her in unflattering poses, as she would describe them, "mouth open, fist clenched." In the *Philadelphia Inquirer*, a young female reporter would write, "she is not as grotesque as the press and the many photographs would have you believe," before allowing that maybe Friedan had a point when she blamed the media for caricaturing her. Although Friedan's looks and her clashes with her NWPC co-founders gave the media fodder, she fought with Abzug to survive over ideological differences. Her feud with Steinem was of a different order. A common explanation for Friedan's rage against Steinem was jealousy. Steinem was beautiful, cool, and did not pay sufficient homage to her Mother. She would never invite Friedan to write for *Ms.* She was sought after: Smith asked Steinem (class of '56) to deliver the commencement speech at the college whereas Friedan ('42) had never been asked. In August, *Newsweek* put Steinem on the cover.[12]

Yet Friedan's animosity toward Steinem came from righteousness as much as envy. In *Newsweek*, Friedan criticized her rival for dismissing NOW as elitist while hanging with the Beautiful People. Gloria should "take the responsibility to go along with the fame," she said. She derisively called Steinem "The Hair," referring to her perfect coif (although she would later deny that she coined the phrase). She loathed Steinem's famous slogan, "a woman needs a man like a fish needs a bicycle," pointing out that "The Hair" attached herself to powerful men like Mort Zuckerman and Mike Nichols. Finally, she felt Steinem lacked political ideas of her own. She "rebelled against *The Feminine Mystique* without an ideology," said Friedan, who deplored Steinem's attempts to include lesbians in NWPC with remarks such as "we are all lesbians now." Ignoring Friedan's beliefs, the press seized upon the feud between the fifty-one-year-old divorced mother of three and the hot, well-connected single (Steinem did not marry until late in life and never had children) to discredit the women's movement.[13]

At the end of the summer, Friedan sent a letter to delegates reminding them of the anniversary of the Women's Strike for Equality and urging them to start actions in their own districts. "Creative actions of a relatively limited scope can be as effective as large marches," she wrote, providing folksy examples such as making men host a bake sale or putting men's photos on the engagement page. There were also theatrical examples such as the "hanging in effigy of several notable 'non sympathizers.'" No action was too small. "Even if your state caucus is not officially launched, card tables could be set up on Main Street," she wrote, sounding like her mother.[14]

She swung between engineering NWPC into a powerhouse female voting bloc and castigating her enemies. She flew to Moorhead, Mississippi, to campaign for NWPC co-founder Fannie Lou Hamer for the Democratic nomination for state senate in Sunflower County. But while there, she told a reporter she wanted Hamer to beat James O. Eastland, the radical right incumbent, in part because two years earlier, he had found her testimony against Harrold Carswell unbelievable. Then she said that Black and white women had to unite, as they had done for civil rights. In the Jim Crow South, that hardly helped Hamer.

Nor did Friedan's escalating strikes against Steinem—the subject of a swooning *Esquire* profile in October—gain her support or popularity. NWPC bounced Friedan from its steering committee and elected Steinem as its spokesperson at the Democratic National Convention (held the following July in Miami). Incensed, Friedan began to attack her rival even more viciously.[15]

Her *McCall's* column by contrast presented a more maternal persona. "Emily blossoms in a way I haven't noticed before," she wrote, stressing how the changes she had made to the zeitgeist improved her daughter's existence. "I would want my daughter to have that part of her life freer of conflict than it was for me for many years," she wrote of Emily's sex life, using the conditional tense, in a column published in November. Other times her daughter seems like a prop for which the central event is a larger statement about how men and women continued to play on an unequal field. In the same column, she visits Emily at camp. On the way, she stops at the Marlboro Music Festival in Vermont to hear cellist Pablo Casals, then married to a woman sixty years younger than he. She comments enviously that Casals "has the freedom to play that only comes from being fully himself."[16]

A *McCall's* column about the fifth annual NOW conference in Los Angeles also began in a reflective mode, registering "an inexplicable dread" about the event but noting her enduring allegiance to the organization. At the conference, she told the story of the founding of NOW as if its success surprised her, then pivoted to attribute NOW formalizing its support of lesbian rights to FBI moles infiltrating the membership. But the central event of that trip occurred outside the conference, when Miriam drove from Laguna Hills to meet her famous daughter for dinner. What happened is not written down, but not long afterward, Miriam gave two rare interviews to the press. In one, she said: "I approve of Women's Lib but I most heartily disapprove of some of the methods Betty used. Like barging into a cocktail bar which is just for men and demanding to be served.

And sometimes I see Betty on TV and I think she puts her cause down. Once I saw her with Senator Percy and she got so excited she didn't let him get a word in edgewise. . . . If Betty had a husband like her father she would be happier. And I guess I would be more proud of her accomplishments if I thought they had brought her happiness."[17]

Friedan replied to her mother in a place she could control her: the *McCall's* column. She used her mother as the genesis for another paradigm shift that she hoped would be as important as the feminine mystique: aging.

> Her third husband died last year. . . . At seventy she started her second career, using her lifelong bridge skill to get licensed as a manager of duplicate bridge tournaments. At seventy-one she took up horseback riding for exercise. Now she has a third career, distributing ecological, biodegradable detergents, cosmetics, and vitamins, which she claims gave her so much energy she has stopped using artificial hormones. . . . I suddenly realize how many millions of men and women must be like my mother, still moving towards life in their seventies and eighties. . . . Will this be the next liberation movement?[18]

By now, Friedan opposed many of the political positions of NOW and NWPC. She countered NOW's support of no-fault divorce in New York, worrying that most wives—because of unequal treatment in the past—would be unable to earn an adequate living for themselves and their children. She did endorse pensions and Social Security for housewives because she knew how hard it was for them to survive. She deviated from the NWPC party line too in her support of Shirley Chisholm, the first Black congresswoman running for president. The standard line was to do what Steinem did: run as a delegate for Chisholm but also endorse George McGovern, the establishment favorite; Friedan ran only for Chisholm. Yet Friedan's support for the congresswoman did not halt the vicious accusations of radical feminists, two of whom had published articles with damning details in them about her Black cleaning woman. As Susan Brownmiller said, "many younger women are horrified . . . that she has a black maid."[19]

The famous author of a manifesto aimed at liberating housewives did not see such a thing as racist. Nor did she seem to calculate the political capital she would squander when she dialed back her initial laudable support of Chisholm. On January 25, 1972, Friedan joined Chisholm on the dais at the Concord Baptist Church in Bedford-Stuyvesant as she announced her candidacy for president on the Democratic ticket. Friedan attended "as a representative of the women's movement," she began. Yet having recently learned that Eugene McCarthy might enter the race, she had begun to think a better ticket would be Chisholm as his vice president. Thus, she told the large and largely Black crowd that "women will settle for nothing less than the vice presidency." Later, she further explained her comment by saying that Chisholm's would be a symbolic win, rather than a real one.[20]

Even before this apparent walk back, Friedan had alienated many on Chisholm's team by hosting her own fundraisers, hiring a PR firm, and enabling the printing of posters and leaflets featuring large photos of herself without Chisholm. Yet Friedan's photo drew attention to Chisholm, whom the mainstream press had written off. Also, despite her chutzpah, she could be shy, and she hated asking anyone for anything. In 1976, all she recalled about her time as a delegate was embarrassment: "I made a quixotic fool of myself, maybe, going into subways at 7 am," she wrote in an uncharacteristic moment of self-deprecation.[21]

Her vendetta against Gloria Steinem muddied the already charged situation with Chisholm. On February 8, at a small gathering with faculty and students after a talk promoting Chisholm for vice president at Trinity College in Hartford, she uttered two damning remarks about Steinem: "The media tried to make her a celebrity, but no one can make her a leader"; and she "was ripping off the movement for private profit." The press picked up these comments and although Friedan told the *New York Times* she was "misquoted," Steinem never forgave her. When, a few days later, Friedan re-upped her provisional support of Chisholm, the candidate replied she did not want half-baked endorsements.[22]

In October, the House had passed the Equal Rights Amendment. On March 22, 1972, the Senate passed the ERA and sent it to the states for ratification. Nixon supported it and only eight more states were needed to make the three-fourths majority needed for a constitutional amendment. Confident about the ERA, Friedan increasingly worried about George McGovern, whom she was convinced would not support abortion reform. At a June 7 press conference at the Ginger Man, her favorite Upper West Side bar, she drank whiskey sours and complained that the Democratic front-runner was distancing himself from it. According to Shirley MacLaine, a McGovern devotee, shortly after that, at a meeting at McGovern's house in Washington, D.C., Friedan confronted him: "Why did you say you believed that the New York State abortion law was too liberal if you believe it is a question of states' rights?" McGovern did not want to engage with her, but she added, "You have got to start asserting yourself in terms of women's issues because you won't win the election without them. If you don't, I couldn't be less enthusiastic about your candidacy. You think you have women in your pocket, but you don't. And you have to have more women visible in your campaign because right now they just aren't there."[23]

Back in New York, Friedan made what many critics consider her worst gaffe since "the lavender menace." She sent out a press release titled a "Traveling Watermelon Feast," promising to drive a truck loaded with watermelon and fried chicken to a Chisholm rally in Harlem. Someone leaked it to "Politics in Black," an influential column in the *New York Amsterdam News*.

The column cast Friedan as a clueless white woman who, having run her press release by some Black friends, densely protested that she "couldn't understand what all the fuss was about." It ended with a question supposedly asked by someone in the know: "Why should we cooperate with a movement that wants to remove racist white men from power and replace them with racist white women?" Though Friedan cancelled the feast, she was not elected as a Chisholm delegate. And the story had legs. Bayard Rustin would write in the *New York Amsterdam News:* "Betty Friedan . . . focus[es] on issues so irrelevant to the personal lives of working people as to appear dilettantish." Nora Ephron would repeat it in *Esquire*, cementing the portrait of Friedan as racist or, at best, "radical chic," as Tom Wolfe's scathing 1970 portrayal of the Bernsteins' party for the Black Panthers had done for Leonard. These stories made older Jewish liberals look out of touch at a time when the Black-Jewish alliance was unraveling.[24]

But why did Friedan, a longtime supporter of civil rights, use the phrase "the traveling watermelon feast"? One theory suggests that her old nemesis, Flo Kennedy, egged her on, although this raises more questions than it answers. It's possible to see Friedan's remark as an expression of her old resentment about the attention civil rights got, as opposed to women's rights. The most generous interpretation would be that she was (cluelessly) trying to help by drawing attention to Chisholm at a time when the white media ignored the politician. "Which Ms. Has the Movement: Betty & Gloria & Shirley & Bella," a piece Friedan's friend Natalie Gittelson wrote for *Harper's Bazaar*, takes this point of view. "Betty makes the hard news and has from the movement's earliest days," Gittelson writes.[25]

Less than two weeks later, Friedan landed in Miami to attend the Democratic National Convention. Like many American feminists, she believed that the DNC, held between July 10 and 13, would demonstrate an unprecedented moment of hope for women's equality. NWPC had promised that 50 percent of delegates would be women and at the DNC, the numbers nearly achieved that, jumping from 13 percent in 1968 to an impressive 40 percent in 1972. Women sported buttons with the slogan: "We're Here to Make Policy, Not Coffee." NWPC members hoped to get equal pay and reproductive rights on the candidates' platforms. Magazines sent feminists to cover feminists. Yet Friedan suspected that sexism and tokenism still ruled, as Germaine Greer also observed in *Harper's*. The female delegates, Greer wrote, did not "have much more bargaining power than they had before."[26]

The National Women's Political Caucus chose Steinem to represent it at the convention; Friedan attended as a reporter/activist. Covering the movement and being its mother superior contributed to, as Nora Ephron wrote in *Esquire*, Friedan seeming "off to the side, just slightly out of the frame." But other factors added to this perception, such as Friedan's complaint to Ephron about the label pinned on her. "I'm getting sick and tired of this mother-of-us-all-thing," she told the journalist. Then too, *McCall's* had booked her into the luxurious Fontainebleau Hotel on the beach, whereas most NWPC delegates stayed in what Theodore White called the "derelict" Betsy Ross Hotel two miles away.[27]

Also, as NWPC struggled to increase the number of female delegates, particularly in South Carolina and Illinois, Friedan defied the organization by refusing to abandon her endorsement of Chisholm as Democratic nominee for vice president. (NWPC supported Texan Sissy Farenthold.) She confronted Black activist Jane Galvin Lewis in a hotel lobby, saying "what kind of Black are you anyway?" after Galvin voted for Farenthold. Friedan promised an adoring crowd, "no politician has women in his pocket anymore," and she continued to be suspicious of McGovern, who, although he had reassured women that he "unequivocally" supported abortion reform, privately worried about "extremist" positions making it more difficult for him to beat Nixon. As Friedan put it later, she was going to bed every night telling herself: "outfoxed again." And in the early morning hours of July 12, during the vote for the abortion plank, McGovern proved Friedan's worst fears correct. Some McGovern aides, including campaign manager Gary Hart, phoned the floor, instructing delegates to reverse their votes, arguing that if the women voted yes to abortion rights, they contributed to McGovern's defeat. Other aides flat-out intimidated female delegates or found men to replace them.[28]

According to Friedan, dog whistles shrieked and fistfights erupted on the convention floor. Although McGovern had promised he would not send in a pro-lifer, St. Louis attorney Eugene Walsh took the podium to warn delegates that "we want our young to live to be born" without giving the Women's Caucus the chance to defend their position. Shirley MacLaine followed, telling delegates that abortion "should be kept out of the political process" and that they should "vote their consciences." Aides had stripped the plank of the word "abortion." Friedan, Steinem, Abzug, and Germaine Greer huddled on the floor to decide what to do. McGovern wanted a voice vote, but Friedan and the North Carolina Democratic activist Martha McKay maneuvered a televised roll call for the issue. "Gloria, Bella, others tell me please not to encourage a roll call vote," Friedan remembered saying. She chased McGovern's political advisor, Frank Mankiewicz, around the hall as he advised women to vote against the plank and she announced: "We have to find out who our enemies are."[29]

At 4 a.m., the vote on whether to include abortion in the national platform came in. It was 1572 to 1101. Nonetheless, women all over the country could see, via the broadcast roll call, who voted for reproductive rights. "Women have to stick together," said Friedan, who claimed that had McGovern aides not intimidated women, reproductive rights would have won. "We were outmaneuvered and manipulated," she said. Not totally. Six months later, in a landmark decision, the Supreme Court decided in favor of Roe, safeguarding women's right to abortion without undue government involvement.[30]

Apoplectic when McGovern chose Thomas F. Eagleton as his running mate (as opposed to a woman), Friedan tore into the presidential nominee as a betrayer of women's issues and railed against feminists who argued that he needed a male vice president to beat Nixon. She confronted Steinem "behind the stadium bleachers." Her rival "sweetly" told her to "get out," she wrote in *It Changed My Life.* (Steinem said this never happened.) Friedan's column for *McCall's* "Beyond Women's Liberation," which hit the newsstands on July 19, is another sort of attack. It begins with her outrage at a *New York Times* op-ed in which a "liberated" woman apologizes for taking time off from writing to wipe the tears from her daughter's cheek. "Why does 'liberation' or 'feminism' imply to her the exclusion of husbands and fathers?" Friedan asks. Challenging the idea that a woman is always the superior candidate, she voices support for William Fitts Ryan, then running against Bella Abzug. Then she singles out Steinem for ridicule, claiming that a nameless male friend turned against the movement after reading her essay "Sisterhood" in *Ms.* and condemning her for having characterized marriage as prostitution in a speech at the League of Women Voters—which Steinem would deny she had done. Friedan downplays race, claiming that she became a Chisholm delegate "to have a voice on all the urgent problems," and she ends with a cry to rid the movement of "female chauvinist boors."[31]

In a press conference and follow-up interviews, Friedan focused on how women's lib scapegoated her. To Frank Swertlow, a young male UPI reporter, in the living room of her 93rd Street duplex, she expressed surprise at how many women dismissed her as a reactionary. But the biggest surprise came when, wearing a caftan slit to her thigh and "sipping" a drink, she described younger feminists' response as a personal affront, calling them ungrateful "daughters." And then she embraced the "mother to the movement" label she had shunned at the DNC, protesting, "I've been more of a Jewish mother to the movement than I have to my own children."[32]

This punitive-funny confession is a performance, a schtick. But it also signals Friedan's continued ambivalence about her commitment to the movement that rejected her and her anxiety that she had scanted her real offspring. She felt guilty. Her brilliant children—Daniel, who had started graduate school at Berkeley; Jonathan, who had dropped out of Columbia in May 1971; and Emily, at Dalton—would soon begin calling her "Betty." Although she adored them, she worried, especially about Jonathan, who had found a job on a purse seine boat, fishing for salmon in the Gulf of Alaska. He was living on Lummi Island, off the Pacific coast, and beginning to take Judaism seriously, flying to Boulder and learning about the Jewish Renewal with a group of like-minded people, keeping Shabbat, and taking account of good deeds each week.[33]

Friedan did not write about Jonathan's newfound interest in Judaism, but she continued to put Emily, a rising junior, into her *McCall's* columns. This made her daughter angry enough to run away. She also drafted a letter to the *New York Times* about her mother "the ogre." (Never sent.) For Friedan, Emily triggered the most guilt about the sacrifice she had made to realize her "passionate journey." The trade-off was the self-involvement it took to change the world. Yet if the collision between Friedan's family drama and her commitment to social change drove her further from the women's movement, increasingly, she had company. That summer the *New York Times Book Review* published Joan Didion's cover story "The Women's Movement," which saw women's lib as a "febrile and cerebral passion."[34]

At the end of August, Friedan returned to Miami to testify on behalf of NOW about repealing laws restricting abortion at hearings for the Republican National Convention. She was one of the few feminists who attended both conventions. She covered the GOP convention for *McCall's* and WOR-TV, infuriating many Democrat sisters by arguing that more Republican women supported equality between the sexes than they thought. "They applaud every mention of abortion reform and equality for women," she told a reporter. But as at the Democratic convention, her optimism proved illusory. Republican women ultimately were unwilling to challenge Nixon's politics. And Friedan, angered that the Republicans gave her less of a platform than the Democrats, scolded them about hesitating to decriminalize abortion. "I am here now to raise the issue to urge women to fight for the right to control our own bodies," she shouted "shrilly," according to UPI's sexist reporting, after seizing the mike from Republican women in a meeting about childcare at the Fontainebleau Hotel. These skirmishes, reported to make Friedan look bad, did not shake one of her core beliefs—that "the amount of sheer discussion on the issue is the important thing."[35]

Friedan and Emily left 9G Co-op and moved yet again, to an apartment on the fortieth floor of One Lincoln Plaza on Broadway and 64th Street. Its views were enviable but as important, given that her youngest child would soon be going off to college, her dear friend Natalie Gittelson lived in the building. Moving seems to have helped her see her dreaded hometown anew. Asked to deliver a speech at Bradley University, she made her first trip to Peoria since 1963, though she worried about "what I might revert to." But mid-speech, she remembered her ancestors coming to America and found renewed gusto for her fight.[36]

As for Emily, she would leave home in the fall of 1973. She got into Radcliffe and Wesleyan, which she preferred. But just as her mother had leaned on Betty to go to Smith, Betty persuaded her daughter to go to Radcliffe. She defrayed the cost of tuition by renegotiating the price of her papers—agreed upon several years earlier—with the Schlesinger Library. She would wipe the top of her desktop into a box so that Sweet'n Low packages and coffee stirrers mixed with NOW memos provided a future for Emily, whatever it took.

By this time, Friedan had been speaking against the idea of women's colleges for several years, arguing that single-sex education was a kind of segregation as detrimental as the racial kind. Then, in the run-up to Nixon's reelection she dropped that crusade and plunged into a series of dramatic struggles with neoconservatives. In one of the most public instances of what would become a decades-long fight, Friedan tangled with Midge Decter on a radio program for housewives, *The Martha Deane Show*. Decter, the wife of Norman Podhoretz, editor of the neoconservative weekly *Commentary*, had published *The New Chastity and Other Arguments Against Women's Liberation*. The first chapter ridiculed Friedan for the hyperbolic phrase "comfortable concentration camp" and railed at what Decter saw as a Commie attempt to destroy the nuclear family: "displaying her bias as a would-be intellectual, Betty Friedan . . . took it upon herself to goad women to *something*." The women's movement, Decter wrote, "does not belong to the history of feminism but to the history of radicalism."[37]

On *The Martha Deane Show*, Friedan responded to Decter by positioning herself as a representative figure. She bragged that she spoke for enormous numbers of women and represented thousands of lawsuits being brought against universities and other institutions for sex discrimination. But then she stooped to her usual insult for those she considered traitors to the women's movement, labeling Decter an "Aunt Tom." And yet, after Nixon won the election, Friedan would, if not take Decter's side, spin the neoconservative backlash as a rebuke to women's lib. In her January 1973 *McCall's* column, she described Decter and Joan Didion as "respected, serious writers" embodying the backlash against women's lib *she* had predicted.[38]

She lost her bid to serve on the national steering committee on the NWPC board (and threatened to sue for fraud, which could never be proven). And then a new enemy came into her sights. Phyllis Schlafly was then a little-known activist, but she had already been mobilizing against the ERA with her organization STOP ERA for several years. Friedan saw a pattern: states Schlafly visited voted against the ERA. She struck back. At NOW's sixth annual convention in Washington, she said she was investigating rumors that a cabal including the John Birch Society, the Catholic Church, and the AFL-CIO funded STOP ERA. Friedan believed, as many feminists did, that the insurance industry, fearing that the passage of the ERA would force it to change underwriting patterns (and lose money), conspired with Schlafly to engineer the amendment's failure. (Scholars and feminists continue to debate these allegations.)[39]

Friedan's March 4 *New York Times* essay "Up from the Kitchen Floor" set out, in her strongest terms thus far, her commitment to ratification of the ERA to ensure "women's economic independence." It used, for the first time in the newspaper of record, the phrase "first stage" feminism to signal the end of the movement that began with *The Feminine Mystique*. Also for the first time in the *Times*, Friedan aired Watergate-inflected attacks on "manhating," "proselytizers," "disrupters," and lesbians and stated sharply her opinions about CIA and FBI infiltration of the women's movement. "Ti-Grace Atkinson took me to lunch in Philadelphia with the wife of a top C.I.A. official, who offered to help us. I told Ti-Grace we didn't want any help from the C.I.A." (Atkinson denies this ever happened.) Throughout, she sprinkled Human Potential Movement phrases like "The New Yes."[40]

The essay caused an uproar. Activists organized a women's movement speak-out against her, which the *New York Times* covered. The *Times* ran two solid pages of letters attacking her. Robin Morgan, Jill Johnston, and Ti-Grace Atkinson were a few of the women who accused her of speaking for the group as opposed to herself, distorting the facts, and being out of touch, narcissistic, racist, and anti-lesbian; only Pauli Murray defended her. Friedan responded in the *Times* by writing "I must . . . speak my personal truth."[41]

Around two months later, in a packed auditorium at Illinois State University not far from the town where she grew up, she told that truth when confronting Phyllis Schlafly for the first time. The two women could not have looked more different. Friedan, then fifty-two, with her salt and pepper hair, wore a black dress; willowy Schlafly, forty-eight, in a blond bouffant hairdo, sported a red pants suit. Suffering from laryngitis, which she blamed on her physical proximity to Peoria, Friedan rasped eloquently: "It is our commitment to our sisters . . . to insist that all women have equality of opportunity." She cited numerous polls showing women wanted passage of the ERA.[42]

Schlafly, who called the audience "girls," stressed that if Congress ratified the ERA, women would be drafted and forced to do manual labor. Still, Friedan had the upper hand until Schlafly directly addressed the crowd, arguing that passing the ERA would not make them happy.

Friedan lost control. She repeated the slur that she had thrown at Midge Decter and others. "I consider you a traitor to your sex, an Aunt Tom." From that point on, Schlafly dominated the conversation, claiming that Friedan "resorted to abusing opponents and hurling epithets at them and making false and phony charges." Friedan took the bait. "I'd like to burn you at the stake," she shouted. "I'm glad you said that," replied Schlafly. "Because that just shows that the intemperate agitating proponents of the ERA are so intolerant of the views of other people."[43]

In the public battle of the mothers, the calm traditionalist emerged victorious over the fiery radical whose critique of motherhood had changed so many women's lives. Yet for all their differences, both women were Midwestern mothers devoted to their children and their movements. Still, only Friedan celebrated when, the following month, after nine years of fighting, the Supreme Court ruled that sex-segregated help-wanted ads were illegal.

# 10

## *"It Changed My Life"*

"This is a momentous day in the massive unfinished revolution of women of the world toward full equality, human dignity, individual freedom and our own identity in the family of man," Friedan proclaimed at the First International Feminist Conference, on June 1, 1973, in Cambridge, Massachusetts. The first hint that finishing the revolution would be more difficult than she imagined came less than three weeks later, on her first trip to Israel. With the World Association of Women Journalists and Writers (WAWJW), she spent ten days in the Promised Land, beginning on June 17 in Jerusalem, where she met Knesset officials and "lady ministers," visited the Israel Museum, explored Tel Aviv, the Golan Heights, and an army base, and went to several kibbutzim in the Galilee. But Friedan did not see women in the young nation seeking gender equality. *The Feminine Mystique* had not been translated into Hebrew. A newspaper editor said to "take the Israeli women's libbers" back to

America. In a year when the Pope would grant her an audience, Golda Meir refused to meet with her. Meir's antipathy toward American feminism, rooted in her belief that Israeli women had already won equality, represented the prevailing view in the country at the time: Israeli women served in the army and worked in the fields, and did not need an American to instruct them. As the feminist Alice Shalvi, who met Friedan during that trip, said, "her work seemed irrelevant to us."[1]

Friedan responded by angrily schooling her hosts. In a talk titled "The Women's Movement for Equality: Dangers, Dividends, Directions Ahead" at the U.S. Cultural Center in Tel Aviv on June 25, she said that Israeli women did not want equality with men and speculated that the polarization of gender roles would only end if war broke out. In New York some months later, after the Yom Kippur War had started, she wrote her friend the Israeli sociologist Dorit Padan-Eisenstark, that only because of the war did she abandon her takedown of the country, "good Jew that I am." For almost a decade, she would express doubts about kibbutzim as an ideal of gender equality. "I'm sure it would not be that easy nor that desirable, to break the tremendous emotional bonds of a family," she told a reporter.[2]

In these years, Friedan did not turn up at meetings of American Jewish feminists working to rewrite the seder. She was suspicious of institutional Judaism. She would sign the revised Humanist Manifesto, which read: "as in 1933, humanists still believe that traditional theism, especially faith in the prayer-hearing God, assumed to live and care for persons, to hear and understand their prayers, and to be able to do something about them, is an unproved and outmoded faith." But she condemned the manifesto's small number of female signatories. She still had faith in Virginia Satir, who had helped her address the pain of her marriage. She attended Satir's so-called "Beautiful People" conferences, some of which used "Parts Parties," exercises where participants interacted with so-called guides and other people playing historical or mythological roles to access apparently lost parts of themselves. In one Parts Party in Sarasota, Florida, Friedan asked a young guide to play Cleopatra, Bette Davis, and Scheherazade, three women of great, though unconventional, beauty and sexuality with the ability to seduce everyone in the room. She felt like an ugly duckling. But she watched with amazement as this guide embodied the beautiful, sexy parts and interacted with other participants playing other roles.[3]

As big a struggle was to balance advancing global feminism and mothering an almost adult daughter. Toward the end of Emily's first year at Radcliffe, Friedan displayed a rare sang-froid on an episode of *Not for Women Only*, the popular NBC television program hosted by Barbara Walters. The topic: famous parents and their daughters. Attempting to seriously explore the tension between Friedan's status as the mother of the movement and as a real-life mother, Walters directed probing questions at Emily, notably asking if her mother embarrassed her. Unblinking, Emily admitted there were some advantages but then said, "I don't consider myself a feminist," a sentence that would be reprinted many times. Friedan did not blink. She regarded Emily as an individual, she said coolly.[4]

The mother to the traitorously unfeminist daughter, the exile by her own design, looked for new targets in her campaign against injustice and singled out her alma mater, Smith College. The Massachusetts Commission Against Discrimination supported two women denied tenure then suing Smith for gender discrimination. Friedan joined the opposition to the school. The following year, she would hesitate when offered an honorary degree, wondering if she should support the institution that contributed to these injustices. But ultimately, she accepted the honor. She could not shun the establishment that had rid her of the feeling that she was a freak.

* * *

In May 1974, a trip to pre-revolutionary Iran reassured her (far more than the disappointing stint in Israel) that her two-sex feminist movement could be global. Though she had read Oriana Fallaci's interview with the Shah, who had lifted the veil but who also claimed he had not been influenced by a single woman, she would nonetheless come to believe that Iranian women would realize Western-style emancipation. The heads of the Women's Organization of Iran—Princess Ashraf, the twin sister of the Shah, and Mahnaz Afkhami, a professor and activist—invited her, Helvi Sipilä, and Germaine Greer. Afkhami recalled later that Friedan was closer to feminists in the rest of the world than Western ones in part because she did not lecture them about abortion, or anything.

Friedan arrived both as a guest and as a reporter for *Ladies' Home Journal.* She would travel to Isfahan, Shiraz, and Tehran, meet the Empress Farah, middle-class Iranian women trying to create their own feminist revolution, and students putting on the veil. Friedan's published piece, "Coming Out of the Veil," was skeptical of Iranian sexism and reverent toward many of the middle-class women who had removed the veil, which she saw as a universal symbol of oppression that "denied women's personhood." She can sound naïve, as when she quotes the Shah criticizing the Communists agitating against him or describes how she tried to locate Vida Hajeb Tabrezi, an imprisoned sociologist who was being tortured. (She could not, but she found the students who had returned to Iran "cynical.") She writes enviously of the generous support of the Iranian state for feminism ("funds beyond our wildest dreams") and childcare. She, like Greer, who would later write two vicious pieces about Friedan on this trip, wondered if the Iranians had staged the trip, at one center for women asking Afkhami, "what if all this has been set up?" And she demanded to interview the Shah. The piece ends as she puts on a chador and writes that women all over the world had "come out of the veil." In the following years, especially after fundamentalism arrived in Iran in 1979, that metaphor would haunt her.[5]

Back in the United States, Friedan spent some of the summer sailing on Sag Harbor with old friends, including David Manning White. She watched warily as Gerald Ford took over from Nixon. She approved of Betty Ford, a Midwestern pro-ERA divorcée, but Friedan was less involved in presidential politics than helping build organizations to address new problems that her revolution had generated due to the economy for example. As one of the initial members of the First Women's Bank and Trust Company, a full-service bank focused on extending credit to women, she attracted investors. She helped start the Women's Forum, a "new girls' network." She began several projects with the futurist Alvin Toffler: The Committee for Anticipatory Democracy, a bipartisan group devoted to finding new solutions to economic problems, including how the rush of women into the workforce shaped the big picture. An Economic Think Tank for Women, launched with Toffler and Amitai Etzioni, would also address the economic impact of the women's movement, including the two-income family, "education sabbaticals" or retraining, and giving housewives Social Security. Some projects were more lighthearted. Friedan and Toffler joined a number of notable New Yorkers in defending the hit nudical *Let My People Come*, then playing at the Village Gate, against obscenity charges. Friedan found the nude ballet in the show joyous and affirming.

The Think Tank for Women dissolved after one White House briefing, and the Women's Bank and Trust fell apart. But Friedan pushed ahead, as usual, managing her chaotic schedule with one part-time assistant who typed, sorted her mail, made editorial suggestions on her columns, tidied up, and witnessed her complaining about Dalton tuition bills, planning parties, and screaming at people on the phone. "She could only keep assistants for a few weeks," said Warren Farrell, one of the first male board members of New York NOW.[6]

Other shocks came at the World Population Conference in Bucharest in August, where she, along with Germaine Greer and Margaret Mead, denounced the proceedings as sexist after learning that men were making all the decisions. Friedan hosted several long pro-women consciousness raising sessions and accused the UN of holding the conference "over the prone body of women." It was also in Bucharest that she first become aware of anti-Semitism in the women's movement. She received several anonymous letters threatening her not to speak the following year at the UN Conference on Women in Mexico City—held to commemorate International Women's Year (IWY)—"where I was not wanted" or she "would be denounced 'first as an American and then as a Jew.'" In the fall, after Yasser Arafat condemned Israel before the United Nations and gained observer status for the PLO, Friedan wondered why prominent assimilated Jews weren't making an outcry as the liberal intellectuals did during the Spanish Civil War.[7]

Derisive attacks from the press continued. The *New York Times* reported that she stomped out of a screening of *The Stepford Wives* at the moment when a visit from a cartoonish Friedan-like character incites the wives to seek fulfillment. Yet in a year when Susan Brownmiller's *Against Our Will: Men, Women, and Rape* argued that the increase in violence against women represented a backlash against feminism, Friedan was rightfully angry at Ira Levin's caricature. She talked more about applying her revolution to what she called "the gestalt"—a total restructuring of society. She had found inspiration once in Europe and she flew to France to interview Simone de Beauvoir for the *Saturday Review*. The trip, however, was mixed. "I felt the thrill of meeting a cultural hero in person," she wrote. But Friedan also found de Beauvoir "cold" and criticized her "Maoist approach."

The wonderful interview contains an exchange between the two women that puts the chasm between them into perspective. De Beauvoir says: "many women think they should not play the game," meaning give in to the patriarchy. Friedan, always wary of separatism, responds: "how are they to eat?"[8]

The same week her de Beauvoir interview came out, Friedan delivered a striking lecture, "The Sex Role Revolution's Impact on Housing," at the International Design Conference at Aspen. (The previous year, attending the conference for the first time, she had attacked Susan Sontag, calling her talk, which suggested citizens develop critical perspectives on society, "garbage.") Here, she sounds like she was channeling the architect Moira Moser-Khalili's just published book, *Urban Design and Women's Lives*, which focused on redesigning Iranian cities to accommodate women's work and lives and reshaping suburban homes to be more like Swedish co-ops. Friedan told the 1,200 conferees—including Frank Gehry (born Ephraim Goldberg), Jonas Salk, and Joan Baez—that architects had a special responsibility to transform her sex role revolution. If they dared. Talking extremely rapidly, she elaborated on her complaint from *The Feminine Mystique* about how open-style suburban kitchens denied women privacy. She imagined feminist architects designing a new type of gender-equal kitchen in a new type of community. But it was never enough for the stormy petrel to just talk. Later that afternoon, for the first fifty men and first fifty women who signed up and at least six architects or architecture students, she scheduled a three-hour game—a competition among the audience to design housing to combat *The Feminine Mystique*. In 1981, she would lament that none of the teams fulfilled her communal ideal. The "individualists" could not get beyond the private home.[9]

With her friend and NOW devotee Mary Jean Tully, she plotted to salvage her two-sex movement for women's equality by founding yet another organization, "Womansurge." However, after President Ford did not name her to the National Commission on the Observance of the International Women's Year, she pitched a story about the UN Conference to the *New York Times Magazine*, casting herself as a Communist and Arab-fighting feminist heroine whom the women of the world needed. Her image of herself as the savior of oppressed feminists everywhere would annoy women globally, as it had nationally. But her effort to impose her liberal, pro-abortion women's movement on the world stage would be more difficult than she thought. Some observers dubbed the first UN Conference in Mexico City—the first of three UN-sponsored women's summits during the so-called decade for women—"the greatest consciousness raising event in history." Friedan saw its potential. But her harrowing experience there convinced her of the necessity for the women's movement to fight despots most of all.[10]

The UN Conference took place from June 19 to July 2 in Mexico City. In addition to the official conference, under the leadership of the activist Mildred Persinger, the UN sponsored the first nongovernmental organization (NGO) symposium for women, known as the Tribune. Centered in Tlatelolco, a neighborhood near the zoo, the Tribune gathered American celebrities such as Jane Fonda, Germaine Greer, and Angela Davis; NOW members; and around 6,000 women from all over the world. Five miles away—accessible by charter buses, by the metro, or by walking—the official conference, at the Juan de la Barrera gymnasium, drew around 1,200 delegates and 1,200 journalists. Shortly after she arrived, Friedan was bogged down in two controversies. The first had to do with her June *Ladies' Home Journal* article about Iran, which incited many American feminists to complain that the flattering portrait of Princess Ashraf Pahlavi, the Shah's twin sister, ignored the country's human rights violations. Friedan defended her as a pragmatist and an optimist who hoped that feminism would liberalize the regime. Then Pahlavi donated a million dollars to the UN conference. It looked like pay for play.[11]

In the second scandal, the radical group Redstockings persuaded Friedan to use IWY to confront Gloria Steinem about her role in the CIA. In May, Redstockings had held a press conference dredging up old accusations that Steinem had worked as a mole; eventually, they convinced Friedan to give a press conference demanding that Steinem respond to the charges. As radical feminist Ingrid Hedley Stone wrote in *Majority Report*, Friedan at first did not want to bring up the issue and "suggested" that *she* distribute the Redstockings press release in Mexico City. According to Phyllis Chesler, Friedan even paid Stone's plane fare.[12]

On June 9, days before Friedan left for Mexico City, the publication of the Rockefeller Commission findings of more government wrongdoings may have boosted her hope that the world was ready to denounce Steinem. But the attack could have been personal too. A few months earlier, Steinem had written a piece discussing the phenomena of women trashing women in the movement. "If she's an old-style Betty Friedan person, she may go power crazy because it's the first time in her life she's had a chance to express herself."[13]

Yet at first Friedan saw Steinem as a side issue. The looming problem at IWY was sexism. The UN had named Pedro Ojeda Paullada, the Mexican attorney general, to be the president of IWY, and too many Tribune delegates—especially those from Communist countries—were men or wives of male officials. Also, despite the fact that the Tribune was supposed to be nonpartisan, Friedan was also upset that Tribune participants lacked access to UN representatives. Shortly after she landed in Mexico City on June 19, she steered NOW members and international feminists staying at Hotel del Prado, in the upscale neighborhood of Bosque del Chapultepec, to organize the Feminist Caucus to protest. She was outraged when, of the three speakers at the inauguration, two men spoke first. She also complained about the decision to hold the NGO Tribune and the official conference five miles apart. Quickly, she coordinated a speak-out. "The Women of the Tribune," as she named her group, would prepare no less than 894 amendments to add to the approved conference document. "All we do at the Tribune is make speeches while at the conference they are drawing up an official world plan of action," she told the *New York Times*.[14]

Her opening remarks praised women of color for launching feminism and blamed capitalism for quelling it. She subsequently held a press conference at which she returned to the subject of how exploitation of women also hurt men. Meanwhile, Black and Third World feminists staged their own protest at the U.S. embassy, accusing UN officials of ignoring them. Wynta Boynes, of the Congress of Racial Equality (CORE), cried, "Where are your Chicanas?" Friedan responded to this provocation by telling reporters, in as plain a defense of her liberal feminism as she ever provided: "The make-up of the delegation is neither here nor there. . . . I'm interested in what comes out of the conference." Then, circling back to Steinem, she argued that some shady government entity egged on these women and that "anyone" should be concerned about efforts to infiltrate the women's movement. "I don't see how she can ignore these charges," she said, referring to her nemesis. The *New York Times* story about the matter did not name Steinem, but everyone knew who Friedan was talking about when she warned of "paralysis of leadership."[15]

On June 23, in a speak-out to address the problems at the official conference, Friedan exchanged jibes with another CORE member, Lorna McBarnette. (A few days later, publicly confronted by Ethel Payne, associate editor of the *Chicago Defender*, and Carolyn Reed, head of a national organization of domestic workers, Friedan would start to weep and deny she had singled out Black women as "agents paid to disrupt the proceedings.")

Complaining about imperialism, a group of Third World feminists attacked Friedan, while she urged them to not air the "internal dirty linen" of their countries. On top of that, according to the scholar Jocelyn Olcott, the Mexican press began to refer to Friedan with a "dizzying array of anti-Semitic names," erroneously reporting that she planned to lead a march similar to the Women's Strike for Equality and alleging that *she* was a CIA plant.[16]

In the major primary source about Friedan at the conference, her exposé, "Scary Doings in Mexico City," she paints herself as a victim of faceless totalitarian agencies. Using words like "horror," "sinister," and "intrigue," she reports radical feminists chasing her, the attorney general of Mexico interrogating her, the government forbidding her from marching, shadowy men "with guns" haunting global speak-outs, following her back to her hotel, and poisoning any chance of women collaborating. "I didn't want to be a coward, but I didn't want to be kidnapped," she wrote. Forty-plus years after the publication of "Scary Doings" there is disagreement as to how much danger Friedan was in. Jocelyn Olcott writes that the police were "almost entirely preoccupied with what Mexicans said and did." But New York NOW president Carole De Saram, who was there, said the U.S. embassy warned them that their lives were in jeopardy. "People were afraid to be near Betty because they heard she was going to be shot," De Saram said.[17]

Leaving aside the question of whether Friedan overstated the peril to her, "Scary Doings" is a strange read because of its lighthearted tone. "Who would ransom *me*?" she asks, as if at a roast. The great details that elsewhere add warmth to her writing here limn the surrealness of the scene. She drinks tequila spiked with sangrita juice, a traditional mixer made of orange and lime juice and chili sauce, and eats Mexican garlic soup. She wears her "slinkiest black evening pajamas" to crash official galas and parties. At a sit-down dinner held at the anthropology museum, she tries to talk to two Chinese women delegates, but their Communist handler shuts down the conversation. But perhaps the most striking fact is her understanding of her own acting out. Reflecting on her weeping and apologizing (to nameless feminists) for her belligerence, she writes, "I guess that made the others feel better."[18]

"Scary Doings" also traces how, while women tussled at the Tribune, an anti-Zionist agenda emerged at the official conference. After attending Leah Rabin's talk at the Mexican Foreign Ministry, watching as much of the audience rose, booed the wife of the Israeli prime minister, and walked out, Friedan writes, "I was outraged." When Egyptian first lady Jehan Sadat refused to speak with Rabin unless the IWY linked women's rights with Palestinian rights and announced that IWY goals could not be achieved "while Arab land remains occupied, while the Palestinians remain homeless," Friedan scoffed that male politicians were behind her and government forces were behind them. "What women really want is not the same as the rhetoric their governments say they want," she told the *Los Angeles Times*.[19]

Back at the Tribune, at yet another caucus meeting, Friedan finally made progress uniting women to demand, among other things, that UN officials rewrite the IWY conference document in gender-neutral language. She accomplished this by letting women speak. Women dropped their anger at each other and began to share losses and tragedies. "We were, finally, just women," Carole De Saram said. According to another attendee, Maxine Hitchcock, roughly 2,000 women approved the changes in the official document through their applause. Standing next to a delegate from China, Sooaka Hang, Friedan presented the list to Helvi Sipilä, the assistant secretary general of the United Nations. (However, a group of Latina feminists protesting Friedan's "manipulative tactics" came up with their own document.) When Sipilä refused to even allow Friedan to voice her grievances to the general assembly—there was no precedent for nongovernmental parties to do so—Friedan complained that the previous year, Arafat had aired *his* grievances in front of the UN, and *he* lacked an official affiliation. But not only did Friedan's argument fail to sway Sipilä, the American press trivialized the ideological struggles as "bickering" among women, as it had been doing for years.[20]

At the official conference, Soviet bloc countries and Arab states had conspired to attach language vowing to eliminate Zionism from the "Declaration on the Equality of Women"—also known as the Mexico Declaration, the document meant to guide global equality for women over the next decade. Only one or two women—none from the United States—joined Friedan in publicly defying anti-Zionism. UN officials refused to allow Tribune delegates to add a statement to the document condemning sexism. The vote on the Mexico Declaration would be 89–3, with the United States, Israel, and Denmark voting no. The anti-Zionist plank would pass 61–23, with 25 abstaining. At the Tribune site, anti-American protests had been going on for several days when, as Friedan awaited the results of the vote, male protesters holding guns and a banner reading "Mujeres y Imperialismo" swarmed in. Friedan's old friend, the labor leader Dorothy Haener, and two other women hustled her out of the room into an empty office. She returned to New York in shock.

Friedan continued attacking Steinem, whom she still believed was a CIA mole. It would take two years for her to backtrack, on the *Phil Donahue Show*, when she claimed that a warning from Steinem's lawyer compelled her to say that Redstockings made her a victim of the situation. "A longer documented thing was issued just before the Mexico conference and that's where, against my own wish I somehow got brought up because people wanted, some people seemed to want me to fan it and I wouldn't." On November 4, when the ERA was routed in New

York and New Jersey, Friedan attributed the losses to government forces. She turned her energies to the UN General Assembly putting Resolution 3379 (based on the Mexico Declaration) on its docket, despite opposition from Ambassador Daniel Patrick Moynihan. To protest the latter, she formed an Ad Hoc Committee of Women for Human Rights. She objected to the racist label being "applied solely to the national self-determination of the Jewish people." Although the committee included such names as Lauren Bacall, Adrienne Rich, and Elizabeth Holtzman, the resolution passed on November 10, the anniversary of Kristallnacht, 72–35.[21]

The following morning, at an anti-resolution rally of over 100,000 people in midtown Manhattan, Friedan spoke after Chaim Herzog, Leah Rabin, and her old critic Bayard Rustin. She identified herself for the first time in a public forum "as a woman, as an American, and as a Jew." Yet she believed that Orthodox Jews rejected her, presumably for supporting the ERA. In a 1976 interview in *Lilith* magazine, she recalled that during her remarks, they booed her. Still, she adamantly opposed Resolution 3379, signing a letter to the editor of the *New York Times* that contained this sentence: "The condemnation of Zionism, an authentic movement for national and ethnic survival, could very well be taken as a signal for further incitements to anti-Semitism." Along with sixty other prominent women, including Bella Abzug, Margaret Mead, and Eleanor Holmes Norton, she signed a protest telegram to Kurt Waldheim, Secretary General of the UN. But nothing could overturn the resolution.[22]

In part as a response to the defeat of the ERA in New York, Friedan circled back to Womansurge, the group of "independent" feminists she had begun thinking about some months earlier to rescue the women's movement from what she saw as the radicalism of NOW. During an eight-hour meeting in a New Orleans airport motel room, she decried NOW and the slogan of her former protégé and then-president Karen DeCrow: "out of the mainstream and into the revolution." She said, "I'm . . . giving my support to younger women who are going to take the lead in unfinished business." Yet she knew Womansurge would not save the women's movement. She did not know what would, except for her leadership, which she didn't want to provide.[23]

Six months later, Random House published her second book, *It Changed My Life: Writings on the Women's Movement.* She hoped it would remind women of what the movement had accomplished, solder fissures among them, and address looming economic problems, such as inflation making it impossible for a single parent to buy a home. But instead, the book exposed cracks between her political persona and her private life, between mothering her daughter and mothering the movement, between what she knew about gender equality and what she could not help knowing. The collection of old essays and lectures with new introductions may have pleased fans, but to Friedan's enemies she seemed like a zealot. The book is composed of five parts. Part One focuses on her time as a young wife and mother before *The Feminine Mystique* and tells of the controversy it sparked. Part Two chronicles the founding of NOW. Part Three includes excerpts of her columns for *McCall's.* Part Four documents her experiences with global feminism, including her gripping 1974 interview with Simone de Beauvoir, conducted around the time she conceded that she "first read *The Second Sex* in the early fifties." Then there is a coda.[24]

*It Changed My Life* reveals two Friedans: the brilliant visionary who pushed for "a sex role revolution" and the paranoid braggart slaying radical enemies and government agents and preaching that the women's movement has gone too far. Although the book contains new flashes of empathy toward her mother—"she . . . generally encouraged me to do the things that she would have liked to do"—Friedan seems devoid of insight when it comes to the women's movement. Not only does she single-handedly take credit for it, she writes many cringe-making paranoid sentences. NWPC "wants to disappear me," she laments, repeating a phrase she used often in this era. She also repeats her warning that sexual politics would lead to fascism. "Scary Doings in Mexico City" is the last essay in Part Four.[25]

The coda, "An Open Letter to the Women's Movement," surprisingly challenges readers to abandon the extremist parts of the women's movement while cherishing its economic and social accomplishments. It also clearly explains what happened. What is remarkable about the movement, Friedan writes, at her most persuasive, is that it gathered women who would not have ordinarily even met. This "letter" also clarifies her infamous opposition to lesbians in NOW. She was not opposed to lesbians, she writes, but "lesbian rights as the main issue is something else." Because of such distractions, she worries that her daughter would have to fight for women's equality all over again. She ends the essay on what seems like a tangent influenced by the Human Potential Movement. Science fiction, she argues, imagines solutions for the second part of the women's revolution where everything else has failed. "Science fiction has fascinated me lately in my search for the new yes," she writes.

She appeared moved by the wave of science fiction inspired by the women's movement, such as the lesbian writer Joanna Russ's novel *The Female Man*, in which four women from different eras—some dystopian, realist, or futurist—meet. At the end of the novel, Russ imagines a world where the so-called female man will be extinct. Friedan also holds up as an ideal Ursula K. Le Guin's 1969 *The Left Hand of Darkness*, in which ambisexual characters alternate as masculine and feminine selves, and only spend a brief time reproducing. In these fantastical musings, Friedan strangely seemed to anticipate what we now call the gender nonbinary.

The book received mixed reviews. In the *New York Times Book Review*, Stephanie Harrington deplored Friedan's rants against Steinem, Abzug, and the CIA, and wrote that she was "too valuable . . . to waste herself"; in the daily *Times*, Christopher Lehmann-Haupt thought that she sounded like "an egotistical Joan of Arc." Reading the sections about NWPC, Audrey Rowe Colom, a Black Republican and national chair of the organization, became furious. She wrangled other feminists including Bella Abzug, Eleanor Holmes Norton, and Gloria Steinem to sign a memo protesting the book. In a letter to Bob Bernstein, then president of Random House, Colom objected to what she characterized as Friedan's "factual errors, self serving fiction . . . and character assassination." She was particularly incensed by Friedan's description of "the cabal" machinating to push her off the NWPC steering committee. Nonetheless, if Friedan was wrong about this specific accusation, her paranoia about government agencies infiltrating the movement proved prescient. In April, the FBI released the final report of the Church Committee, which revealed that J. Edgar Hoover had surveilled the women's movement and ordered agents to infiltrate it since 1968. Still, no records exist proving her claim that the moles were lesbians dispatched to seduce her.[26]

By this time, the market was flooded with books influenced by *The Feminine Mystique.* The psychologist Dorothy Dinnerstein's 1976 *The Mermaid and the Minotaur: Sexual Arrangements and Human Malaise* amplified Friedan's anti-Freudianism, focusing on the harmful effect of gendered parenting roles; two years later, scholar Nancy Chodorow's *Reproduction of Mothering* went further: if gender roles in parenting were changed, Freudian theory itself might be reimagined. Dinnerstein mentions Friedan in a footnote; Chodorow not at all. Nor did Adrienne Rich refer to Friedan, even though *Of Woman Born* (also 1976) contained sentences that owed much to *The Feminine Mystique.*

Friedan did not complain (in public) about scholars and poets writing as if she had never existed. She was consumed with worry that no new states had ratified the ERA. By this time, Phyllis Schlafly had swayed many Orthodox Jews to her side by proclaiming that ratification of the amendment would force women to be conscripted. Some observant Jews remembered *The Feminine Mystique*'s anti-volunteerism and disdain for housewives, and others worried that the equality that Friedan supported would destroy Jewish life in America. Yet as *It Changed My Life* tanked, Friedan started a countereffort to persuade her fellow Jews that the ERA—and feminism itself—would be good for them. On June 29 in Louisville, in front of 250 delegates at the National Jewish Community Relations Advisory Council, she talked about her identity as a Jewish woman and said that the ERA's effort to "liberate and attain full equality for women would have a positive effect on strengthening Jewish family life in contemporary society" and that "the ERA is closer to the Jewish tradition than most people think." She joked: "No longer do you bring up your daughter to marry the doctor, you bring her up to be the doctor." But she also defended the women's movement against naysayers who blamed it for the rising divorce rate and delayed marriage among young Jews.[27]

Shortly afterward, in an interview with the journalist Amy Stone in the premiere issue of the Jewish feminist magazine *Lilith*, she strongly criticized the obstacles organized Judaism placed in front of women: "If you want Jewish women to have more children, you have to be strongly supportive of institutional changes so women don't have to choose between professional advancement and political participation and child-rearing." Regarding the Young Leadership Cabinet, a UJA fundraising group for Israel then excluding women, she was even more adamant: "It's absolutely incumbent on Jewish women to protest and to withdraw their support from any Jewish organization that doesn't take action against sex and race discrimination." (Her remarks caused UJA to scramble to both defend itself and protest.) She also took offense at the rise of the sexist phrase Jewish American Princess (JAP), referring to a spoiled Jewish gold digger. But instead of condemning men for this phrase, she held accountable JAPs themselves, "the woman that's bred to take advantage of this female role in a way that I think is outrageous," she told Stone.[28]

She agreed to sit for a portrait by the Jewish painter June Blum. The result, *Betty Friedan as the Prophet,* would become part of the Sister Chapel, a feminist hall of fame in oil. Created by eleven female artists, the Sister Chapel was comprised of nine-foot portraits of twentieth-century female icons, including Frida Kahlo by Shirley Gorelick and Bella Abzug by Alice Neel. It would be exhibited to much acclaim in 1978. *Betty Friedan as the Prophet* was the only portrait in the series depicting a feminist icon as an Old Testament sage. Blum painted Friedan in a floor-length red gown with a low ruffled V-neck standing in the desert. As Moses might have looked sternly to the Promised Land, Friedan gazes severely at the viewer, a copy of *The Feminine Mystique* under one arm as she descends from Sinai.

She seemed to bring that persona to the 1976 Democratic Convention, held in New York City, by arguing that President Jimmy Carter should "promote" equal representation of women by 1980, as opposed to "requiring" it, language that NOW and NWPC officially supported. She did not want it to seem like women were receiving special favors, she said, adding that "as a Jew I belong to a minority that has been persecuted by quotas." She was influenced by the controversial case of Marco DeFunis, a Sephardic Jew who in 1971 sued for discrimination after the University of Washington Law School denied his application twice, admitting less qualified candidates, many of whom lived out of state. The Superior Court of Washington State ruled in favor of DeFunis. In February 1974, the case reached the Supreme Court, which ruled it moot because DeFunis, then in his last year of law school, would shortly graduate. But the DeFunis case divided many liberal organizations, a number of which contributed amicus briefs. The National Organization for Women argued against DeFunis, maintaining that affirmative action was necessary whatever the means, whereas some Jewish organizations took his side, worrying that the court's decision would lead to widespread anti-Semitism. Several opinion pieces appeared in *Commentary*, speculating about the damaging effects affirmative action would eventually cause.[29]

Always on Friedan's mind was the fate of the ERA, whose purpose she movingly described to a reporter from her home state as "not only the symbol but the substance of all we have won. Do you think they will fight for rape victims, for displaced homemakers in the legislature, to enforce laws against sex discrimination [if the ERA is not ratified?] consciousness is a very fragile thing." It upset her that Illinois—the state where she was born—had become an ERA battleground. Every year between 1972 and 1982, the ERA, which required a three-fifths majority to pass, was either defeated in the House or in the Senate. In 1977, Friedan flew to Chicago and urged demonstrators to ignore "phony" arguments against the ERA, by which she meant Schlafly's assertions that passing it would lead to women being drafted and unisex bathrooms. In June 1977, when the ERA was defeated (again) in the Illinois House, she flew to Springfield. She argued that politicians were treating women like second-class citizens and called for a new phase of campaigning—"days of outrage." She said women "do not accept defeat." She planned Father's Day "gifts" of demonstrations on each senator's lawn. Delivering an unofficial press conference at an IWY symposium in Normal, Illinois, she expressed fury that the ERA was tanking as the UN was celebrating International Women's Year.[30]

Amid the contradictions of the post–*Feminine Mystique* world, she looked back searchingly. After David Manning White was in a bad bicycle accident in Virginia, Friedan flew into Richmond where his wife, Catherine, picked her up. That summer, in a first-person *New York Times* story, "Cooking with Betty Friedan," she asks: "Why did I lose touch with . . . those generations of women who expressed their love with chicken soup?" Around the time her son Jonathan made plans to leave for Israel, where he would study with Shlomo Carlebach, a leader in baal teshuva, a movement helping secular Jews seeking to become observant, Friedan accepted an offer to deliver a keynote in October at Arcosanti, an intentional community on a nine-hundred-acre plot in the Arizona desert near Sedona.[31]

Friedan found pleasure there, as she had at other such communities. Founded by Italian architect Paolo Soleri as a counter to urban sprawl, Arcosanti embodied Soleri's concept of "arcology" (architecture plus ecology)—car-free and civic-minded. Seven buildings of varied shapes and sizes connected by twisting paths clustered at the foot of a twenty-five-story structure designed to house 5,000 people. Mel Roman, Friedan's neighbor from 9G in New York and now involved with Arcosanti, helped arrange her invitation to a conference on the arts and healing; there was also a concert, where Jackson Browne, McCoy Tyner, and Native American and mariachi groups played. Friedan and Arthur Blaustein, chairman of the National Advisory Council on Economic Opportunities, were keynote speakers. Psychiatrist Leonard Duhl, Dr. Andrew Weil, medicine men, herbalists, nurses, social workers, nuns, and experts on Black and Navaho health also spoke. In the giant amphitheater known as the Vault, Friedan's talk, "Wholeness Is Woman And/In Equal To Man," elaborated on how women's lib had corrupted her revolution by misunderstanding the uses of rage: "The rage of our own powerlessness as women in the office or as housewives or as volunteers has been misunderstood, misapplied too literally as class warfare or race separatism: women as-an-exploited-class rising up to take the power from men as-an-exploiter class."[32]

Friedan flew to Lummi Island to visit Jonathan. She admired him, even considered him a model for a new type of man. But she also worried that he blamed her for what had happened to him—and his generation. Nor had she ceased raging at what she saw as Jimmy Carter's tepid support of women, the stalling of the ERA, and the Houston National Women's Conference (NWC), which she considered a distraction. Held in the Sam Houston Coliseum from November 18 through 21, the NWC conference aimed to create action items for women that Carter's administration would put into place, enable the ERA to become part of the Constitution, and make reproductive rights a reality. But Friedan, now alert to surging anti-feminism and far-right activity from Schlafly's organization, called the NWC "an artificial happening." When the *New York Times* asked her about the possibility that the Klan would be in Houston at the same time as NWC, she amplified the warning she had first delivered three years earlier—an anti-Semitic plot from the Right threatened the ratifying of the ERA. She dramatically characterized the counter-event to reporter Judy Klemesrud as a "female Nuremberg fire."[33]

Schlafly did host her own anti-ERA conference at the Astro Arena in Houston at the same time as NWC, and the KKK did threaten to attend. But although anti-Semitic protesters carried hateful banners at Schlafly's conference—"Kikes for Dykes" was one—NWC would not burn up. Washington-sponsored to the tune of five million dollars, it was attended by three presidents' wives, two of whom—Betty Ford and Rosalynn Carter—supported the ERA. It was the biggest American feminist conclave since the Seneca Falls Convention in 1848, with 2,000 delegates and around 20,000 observers. NWC Houston also attracted the most diverse group of women thus far, including Latinas, Asians, Blacks, Jews, lesbians, straight, old and young. Historians regard the final stop for thousands of runners carrying the torch from the historic site of the founding of modern suffrage as both the zenith of the second-wave women's movement and the genesis of the Right's successful family-friendly anti-feminist program. Schlafly called NWC "our boot camp" and brought 20,000 anti-ERA supporters to her counter-event, where she reinvigorated the Right. The ERA, then three states away from ratification—and set to expire in 1979—gave her a platform.[34]

At first Friedan slipped into the background. Part of it was organizational: whereas Bella Abzug served as the NWC Commission's presiding officer, Friedan was merely the New York delegate "at large." Part of it was that journalists ignored her. A photo taken of the torch finish line captures Friedan, standing beside Abzug, Susan B. Anthony (grandniece of the suffragist), female runners, and Billie Jean King, glowering and looking off to the side. Friedan was "off to the side" as well when, during discussions about the ERA, she agreed with Dianne Edmondson, the Oklahoma NWC Citizens Review leader, about not extending the ERA timeline. Friedan feared that if the ERA did not pass immediately, it would not pass. But part of her ostracism arose from animosity from other feminists.

She hosted a press conference where she said, "We don't intend to let Phyllis Schlafly take over family, love and God," and expressed her dislike of Steinem and Abzug's platform. But her most impactful turn came on Sunday night, at the plenary on Sexual Preference, when she apologized for her 1969 "lavender menace" remark. "Friedan's fierce voice and tender words came from somewhere far back in the hall," wrote the journalist Anne Taylor Fleming. "I am considered to be violently opposed to the lesbian movement and in fact I have been. This issue has been used to divide us and disrupt us and has been seized on by our enemies to try and turn back the whole women's movement to equality and alienate our support. As a woman of middle age who grew up in Middle America—Peoria—and who has loved men maybe too well."[35]

Lesbians in the audience began to laugh, but Friedan pressed on: "We've all made mistakes in our view of the issue, but we all have learned . . . it's the duty of the women's movement to help [lesbians] win their civil rights." Balloons stenciled with the phrase "We Are Everywhere" flew to the ceiling. Women—many of them lesbians—jumped onto chairs and cheered. Friedan's biographer Judith Hennessee explained that she retracted her "lavender menace" slur because Dolores Alexander, NOW executive director, persuaded her to make peace and because she longed to regain her sway over the movement. Friedan herself claimed that she wanted to quash any distractions from the ERA. She would continue her apology tour for the rest of her life.[36]

The end of the Me Decade found Friedan trading old animosities for new priorities, some of which involved apologies or reexaminations of cherished principles from the 1960s. When Jimmy Carter fired her old nemesis, Bella Abzug, from the National Advisory Commission for Women, for criticizing his budget and his increase in military spending at the expense of social programs benefitting mothers, Friedan defended her. She became friendly with the Modern Orthodox feminist and writer Blu Greenberg, who had fought to reconcile gender equality and Jewish law since reading *The Feminine Mystique.* Greenberg got Friedan involved in "the federation world," as she put it, recalling her friend cringing after she joked that the book had caused the birthrate of American Jews to decline "as if I had stung her with my comment." Friedan also made an alliance with the activist and editor Michael Lerner, a founder of the Seattle Liberation Front then living as a religious Jew. He tapped her to lead an organization and host a conference to study the stress of work on family life for ordinary people, which he wanted to call "Friends of the Family." Friedan challenged him to use the more inclusive word "families," to reflect diverse households of the era—such as her own.[37]

She paid more attention to younger feminists she thought of as her adopted daughters, such as Laurie Goldstein, her brother Harry's daughter, who had been suffocating in Peoria.

Friedan got Laurie a job at NOW Legal Defense and Education Fund and let her stay at her New York apartment. They would talk all night. Yet her relationship with her biological daughter remained tumultuous. After Harvard Medical School accepted Emily, Friedan wrote an essay lecturing her daughter about feminism. She had begun *The Feminine Mystique* when Emily was one year old. Thinking of the fate of the ERA, despite two decades of progress since that time, she worried that "The things we have fought so far, are, one by one, being whittled away." She concluded by wishing that she lived in a world that could respect Emily's rejection of feminism which, articulated a few years earlier, sounded like her young self. "I'm not a feminist, I'm a person," Emily had said. Yet instead of pointing out that she had used a similar phrase in 1960, before her famous book, Friedan wrote that the world still needed her feminism.[38]

She continued to research the relationship between aging and changing sex roles. She had begun to think of aging as a problem in need of a paradigm shift. But she now also considered it as a change that the women's movement had initiated—for one, "the vanishing menopause," as she called it. She wondered if true equality between the sexes could only come to fruition in the so-called "third age." She imagined an enormous project with twenty investigators, twenty practitioners, and a hundred participants. She planned five research trips, traversing the United States to explore the "transcending of role polarization" in late life.[39]

One such trip brought her to Peoria in the summer of 1978, a few months after the National Conference of Catholic Bishops voted not to support the ERA because it might "pave the way for more abortions." The putative occasion for Friedan's trip was her fortieth high school reunion, which she agreed to write about for the *New York Times Magazine* only because the local NOW office arranged a march to show their support for the ERA in Illinois. A thousand people showed up, which Friedan saw as a positive sign. But what meant as much to her was discovering the good in her hometown. The housewives who ostracized her in 1963 welcomed her, and she returned the sentiment. She saw that in marriages of thirty-odd years "there seems to be a lot more equality and a lot more mutual dependence than the laws or the images of women's lib recognize." About her classmate John Parkhurst, now a Republican state legislator, "the roots of his activism and mine are the same, and in the last few years the political realities impinging on his life in Peoria and on mine in New York have defied that simplistic left-right polarization." She even waxed sentimental about the Peoria Country Club, which once denied her family membership because they were Jews. Now, she, Harry, and the Parkhursts had a drink there. The *New York Times* story ends in Washington, where Congress extends the deadline for ERA ratification. Since Illinois had failed to ratify, Friedan now supported the extension. "Congress saved the E.R.A. because it heard from the Peorias everywhere," she said.[40]

She bought a clapboard house on Glover Street in Sag Harbor, where she finally felt rooted. Then she found another kind of root. Laura Geller, whose brother, Michael, had been the best friend of Friedan's son Jonathan at Dalton, called her. Geller, who had just become the third woman to be ordained as a Reform rabbi, learned that the yearly meeting of the Central Conference of American Rabbis, the rabbinic arm of Reform Judaism, was scheduled to take place in Arizona, then against the ERA. Unsure as to whether she should boycott, the young rabbi asked Friedan for advice. Friedan not only told her to attend, she volunteered to speak. "We had a rump convention with her that was totally packed," Rabbi Geller said.[41] Connecting the restrictions her mother felt to writing *The Feminine Mystique* and the overrepresentation of Jewish women in feminism, Friedan told the rabbis:

> And if I've had strength and passion, and if that somehow has helped a little bit to change the world or the possibilities of the world, it comes from that core of me as a Jew. My passion, my strength, my creativity, if you will, comes from this kind of affirmation. . . . I knew this, in some way, though I was never religious as a Jew, and did not feel alien in the male culture of Judaism at that time . . .
>
> You can see why so many Jewish women particularly gave their souls to feminism, when you think of all these girls brought up by the book, brought up to the book, to the worship of the word, as our brothers were. When you think of all the passion and energy of our immigrant grandmothers, in the sweatshops without knowing the language! When you think of mothers rearing sons to be doctors, and coping with all the realities of life! When you think of all of that passion, all of that strength, all of that energy, suddenly to be concentrated in one small apartment, one small house as happened with Portnoy's mother! . . . A lot of women realized they were not alone and we broke through the feminine mystique.[42]

Although she more explicitly linked her fight for women's rights and her Jewish identity, she had hardly abandoned the Human Potential Movement. Since Esalen, she had become a patient of John Pierrakos, a Greek-born, Columbia-educated analyst and student of Wilhelm Reich. She took up Bioenergetics, a therapy developed at Esalen by Pierrakos and another Reichian, Alexander Lowen, using movement to overcome psychological blocks. It was not for the faint-hearted. The historian Martin Duberman, also Pierrakos's patient, recalls a session where he stripped to his underwear and lay on his back on a sawhorse. Only after he kicked his legs in the air so violently that he broke into sobs did the psychiatrist observe, "The more you feel the pain, the less its hold on you."[43]

Friedan often visited the Center for the Living Force, Pierrakos's three-hundred-acre retreat in Phoenicia, New York, sometimes known as Esalen East. She swam naked in the pond, sweated in the sweat lodge, ate in the communal dining room, danced, and did yoga and primal scream therapy. In the city, she did sessions with "helpers," as the therapists of Pathwork, the spiritual coaching branch of the Center for the Living Force, created by Pierrakos's wife, Eva Pierrakos, were called. One helper, Judith Garten, remembered Friedan recounting a dream involving the foundational Jewish prayer. "She woke up with the Shema on her lips," Garten said. And "she was tearful."[44]

# 11

## *Her Second Stages*

Despite the setbacks, Friedan still believed, as she told the *New York Times* in August 1979, that "women have a place in society . . . the question . . . is how to put it all together." On November 19, in her keynote at the National Assembly on the Future of the Family, at the Hilton Hotel in New York, she elaborated: Capitalism was a destructive force, albeit one targeting not just the housewife but the entire family. The first stage of feminism had ended, and she was concerned with how to support the second stage. At the conference, sponsored by NOW Legal Defense and Education Fund, architects speculated about how to design new, more gender equal forms of housing; geriatric specialists clarified what the rising numbers of old people would mean. Alvin Toffler spoke about feminism's bloodless revolution, and Isaac Asimov imagined a unisex future where machines did the housework. Benjamin Spock (whom Friedan bashed in *The Feminine Mystique*) attended, as did Bess

Myerson. "Living Equality," a panel of two-career couples led by Norman Lear, explained how such marriages worked. But the press focused on Friedan's outbursts, such as the moment when, during the question-and-answer period, she shouted from the audience: "what's in it for the men?"[1]

Predictably, the conference incited many younger feminists to write angry letters to the *Times.* The radical activist Andrea Dworkin, thirty-three, already established as an anti-pornography feminist, accused Friedan of focusing too much on "issues of privilege and comfort." But opposition spurred Friedan on, as usual. She signed with Random House to work on a book about her beloved second stage.[2]

For Friedan, *The Second Stage* would fill a void. She broke up with David Manning White, whom she would refer to as the great love of her life after Carl. Their affair had lasted for over ten years. They had traveled together, and she had met his sons. According to Judith Hennessee, as the relationship went on, she became uncomfortable with his refusal to divorce his wife, Catherine, although she continued to care about him. Yet *The Second Stage* also put to paper the utopian ideas she had begun to develop at least a decade earlier. As she was writing, she continued to put into action her recent discoveries about the link between her feminism and her Jewish identity in her activism. She accepted Blu Greenberg's invitation to join a Task Force on Jewish Women in a Changing Society sponsored by the United Jewish Appeal-Federation of New York. At an early meeting, she confronted the group about how UJA-Fed lobbied for feminist issues, such as abortion. There is no record of a reply. Later, she would complain that rabbis obstructed women's fight for equality when they said:

> Now how are we going to get the Jewish women to stop this nonsense about careers and professions and go back home and have children again, and we would look at each other,

> the women rabbis, the women heads of Hadassah, and myself and some of the academics, . . . and . . . We would very patiently try to explain, that if you want the new generation of Jewish women to continue to choose to have children, and we do want that, then we have to deal with the reality that she is going to need education, participation in modern life.[3]

Nonetheless, fearing a backlash against feminism, Friedan fought for women's equality in the Jewish community. At an April 1980 UJA-Fed meeting, she "stressed the need for involvement and awareness of the Jewish organizations of this new threat [anti-Semitism] and urged Task Force members to assure that this information is conveyed to the appropriate structures." The following month, at the White House Conference on Families in Washington, she defended diverse families, then delivered a fiery speech about abortion and the ERA. But on the advice of the American Jewish Congress, she modified the language she used to support abortion to satisfy moderate Catholics, although she refused to stop speaking about the issue. Her concession failed to sway the hardliners and the conference ended in a stalemate.[4]

Disappointments piled up. In her home state of Illinois, the ERA fell short of the three-fifths majority required for constitutional amendments by five votes. The United Nations Second World Conference on Women, held in Copenhagen in July, ended, like the first one, by attaching anti-Zionism to feminism. Although Copenhagen attracted 10,000 women, almost double the number of Mexico City, it supported anti-Zionist politics more viciously than the earlier conference. Aliza Begin did not attend. Leila Khaled, who had hijacked a TWA plane in 1969 and an El Al plane in 1970, organized walkouts during the speeches of Jehan Sadat and Hava Hareli, the chief Israeli delegate, and gave anti-Israel interviews to the media in which she spoke about Palestinian rights. Many Arab women and their allies openly proclaimed their anti-Zionism. In her account, Letty Cottin Pogrebin quotes Mormon activist Sonia Johnson: "I heard people say that Gloria Steinem, Betty Friedan, and Bella Abzug all being Jewish gives the American women's movement a bad name." Pogrebin also quotes a source reporting that Black women sided with Arab activists to decry Jewish women, refused to recognize Judaism, and did not see what "was wrong with saying Zionism is racism."[5]

Friedan's NGO forums workshop "The Future of the Family" and her consciousness raising group about feminism—according to her the only one at the conference—decried the blurring of global politics and women's rights and railed against the collaboration of fascists and anti-feminists. "I don't buy the idea that the Third World women are content with the chador and genital manipulation," she said. She signed an international petition, which read "politicizations have no place in this encounter," and stressed the importance of fighting setbacks to women's rights. She told *Time:* "There must be some way we can use our power to make this conference come up with something to advance the welfare of women." She told *Newsweek:* "The airwaves have been polluted by political issues." She could not believe that women were responsible, and blamed men and Communists. The final UN document included the "Zionism as Racism" clause, again linking women's equality and the smearing of the State of Israel. The vote was 94 to 4.[6]

After Ronald Reagan was elected, Friedan stepped up her appeals to observant Jewish women. At the national convention of the Women's League for Conservative Judaism she even adapted the famous words of Hillel to reconcile the family and feminism: "If a woman is not able to be for herself, how can she be for her family?" Yet this commitment to family-friendly feminism sometimes left little room for individual consciousnesses, even those she loved. At her sixtieth birthday party, she complained, her friends treated her as though she—and feminism—had died. She began a cover story in the *New York Times Maga-*

*zine* by quoting an unnamed friend declaring feminism "over" and worrying that the ERA would tank. In March, desperate, she attended the Gridiron Club dinner in Washington. There, she appealed to Nancy Reagan, who had graduated one year behind her at Smith (they did not know each other there), to help. According to her, Nancy responded, "Oh Betty, Ronnie and I are for equality and Ronnie and I are for women's rights, we're just not for amendments." To be sure, a few months later, Reagan nominated the first female Supreme Court justice, a pro-ERA, pro-choice Republican—Sandra Day O'Connor. But Friedan continued to worry about Schlafly, whose STOP ERA had gained force. To counter her rival, Friedan had increased her protestations of regret for condemning housewives in *The Feminine Mystique* and pointed out that the conservative leader, who had recently graduated from law school, would not have been admitted if not for the women's movement.[7]

Jonathan had gone back to school, gotten his BA, and started an MA in engineering. On October 25, 1981, then twenty-eight, he would be the first of her children to marry. The Jewish ceremony with his wife-to-be, Helen Nakdimen, a teacher who would become a rabbi, was held in Betty's backyard in Sag Harbor. The glass was smashed. At the party, held at nearby Baron's Cove Inn, Carl got drunk and made a misogynist joke: "Never marry a woman you can't knock out with one punch." But according to one friend who was there, Betty didn't get upset. She looked at him as though she was humoring him, as if she was saying to herself fondly, "Oh Carl, come on."[8]

*The Second Stage* was published shortly after the wedding. Friedan hoped the book would help get the ERA passed and beat back conservatives. It did neither. *The Second Stage* functioned somewhat successfully as a letter about her "daughters," to whom she apologizes for having to "speak the unspeakable and accept new uncomfortable realities and secret pains." But like *The Feminine Mystique, The Second Stage* strikes at prevailing orthodoxies as a poetic, individualist claim more than a collective, activist one—the epigraph, from Rilke, contains the line, "be patient towards all that is unsolved in your heart." There is a good deal of repetition, including about her personal life. Friedan apologizes yet again for the gap between her public courage and her shame about her violent marriage. "My own brave words in the early days of the women's movement hid a certain abject terror of making it on my own in the last days of my self-destructive marriage."[9]

*The Second Stage* is divided into two parts. Part One is a documentation of the collapse of the women's movement and an apologia for Friedan's struggle against it. She dismisses pornography and registering women for the draft as distractions from equal pay and, for the first time, argues against the welfare state. She blames the anti-family direction of women's lib for alienating American women who would otherwise have joined the movement even as she admits she spent too much time fighting over it. She wishes to move forward. She defends her use of hyperbolic language in *The Feminine Mystique*, citing its necessity even as she apologizes—especially for the phrase "comfortable concentration camp." Then she coins another incendiary phrase, "the *feminist* mystique," which condemns women's lib for the movement's failure.[10]

In a rare moment of self-reflection, she confesses that her uneasiness and fear about motherhood not only shaped her 1963 masterpiece but hollowed out "the way I felt about being a mother." Time and the easing of her daughter's hatred allowed her to break through. But then, like some female Lear, she only praises movement "daughters" who echo her idea that family is as important for women's equality as external fulfillment. She concedes that she understands why the conservative writer Jean Bethke Elshtain caricatures the women's movement and she chastises Ellen Willis for defining the family "as the main source of women's oppression." She commends Linda Gray Sexton, the daughter of the poet Anne Sexton and author of the 1979 book *Between Two Worlds: Young Women in Crisis*, for deftly representing the tension between feminine and feminist mystiques. Yet Friedan distinguishes herself from conservatives by defining family not as the nuclear family of the 1950s, but as chosen ones fought for by liberal gay men, women, and feminists. Of course, many of these individuals found her perspective antiquated. On reading *The Second Stage*, the gay Jewish activist Eric E. Rofes, Emily's friend, wrote Friedan: "At some point we should sit down and talk out some stuff about gay people. I've learned a lot from you about feminism and I only wish you had a better understanding and feeling for gay people."[11]

Chapter Two is notable for Friedan's critique of the "superwoman"—the word signifying the pressure women had experienced since second-wave feminism to "have it all" without any systemic support. Despite the sex role revolution, women still had to choose between success in the home or the office. In Chapter Three, Friedan returns to a solution she has been suggesting for decades—federal- or company-sponsored day care—to help women crushed between motherhood and work. She reviews statistics that show that few people live in the kind of family arrangements that are supposedly the norm. Finally, she avows that her new focus on the family does not diminish her fight for how "to live the equality we fought for"—a fight whose path had become unclear. Awkwardly navigating the distance between what she imagined and what existed, she quotes Joan of Arc: yet whereas in *The Feminine Mystique*, Friedan used the saint's words ("*all that I am*") to defend women's choices to fulfill themselves outside the home, she now does so to defend their choice to be housewives and mothers too.[12]

Recalling the White House Conference on Families the previous year, she blames its dispiriting outcome on polarizing media coverage. But she does celebrate the unexpected coalition that emerged among liberal and right-wing groups. In one of the moments that most angered progressives, she modifies further the language she used to describe her position on abortion. "I am not *for abortion*—I am for the *choice to have children*," she wrote, putting to paper her agonizing feelings about the impossible choice for women she now believed this issue represented. She hoped that her softer language would reverse the Right's successful co-opting of the pro-family position. Privately, she questioned whether abortion should be the central issue of the women's movement. But she never stopped fighting for women's right to have it.[13]

Other things upset readers. *The Second Stage* does not mention any of the generation of Jewish women writers who, after reading *Feminine Mystique*, made sense of their relationships with their mothers: Grace Paley, Tillie Olsen, Erica Jong, and Nancy Friday, whose bestseller, *My Mother My Self* concluded that feminism gave women "alternatives her mother did not." Friedan loathed the grim books and movies of this age, "objecting" to the endings in which the heroines wound up dead or walking on the beach by themselves. At the same time, she attacked male novelists, including Philip Roth, who, she writes, "have created 'heroes' who go to desperate lengths of violent or covert aggression against women because they fear their own passivity." She dismisses one of the most contentious issues the ratification of the ERA raised—the introduction of female cadets at West Point—as a distraction.[14]

Part Two starts with an analysis of recent failures of the women's movement and ends by arguing that women could address those failures by refusing to give in to the "either/or" conversation (either home or career). Reasonable enough. But Friedan mars these chapters by frequently falling into a tone that is alternately corporate, reactionary, New Age-y, odd, mean, or tone deaf. When she approvingly cites Stanford researchers on the necessity of rebalancing leadership styles between alpha (macho, dominant) and beta personalities (submissive, female), she identifies with the latter, like a throwback to pre–*Feminine Mystique* days, not to mention clueless about herself. The most difficult chapter to read, Chapter Eight, "Take Back the Day," dismisses the fight against sexual violence and blames anti–sexual violence activists for contributing to the twilight of second-wave feminism: "Obsession with rape, even offering Band-Aids to its victims, is a kind of wallowing in that impotent rage," this chapter begins.[15]

Such off-putting ideas obscure the book's centrist politics, as well as its faith in Gestalt psychology and feminist architecture. For the first time Friedan uses the word "generativity"—the penultimate of the eight stages of life, as defined by psychologist Erik Erikson, with whom she had studied in 1943. To Friedan, generativity meant "passing on" wisdom to the next generation. But she also used the word to combat the idea that feminism was selfish or narcissistic, to convince readers that although Erikson did not say so, women could be leaders in "generativity." The underdiscussed Chapter Nine, "The House and the Dream," elaborates on her long-held ideas that the sex role revolution demands a spatial one. She dismisses kibbutzim—where she saw women reprising the role of housewife—as a model. But she holds up intentional communities like Moshe Safdie's Habitat 67 and Paolo Soleri's desert laboratory Arcosanti, as well as Dolores Hayden's groundbreaking book *The Grand Domestic Revolution*, published earlier in 1981. In her feminist classic, Hayden puts to paper an idea that Friedan had been talking about for decades: that the sex role revolution would stall until architects and urban planners redesigned housing. Friedan used Hayden to write about how her ideal "family of choice," united by a common fight for equality and justice, lived.

The last chapter, "Human Sex and Human Politics," adds to accusations she had voiced since 1973—that the Klan and John Birch Society were funding STOP ERA. Here she recounts the ugly incident she had learned of in her home state two years earlier: "A leaflet sent to each state senator just before the legislature voted on ratification of ERA in May 1980, reproduced a newsclip of a Hollywood fundraising party for ERA with arrows pointing to all the Jewish names. The leaflet said: More proof that ERA is a plot to wreck Christian homes—and is promoted by anti-Christians, Jews, anti-Americans, and subversives."[16]

From there, Friedan addresses the charges of racism that critics had leveled at *The Feminine Mystique* and then NOW. She argues that what she called "her" movement had "more vitality than most movements because we were truly acting *for ourselves.*" Thus she "inspired minority groups of women" to move forward, she writes, echoing Dr. King's "we cannot be what we ought to be until you are what you ought to be." She quotes Rabbi Hillel: "If I am not for myself who will be for me? If I am only for myself, who am I?"[17]

*The Second Stage* flopped. The *New York Times*'s John Leonard called it "flim flam." Simone de Beauvoir, then seventy-three, threw the book across the room. In the *Nation*, Bella Abzug criticized it for trivializing collective action, and Ellen Willis wrote that Friedan was "blaming the victim," holding women's liberationists responsible for the patriarchy even as she presented a "vulgarized rehash" of their arguments. In *The Radical Future of Liberal Feminism*, Zillah Eisenstein wrote: "Friedan inadvertently denies male privilege by denying that antagonism exists between men and women as sexual classes." Yet several major women writers, including Mary Cantwell and Erica Jong, praised the book, and in a second *New York Times* review, the legal scholar Herma Hill Kay wrote about how by seizing the idea of family from conservatives, Friedan's book accomplished an important win for liberals.

At the same time, conservative writers approved. Perversely, Phyllis Schlafly applauded it for destroying feminism; in the

*New Republic*, the political scientist Benjamin Barber gave it one largely sympathetic treatment and the writer Megan Marshall another. A Jewish Orthodox newspaper hailed it for retracting *The Feminine Mystique*'s condemnation of housewives and "passionate volunteerism." The sociologist and critic Judith Stacey would point out that Friedan, with her emphasis on families and abhorrence of sexual politics, now shared more with neo-conservatives than radicals and, however inadvertently, may have helped fuel anti-feminism.[18]

The drubbings hurt. Friedan wept at a 1982 pro-choice march after organizers excluded her from the roster of speakers. Perhaps it consoled her that the book succeeded to the extent that it did as a message to Emily. Whereas she had written *The Feminine Mystique* to understand her mother, she wrote *The Second Stage* to broker a reconciliation with her daughter. This time, the tactic seemed to work better. Emily reversed her anti-feminist position of a few years earlier. And when Friedan returned to Israel in March, her daughter accompanied her.

Friedan now found Israeli women more sympathetic to her ideals. Since the Yom Kippur War, they had recognized that they "were living in a kind of fool's paradise" where gender equality was concerned, and needed American feminists such as Friedan, said the Israeli feminist Alice Shalvi. Of course, it helped that instead of denigrating Israeli women, Friedan struck a more inviting note at Mankind 2000, an international futurist conference at the University of Haifa attended by her cousin, the judge David Bazelon, and notables such as Joe Papp and Elie Wiesel, whose speech, "Never Again," struck the crowd into silence. As for Friedan, her talk, "The Future of Women," traced the monumental changes in family and career she had inspired. She worried that men were suffering less from her unfinished revolution than from the capitalist boot. Yet she pointed to the Israeli Canadian architect Moshe Safdie, then forty-three, in the audience holding his baby, as proof that *her* movement had altered male and female sex roles in a positive way. Of course, she still had to beat back male chauvinism. After the South African heart surgeon Christiaan Barnard answered his own rhetorical question "Why did God create women?" with "To be a companion to men," Friedan snapped that the Old Testament's use of the verb "to know" describing sex from a male perspective ignored Jewish women.[19]

She did not spend all her time in Israel talking about feminism. According to Lennart Levi, a Swedish professor of environmental medicine also participating in Mankind 2000, one Friday night, the participants took a field trip into the desert. Suddenly, their transport broke down. Everyone got off and sat down under a fig tree. After some time, a local bus stopped but could not fit everyone. "Women and children first," Friedan joked, as she climbed on.[20]

After Mankind 2000, she went to Jerusalem, where she wandered through the Old City, pausing at the Western Wall to pray for the safe delivery of Emily's baby—her new grandchild.

June 30, 1982, marked the deadline for the extension of the ratification of the Equal Rights Amendment. Thirty-eight states were needed to add the ERA to the Constitution, but only thirty-five voted for the amendment. Despondent, Friedan wrote: "So diverse have the choices and patterns of women's lives become that there is no single issue now that could hold us all together as firmly as the battle for our constitutional rights." At the same time, she predicted that the women's movement had learned from the loss. "Their new political energy will turn the country around," she said. Yet she explained Reagan by saying that in the next election more women would vote for better female candidates: "changes will take time. We're still electing women who are imitation men."[21]

Yet although she was hopeful about the ability of the women's movement to weather these political setbacks, she would remain silent on questions emerging out of the so-called culture wars with which her American "post-feminist" daughters grappled, such as how multiculturalism intersected with Judaism, anti-Semitism, and anti-Zionism. Nor did she publicly answer feminists of color like bell hooks bringing anew the charge of racism against *The Feminine Mystique.* She hated to read anything negative about herself and saw such questions as "diversions" from the fight against Reagan, who had declared war on reproductive rights and the women's movement.

Instead, she again turned to her own experience. In "Thoughts on Becoming a Grandmother," the epilogue to the twentieth anniversary edition of *The Feminine Mystique*, she writes with optimism about gender-equal sex roles in families, as demonstrated by her children. She joyously recounts the birth of her first grandson, Rafael, although she expresses regret that her daughter-in-law, like her, had to deliver by cesarean. She takes pleasure in reconnecting with her ex-husband, Carl, for the first time in years. She calls her son a *Second Stage* man and her daughter-in-law, who takes time off from work for the baby, a *Second Stage* woman. Being "second stage" advances "chosen motherhood," she writes. She is still reshaping women's roles. "I have no role model as a modern, feminist grandmother," she writes.[22]

She did, however, have her mother. Since the early 1960s, when she was in her sixties, Miriam had been living in Leisure World retirement home in Southern California. Betty visited her in the 1980s, after she returned to working on *The Fountain of Age*, the book about aging she had sold a few years earlier. Using her mother as an "impetus," she hoped to explore how women and men transcended sex roles as they aged and to investigate questions such as whether feminists suffered less from menopause or heart disease than unliberated women. As she had been doing for decades, she connects the design of living structures to the well-being of their inhabitants. Clustering old people together, institutions such as Leisure World protected them from the isolation that can crush people late in life and yet alienated them, she writes. Whereas years earlier she had made Miriam stand in for the evil of housewifery, now she used her mother to symbolize the social ill of agism. Just as many housewives in *The Feminine Mystique* succumbed to depression and shame behind closed doors, so did many of the 21,000 senior citizens in Leisure World. And like the postwar suburbs, Leisure World discouraged its residents from holding honest conversations about what mattered, which Friedan suggested generated rage. She saw it in Miriam, who, despite taking up horseback riding and becoming a duplicate bridge player, recounted how bridge players came "to the bridge table hooked up to IV equipment." Miriam kept dealing hands when one of the players got a nosebleed and two people died during the game, she told her daughter. The players carried on as paramedics carried out the bodies. "That's the way I'd like to die, in the middle of a good bridge game," Miriam said.[23]

In the summer of 1984, she threw Emily, now a pediatrician, a wedding in her backyard at Sag Harbor to celebrate her marriage to Eli Farhi, a Jewish doctor whose father fought for the Haganah. And she devoted herself to Walter Mondale's campaign for the presidency. Virulently opposed to Jesse Jackson after he referred to New York as Hymietown, she believed that with Geraldine Ferraro as the first female vice presidential nominee, Mondale would usher in a gender-equal future. And yet, that summer, with the defeat of Mondale still in the future, Friedan uttered her most inspiring remarks in Jerusalem. The members of the American Jewish Congress Advisory Committee on the twentieth annual AJC Dialogue—"Woman as Jew/ Jew as Woman: An Urgent Inquiry"—had "unanimously recommended" that she deliver the keynote for the Americans; the

Israeli feminist socialist Rivka Bar-Yosef was her counterpart. Held from July 30 to August 2 at the Van Leer Institute in Jerusalem, the Dialogue also hosted Cynthia Ozick, Elizabeth Holtzman, then district attorney of Brooklyn, and many Israeli journalists and scholars. But Friedan was indisputably the star.[24]

On the evening of July 30, three hundred people crammed into the auditorium to hear her keynote, "Women and Jews: The Quest for Selfhood." The AJC had to set up closed-circuit television in the lobby to make additional audience space. By all accounts, Friedan exceeded herself. According to the *New York Times*, she repurposed a scholarly lecture as "a rap session." Anne Roiphe later described how "like a Hasidic rabbi she rides her thoughts through fields of association, jumping over matters of structure and logic." Friedan riffed on the decades-old idea that anti-Semitism was as toxic as misogyny, delivered a "biting account" of the American women's movement, critiqued Israeli sexism, and defended "potluck Seders" and universal day care. She complained about materialistic American rabbis and gender wage inequity and asked: "Despite the fact that Jewish women like myself have given a lot of the ideas and the vision to the leadership of the modern feminist movement, the Jewish community, as represented by the male heads of organizations, has been a bit threatened by us, the same as the leadership of Israeli society. Why was this threat more profound among Jews than elsewhere in American society? Or did it just pain me more, because after all I was and am Jewish?"[25]

Friedan felt her Geiger counter—the internal device that years earlier made her see that one housewife suffering was a mass affliction—clicking. Feminism was "essential for the survival of Judaism," not "selfish," as some rabbis claimed, she said. She retold the story of how anti-Semitism in the women's movement and global anti-Zionism had spurred her reimagining of the link between her Jewishness and her work on behalf of women. She proclaimed that Israel and America needed to unite to fight anti-Zionism at the upcoming UN-sponsored Third World Conference on Women in Nairobi. She again mentioned Erik Erikson's idea of generativity, the stage of life in which older people pass down their wisdom. She imagined a feminist utopia that included female rabbis and generals alike and said that whereas she had once answered questions about her identity by answering "agnostic" she now answered "Jew." She emphasized the importance of bringing women from the margins to the mainstream, echoing the Jewish reverence for humanity, repeating Elie Wiesel's phrase—"in the interest of life."[26]

Over the next few days, Friedan participated in a series of lively conversations about Israeli feminism. As usual, she made some women in attendance uncomfortable. The writer Rochelle Furstenberg would raise a difficult subject: in the United States, had Friedan made it possible for women to pursue their "passionate journey" or had she merely displaced women's enslavement from housework "to their professional functions."[27]

That's a fair question to ask. Yet in Jerusalem, as at other times, Friedan was less concentrated on the past than generating new actions, such as the launch of Israeli feminism. On the evening of July 31, along with other women from the conference, she attended *Maasah Bruria*, a piece created by the all-female troupe Theatre Company Jerusalem. *Maasah Bruria* told the story of Bruria, the most esteemed female sage in the Talmud. She kicks a student to show that Judaism needs to be physically enacted, said co-director Gabriella Lev. Afterward, Lev remembered, during a post-show talk back, some of the women in the audience argued that *Maasah Bruria* should have offered an action plan to combat gender inequality in Judaism. Friedan countered that the play was a work of art—not a manifesto—and as such had its own language. "For her, feeling and passion made protest," Lev said.[28]

Thus the following morning, at a colloquium titled "Women

in the Family," when the Israeli sociologist Michal Palgi speculated that, because of required military service in Israel, it might be difficult transplanting American-style feminism, Friedan responded with a speech that sounded like something Bruria herself could have said:

> So what is missing? What is missing is the question that you have to ask of yourselves, and even more important, of Israeli society, just as we asked of American society. Are you proceeding from the assumption that the values of equality are shared by the larger society? Can you assume that Israeli society accepts these values on behalf of Israeli women, or do you have yet to go through that first stage of making the perception of equality be heard louder and clearer, in your own minds and in the minds of society?

Chaired by Alice Shalvi, the next session, "Women in Jewish Religious Practice," discussed how the ultra-Orthodox impeded Israeli feminism. After listening, Friedan again urged Israeli women to start their own movement. She additionally explained, for the first time in public, why she had excluded the details of her Popular Front past from *The Feminine Mystique*. "It was also the end of the McCarthy era and it was really risky for wornen [*sic*] in government and in the labor unions to take part in our activities." Before the Thursday morning sessions, Friedan participated in an all-female minyan led by Naamah Kelman, at the time a young activist and founding member of the Egalitarian Minyan, the first of its kind in Jerusalem. In Friedan's hotel room in the King David, Kelman called her to the Torah, she recalled, adding that Friedan said that it was *her* first time. Kelman added: "She said 'I'm listening to the words of the prayer, hear o Israel lord our God, the lord is one. And "one" is Man, woman, and child.'" About this humane rejection of the patriarchy, Friedan would write, "Tears came to my eyes."[29]

That afternoon, at a session in which Israeli women whom

the rabbinical court had penalized streamed into the room, she was both moved and impatient with all the talking. She took charge, again encouraging the Israelis to protest. "You have to put your bodies where your mouths are," she said. That line was "a catalyst," Anne Roiphe wrote. Elizabeth Holtzman and the Israeli legal scholar Frances Raday drafted a statement calling for Israeli women to form an independent feminist organization and the Israeli Women's Network was born. Cynthia Ozick gave a soaring valedictory speech that praised Friedan for her definition of feminism. "She encapsulates it in a word—the 'personhood' as she puts it, of women." The next morning, Friedan walked with—not in front of—one hundred women who had embraced their personhood down Jabotinsky Street to the King David Hotel, where Yitzhak Shamir and Shimon Peres (through a coalition, sharing the Israeli prime ministership) were meeting. She wanted the Israelis to be in front so they could make a case for the independent Israeli women's organization to the prime ministers. Friedan described the event as a victory. Yet only after the women waited for hours and sent the leaders a note reminding them who elected them did Shamir and Peres open the door. They let in two protesters, then conceded that they "would take serious note" of the feminists' concerns. Nonetheless, "many women felt elated by the government's acknowledging them for the first time," Alice Shalvi recalled.[30]

Israel changed her. In a *Voice of America* interview, Friedan talked openly about the absence of Black women in NOW and speculated that the second stage would do a better job including all women. And although she did not see herself as "part of the Jewish establishment," as she wrote to her friend A. M. Rosenthal, executive editor of the *New York Times*, she agreed to co-chair the American Jewish Committee's National Commission for Women's Equality (NCWE). Her first move was to explore the intersection of religious freedom and women's rights.

But she also used clout to address inequality. According to the legal scholar Frances Raday, Friedan helped end Hadassah Hospital's policy requiring women to retire at sixty, five years younger than men. Friedan and Elizabeth Holtzman met with Ruth Popkin, president of Hadassah in the United States. If Popkin wanted to ignore her, *fine*, Friedan said. They were meeting with a *Times* editor the next day. Presto! The policy changed.[31]

At sixty-three, Friedan remained unconvinced that gay rights were as important as those of women. But what wounded her as much as the distance women still had to go to achieve equality was their declining romantic possibilities as they aged. In *The Fountain of Age*, she would write matter-of-factly about the loss of her sexual appetite, the diminishing chances of meeting a life partner: "How to face the reality that there might never again be a man to fill that longing for romance, sexual passion, transcendent bliss?" She was no less consumed by the declining political possibilities for the women's movement. After the defeat of Mondale and the reelection of Ronald Reagan, she took an assignment from *Harper's* to cover a junket to Nicaragua led by Abbie Hoffman and his wife, Johanna. The idea was to spend a week during Christmas to introduce Americans, including Art D'Lugoff, owner of the Village Gate, and his wife, Avital, writer M. G. Lord and her soon-to-be-husband, book dealer Glenn Horowitz, to liberation theologists Ferdinand and Ernesto Cardenal and the Sandinistas. It was a difficult trip. Vegetables and fruit were scarce. The group, which Friedan dismissed as "religious do-gooders," visited Managua, the port town of Corinto, and a farming collective. A draft of the *Harper's* piece criticizes the male rebels, who, she wrote, discouraged their women from pursuing an education, made them wash clothes by hand, and neither elected them to leadership positions nor affirmed reproductive rights. Friedan was distracted. She drank too much. According to those who were there, when the group met the Cardenals, she dozed off. When they stopped at a women's collective run by the Sandinistas, the woman who had famously critiqued the commercialization of domestic labor demanded to know why the female laborers had sewing machines, not computers. This outraged many of the "do-gooders," who felt her remark was imperialist. She was upset that the trip was not the kind of high-level delegation she was used to. What did she expect? asked M. G. Lord.

"Well not exactly Elaine's, but just a place where people like *us* would go!"[32]

She was more in her element fighting Reagan. To commemorate the end of World War II and make a gesture of reconciliation with Helmut Kohl, the president had scheduled the laying of a wreath for German soldiers killed at Bitburg, the cemetery where forty-nine members of the SS were also buried. Despite protests from the Jewish community, Reagan refused to back down, even when Elie Wiesel staged a dramatic dissent during his acceptance of the Congressional Medal of Honor. "Mr. President, that place is not your place," he said. Reagan would not reconsider.

On May 2, Friedan flew to Germany with a group sponsored by the American Jewish Congress (AJC) that also included Dick Gregory and David Dinkins, then New York City Clerk. The flight landed in Munich and on the first night, the group dined with surviving relatives of Hans and Sophie Scholl, and members of the White Rose—Christian students led by the Scholls and their philosophy professor—who disseminated anti-Nazi leaflets before they were beheaded in 1943. Echoing Wiesel, Friedan said, "It is in the interest of life that we must remember the Holocaust. We must not forget." The next day, at Perlacher Forest Cemetery in Munich, Friedan and Dick Gregory laid a wreath of white roses on the Scholls' graves. The group then traveled to Dachau, where Kaddish was recited. Ernest Michel talked about his time in the camps. Friedan, Gregory, and Henry Siegmann, the director of the AJC, gave speeches demanding that Reagan cancel his visit to Bitburg. To their horror, the president only conceded that he would shorten it from thirty minutes to ten. On the flight home, Friedan, Gregory, and Dinkins huddled in the back of the plane, plotting their survival of the Reagan years. Friedan later used strong language to condemn him: "Americans, after Bitburg, have to wonder whether a president . . . who can gloss glibly over fascist evil in history might have to be watched closely for signs of acquiescence to evil."[33]

In New York, confronted with the so-called "feminism sex wars"—the fight roiling feminists about whether pornography should be banned—Friedan sided with the "pro sex" camp, including Ellen Willis. She condemned anti-porn feminists, such as Steinem and Andrea Dworkin, for supporting censorship and linking the women's movement to the religious right. Further, as co-chair of the American Jewish Committee's National Commission for Women's Equality, she tapped the Playboy Foundation for money to help fund a conference on women's rights and religious freedom. Although this venture alienated many Jewish anti-porn feminists, Friedan believed it would help the conversation about women's equality continue robustly.[34]

The American Jewish Congress conscripted Friedan (along with Bella Abzug) to Forum 85, the nonprofit symposium of the Third UN World Conference on Women, to be held in Nairobi between July 15 and 26, 1985. Friedan worried that Nairobi, like the first two UN conferences on women, would link anti-Semitism and the women's movement, resulting in the eruption of "a new assault on Israel." But rather than dive into the fray and lead a march or walkout, she wanted a less confrontational way of being. A "Geiger counter" moment led to her sitting under a tree on the University of Nairobi campus and dispensing wisdom:[35]

> Never did find out for sure whether it was a banyan tree or a baobab a fig or pepper tree, or maybe an acacia. But it was tall, with spreading leafy graceful branches, with shade enough for 30 people as I'd asked on a grassy knoll behind the peace tent. Though after the word spread that there every noon, we were sitting having "dialogue on future directions of feminism," the circle under the tree spread, until the last few days maybe a hundred of us were sitting cross-legged on the grass, with a circle of African men, standing behind us, leaning in to listen. The dialogue under that tree kept evolving, and the tree itself changed, just like the women's movement.[36]

The conference, which would attract over 15,000 women, many from outside of America, started with a pedestrian concern—a lodging shortage, of all things. After it became clear that there would not be enough room for official delegates, luxury hotels in Nairobi claimed they had not invited so many women to the Forum. An offer was extended to resettle Forum attendees in university dorms far from the city center. Outraged, Friedan saw this as a continuation of the sexism that had plagued Mexico City and Copenhagen. She urged the women to stage sit-ins and to quadruple up as a way of negotiating with the Ministry of Tourism. After singing a round of Mavis Staples's "We Shall Not Be Moved" in the lobby, they won that battle. Friedan subsequently spent most of the conference holding court beneath her tree, where she saw not unity—but commonality—among women from diverse backgrounds. She urged all women to do battle in "the theatre of life" and to consider the many faces of feminism emerging all over the world. Swerving from her concern that geopolitics would crush the women's movement (as in Mexico and Copenhagen), here she applauded the progress women had made in their countries. She noted approvingly that whereas at the Copenhagen conference many radical women equated Western feminism with imperialism, at Nairobi a new, more complex relationship among First and Third World countries had been accepted. But as one of around 250 Jewish women among the attendees at the forum, she found herself in a tricky spot. While loathing many of Reagan's policies, she aligned with his support of Israel. She had not protested when Reagan appointed his daughter Maureen—the women had fought together for the ERA in Florida—and hard-liner Alan Keyes to the U.S. delegation. She thought Reagan, especially, would prevent a repeat of Mexico City's anti-Zionism. "Maureen worked a lot harder than daddy wanted her to," she said.[37]

Not in all arenas. As Friedan had also predicted, Reagan and Keyes whitewashed Reagan's anti-feminism and ignored the Houston Plan of Action—the agenda that women at the 1977 Houston IWY meeting agreed to pursue. But in contrast to her fiery activism at the previous two UN conferences, Friedan had "determined not to be confrontational," said Sandra Featherman, a university administrator and activist taking notes for her. She "did not want things to go negative," Featherman added, explaining that they were among a group of women who met each morning to try to "cool the anti-Jewish message." Otherwise, Friedan sat under the tree and participated in a few forum activities, kept to herself in the peace tent—the designated area for controversial speech about geopolitics—even when, after Bella Abzug defended Israel in an Israeli-Palestinian speak-out, an Arab woman blamed Jews for Palestinian suffering. Some Israeli feminists misread her uncharacteristic reticence as holding court, but she maintained her distance from the fray. Mostly—she could not refrain from scolding the anti-Zionist Egyptian feminist Nawal El Sadaawi (whom she admired) for bringing up the West Bank, fearing that this would rouse a reprise of Copenhagen. And she castigated a Mexican woman for her "politics," an exchange captured by a *Washing-*

*ton Post* reporter, which to many women made her look out of touch, at best.[38]

During the final week, Palestinians and the Soviet bloc walked out of negotiations over the official conference document. But Maureen Reagan and Alan Keyes refused to sign until administrators removed the phrase "Zionism as Racism." Behind the scenes, according to the activist and writer Shirley Joseph, Friedan urged everyone to go back to the negotiating table. "There is a *will* to make it work. Keep trying," she said. As they did. Thus, on the Israel front, Americans won. However, in terms of women's issues, Friedan concluded that America had lost. "We are no longer the cutting edge of modern feminism," she wrote, thinking of the countries whose governments supported women to whom the United States had turned its back.[39]

When Friedan returned to her position at American Jewish Congress, she abandoned her efforts to persuade *Playboy* to fund the conference she had been planning on women's rights and religious freedom "due to the divisiveness of the issue." She dialed back her involvement at AJC to focus on fighting Reagan. In her *New York Times* essay "How to Get the Women's Movement Moving Again" she decried the president's dismantling of gender equity laws, denounced female athletes wearing skimpy sequin tops, condemned the reversal of legislation prohibiting businesses from discrimination in hiring, ridiculed the idea of a "postfeminist" generation, and quarreled with leftist critics. She ended with suggestions, including "get off the pornography kick because the real obscenity is poverty" and "do not surrender to the far right." Although fighting anti-Semitism was not on the list, Friedan had not forgotten the dangerous links between that scourge and misogyny. In a talk at Hebrew University that year, she returned to her old caution that listeners should "systematically analyze the similarities between anti-Semitism and sexism."[40]

# 12

## *"Here I Am! This Is Me! This Is How I Am!"*

In 1986, the University of Southern California offered Friedan, sixty-five, the chance to run what she called "a think tank" at the Institute for the Study of Women and Men (SWMS), then chaired by the historian Helen Lefkowitz Horowitz. Friedan rented a condo at the Sea Colony, an elegant beachfront building in Santa Monica, and began to enjoy California life. The think tank, which would last for seven winters, became, the publisher Sara Miller McCune observed, "one of the more unusual spoken dialogues to be developed under university auspices." Supported by a coalition of academic programs and funded by philanthropist Diana Meehan, the think tank was co-hosted by Rabbi Laura Geller, who had become head of USC Hillel. The feminist political scientist Judith Stiehm and the feminist legal scholar Judith Resnik helped shape it early on.[1]

The group met around once a month, usually in a room at the Hillel building on Hoover Street. Mostly women (and a few men) sat at a round table. Sometimes people crouched on the floor or women sang. Friedan was a terrible listener, so one of the scholars attempted to make sure that everyone got to speak. Over time, the think tank would cover an impressive range of topics, including women's lives, pornography, media representation, feminist platforms of the presidential candidates, legal issues, gun violence, and feminist architecture. Scholars debated what Friedan called "public members"—people from film, music, journalism, politics, architecture, the armed forces, education, and business: for instance, Wallis Annenberg, Barbara Boxer, Dianne Feinstein, Anne Taylor Fleming, Gloria Goldsmith, Ann Reiss Lane, Susan Anspach, and Norman Lear, whom Friedan had met in the 1970s and whom she hoped would make a film about *The Feminine Mystique* and *The Second Sex.* Barbra Streisand attended several sessions, including one on intimacy. According to Friedan, she wanted to know "what happens to relationships when women have power." But she hardly spoke and when she did it was only a whisper. The executive director of the American Jewish Congress and a board member of the Jewish Federation Council showed up, as did a female rabbi in training. As usual, Friedan welcomed men. John Doyle, a Cal Tech mathematician, swore that the seminar "helped me reshape mathematical thinking."[2]

Friedan often arrived frumpily dressed "with an interesting scarf," recalled the architect Dana Cuff, a frequent attendee. She sometimes opened a session with a monologue or a joke. Other times she yelled. She craved the approval of the celebrities in attendance even as she cast herself as an ordinary American woman fighting radical feminists who had hijacked the movement two decades earlier. Once, during a session in which a scholar was talking about feminist theory, Frieda Caplan, founder and then CEO of Frieda's, a produce company that, in her words, "introduced kiwis to the world," whispered, "I don't understand what these people are talking about." Friedan replied, "Neither do I."[3]

At best, the think tank served as a laboratory where diverse people could work on new problems that Friedan's "sex role revolution" had created. "That seminar led me to believe that as a woman in a male dominated field, I could do something significant," said Cuff, who was told to draw a blueprint for a feminist city. It was also, said the late TV writer and comedian Emily Levine, who developed a show from the discussions, a place to hear different perspectives and to stretch your intellect; consensus was not the goal. Friedan used the think tank to hash out positions on new legal cases redefining motherhood and work for women. In 1986, *California Federal Savings & Loan v. Guerra* addressed the issue of whether a California law violated an individual's civil rights (and Title VII) if it required employers to rehire women after maternity leave. While NOW attorneys contended that giving birth should be defined as a disability to ensure that employers did not discriminate against women, Friedan, adding her name to a brief filed by Planned Parenthood, the International Ladies' Garment Workers Union, and groups supporting working people, wanted to distinguish between pregnancy leaves and those granted due to disability. She told the *New York Times* that "there has to be a concept of equality that takes into account that women are the ones who have the babies." In 1987, after the Supreme Court ruled 6–3 that pregnancy should not be regarded as a disability and required states to give mothers their jobs back after pregnancy leaves, Friedan was cautiously optimistic.[4]

That same year, the "Baby M" trial split Friedan between competing visions of motherhood: one limiting the definition of a woman as someone who would write a contract to gain a child; the other creating a class of poor women who might be exploited for their childbearing capacity. In the case—the first one involving a surrogate mother—Mary Beth Whitehead, a twenty-nine-year-old high school dropout homemaker, was suing to void the contract she had signed to sell her baby to a middle-class family, the Sterns. Richard Stern, a biochemist, and Elizabeth Stern, a pediatrician who had delayed childbearing because of her career and because she had MS, fought back. At first, Friedan sided more with Whitehead, the surrogate and biological mother, yet she worried that a surrogacy industry would commodify motherhood. In March, she joined the Committee for Mary Beth Whitehead, a group of around one hundred feminists including Gloria Steinem, Meryl Streep, Carly Simon, Susan Sontag, and Grace Paley outraged at the sexism of the media and that of Judge Harvey R. Sorkow in the New Jersey State Superior Court.

In April, Friedan both railed against Judge Sorkow's ruling in favor of the Sterns as having "frightening implications for women" and defended the couple, writing, in the *New York Times:* "the only reason the child is on earth is because of the Sterns." Her foe was capitalism. Her think tank in California that month on the subject attracted the biggest turnout of any in the meeting's history. Friedan took the floor to talk about family, condemning for-profit surrogate agencies, worrying that poor women would be "uteruses for hire," victims of "procreative pimpery" and a "breeder class of women." She wanted to defend women who were infertile and sought help conceiving, but those women who were not in that category yet sought a surrogate "offended her," she conceded, making a rare acknowledgment of her own biases. Her best impulse was to avoid either/or thinking about the issue and later, along with feminist writers Phyllis Chesler, Marilyn French, and Letty Cottin Pogrebin, she would sign another amicus brief affirming the dignity of the biological mother. The following winter, the Supreme Court of New Jersey invalidated the contract between Whitehead and the Sterns and the case moved to family court, which ruled that the Sterns could keep the child and Whitehead could have visitation rights.[5]

Friedan had, as Rabbi Laura Geller would say, "come to see some of the richness and healing in Jewish tradition." She participated in Peace Now benefits, attended feminist Shabbat dinners at Geller's home, and joined a Torah study group. In New York, she would appear at a commemoration of the first bat mitzvah—that of octogenarian Judith Eisenstein, the daughter of the founder of the Reconstructionist movement. She became a member of the editorial board of the progressive Jewish magazine *Tikkun*. In an interview, she dismissed women rejecting Judaism for its patriarchal slant, scolding, "You don't throw away the baby with the bath water." And she scorned feminist scholars who wanted to rewrite Jewish texts as matriarchal ones. She now saw these efforts as an extension of the polarization she had fought against. She "was intrigued by and suspicious of the Judaism I was involved in," said her friend Michael Lerner, then *Tikkun*'s editor, who suggested she read Abraham Joshua Heschel's 1962 book *The Prophets*, because, as he put it, "This was the Judaism that made sense to her."[6]

Visiting the Brandeis-Bardin Institute, a center devoted to all forms of Judaism located in a beautiful spot in Simi Valley, she listened to students reading the section of the Bible about Moses breaking the tablets to punish the Israelites for worshipping the golden calf. For her, the story recalled her fight for feminism and made her reflect upon her own struggle as part of Jewish history: "I would not be the first in the history of the Jews to play the role of a visionary . . . a female Moses leading women out of the wilderness," she said. She continued. "It is dangerous to make a graven image of feminism. . . . The answers of the 70's will not satisfy the questions of the 80's."[7]

Nor would the romances of the 1970s satisfy her needs in

the 1980s. She had first met Roy Walford in 1981, when she was sixty and he fifty-seven, at the New York salon of the literary agent John Brockman. Walford, a professor of pathology at the UCLA School of Medicine and pioneer in calorie-restricted diets as tools for longevity, was a man of paradoxes—a Jew who hid his Jewishness, a respected scientist and a dandy who shaved his head and grew a Salvador Dali mustache, a shy hedonist who wore a tie-dyed jacket handmade in India, where he had gone several times to measure how swamis managed to lower their body temperature and stay alert. Walford loved fine scotch and pot, acted in Living Theatre spectacles, and befriended Timothy Leary. Their affair heated up in Los Angeles where he introduced Friedan to "feminist porn art" and shared his dope, his gin, his apartment, and his ideas about how eating less could stop aging. She took him to Shabbat dinner at Rabbi Laura Geller's house and to Le Dome, the see and be seen restaurant co-founded by Elton John. In New York, Walford, Friedan, and another couple went dancing "wildly" at Studio 54 and Area, a louche celebrity nightclub on the far West Side of Manhattan. Walford called her his "leading lady," but he dated other women too. Still, when he published *The 120-Year Diet* in 1987, she helped get out the word.[8]

She returned to her beloved Sag Harbor every summer, where she lunched at the Dockside Bar & Grill, across from the boat ramp. She drove a Rambler whose dashboard she could barely see over—she was still a terrible driver. Jon Slon, Jonathan Friedan's friend, recalled going with her to the beach one day. They pulled into the nearly empty parking lot and Friedan headed straight for an old man standing next to his car. When they got close, it was E. L. Doctorow, who began to get mad. "Oh hello," she said. "I almost ran over one of America's eminent writers." He smiled.[9]

To make her house, which backed onto the water, more

amenable to the parties she adored throwing, she bought a long dining room table around which guests could gather. And she revived the hyper-local activism she had embraced decades earlier in Rockland County. With Doctorow, the Black writer William Demby, William "Bill" Pickens, grandson of one of the founders of the NAACP, and his wife, Pat, as well as other distinguished figures, she launched the Sag Harbor Initiative. Its goal was to create an agenda for politicians, as Pickens put it, "to give America the dialogue it deserved," and to end the segregation of the South Fork and the invisibility of Blacks at white cultural events. The first dialogue, held on Columbus Day weekend of 1987, included panels on race, aging, housing, and sexism. It drew media coverage and celebrities. Karl Grossman, a journalist who chaired a panel on nuclear energy, thought "it was a real example of diversity in action."[10]

Two subsequent dialogues returned to the goal of giving liberals a program to fight the anti-feminist, anti-humanist, anti-reproductive rights agenda of the Reagan era. At one, "Retreat from Equality," Friedan moderated a panel of luminaries with the skill of a lion tamer, sometimes defaulting to her old strategy of attacking her attacker. Yet some critics found her dialogue a stale repeat of her tone-deafness on race and class and pointed out that few Blacks or working-class people attended. Others complained that she brought no new solutions to the insistent gender inequities, instead repeating talking points from *The Second Stage*. She still counted on Congress ratifying the ERA, rightly still complained that the United States was the only industrial nation "that doesn't have a national policy on parental leave and childcare," and blasted the solution Republicans proffered to women in the workforce—so-called "sequentialism," which put the onus on individual women to divide their lives into chunks—raising children and then returning to work.[11]

She co-founded a watchdog group, Women, Men, and Media

(WMM), which released a yearly count of male and female bylines and mentions on page one and convened many symposia on gender inequity in the media, illuminating media biases and the inability of women to break the glass ceiling. She called the numbers "a symbolic annihilation of women." She even used the Gary Hart scandal to talk about feminism. After the media caught him with Donna Rice, Friedan called an emergency session at her think tank and swore, in front of the press, "this is the last time a candidate would be able to treat a woman as a bimbo." If only. Yet if she worried about Hart, she worried that the economic downturn had already ushered in a second feminine mystique.[12]

The twenty-fifth anniversary for *The Feminine Mystique* showed how divided women remained about it. On February 9, 1988, at a party for the book at Chasen's, the legendary Beverly Hills restaurant, the deputy mayor of Los Angeles, Grace Montanez Davis, proclaimed it "Betty Friedan Day." Stephen Spielberg, Norman Lear, Valerie Harper, Alvin Toffler, Los Angeles mayor Tom Bradley, and ex-governor Edmund G. Brown Jr., listened as Helen Reddy confessed that *The Feminine Mystique* had inspired her to write the song "I Am Woman." The comedian Emily Levine, a devotee of the think tank, said: "If Betty had not written that book, I would not know who I was." Friedan spoke, acknowledging that women's lives had improved but cautioning that everyone needed to accept the Second Stage. However, in New York, the anniversary of *The Feminine Mystique* incited fewer laudations. Friedan appeared on *The MacNeil/Lehrer NewsHour* with three generations of feminists—Eleanor Holmes Norton, Anna Quindlen, author of the *New York Times* column "Life in the 30's," and Garret Weyr, who had recently graduated from the University of North Carolina at Chapel Hill. Holmes Norton called *The Feminine Mystique* the "*Uncle Tom's Cabin* of the twentieth-century women's movement," although she credited Friedan with describing a "universal" phenomenon. Quindlen talked about how much Friedan meant to her and her family. Then Weyr spoke. When she complained that she didn't know how to be a feminist, Friedan barked, "Read my book, *The Second Stage*, see what the next step has to be."[13]

Although she failed to satisfy her daughters' need for her to address the challenges of their generation, she did reach out to Gloria Steinem to effusively thank her for her birthday card and to apologize. She wanted to salute "the transcending of previous hostilities, misunderstandings, or real differences between us . . . I am grateful for your continued contribution and commitment to the women's movement." There is no record of a reply in Steinem's papers.[14]

Three years earlier, Miriam, then eighty-seven, had fallen and hurt herself badly; then she developed heart trouble. She moved from her cottage in Leisure World to "the tower," a building in the same complex with more services. Her doctor recommended that she stop playing bridge, advice Friedan would always regret heeding. After that, Miriam seemed disoriented. At a family lunch celebrating Miriam's ninetieth birthday on February 13, 1988, Friedan, her brother, Harry, and his daughter Laurie broke it to their mother that they needed to move her to a nursing home in Wisconsin, near Harry's other daughter, Nancy. Friedan had "a severe asthma attack, the first one in years." She knew her mother would not want this end. She next saw Miriam in late March, after she gave a lecture on aging in Windsor, Ontario. From there, she detoured to spend "about five hours" with her. When she put her arms around Miriam and told her that she loved her, her mother replied, "I know you do, darling. And I love you too." Then she watched as her mother spoke to another resident in the same saccharine tone of voice in which the aides spoke to her. "God knows, I had been fighting against my mother almost all my life; it seems that love-hate never dies . . . but I had come to admire her guts," she wrote.[15]

Miriam died on April 4, 1988. Rabbi Laura Geller led a memorial service for her in California. There, in front of a group of mourners, Betty expressed gratitude that she had the chance to share her love with her mother at the end. "That was such a blessing," she said. The author of the famous book about how housewives should liberate themselves from their mothers teared up about losing hers before pivoting to the sentiment that drove her to write her great book: "I didn't want to be like my mother," she said.[16]

Rabbi Geller smoothed Friedan's contradictory remarks into a universal story about Jewish lineage: "Miriam was not . . . a religious Jew and yet her daughter has come to see some of the richness of Jewish tradition and . . . to feel that there is a great deal of healing that Jewish tradition has to offer," Geller began. She went on to talk about Miriam as a symbol: "she represents all of our mothers" and then started reading a poem for the Yizkor service by Rabbi Morris Adler: "Shall I cry out in anger, O God, Because Your gifts are mine but for a while?" Geller also read the poem "From My Mother's Home" by the Israeli poet Leah Goldberg, about a granddaughter looking into a hand mirror, the sole possession of a woman she knew only by imagining her. When Betty's friends spoke, they echoed the poem's sentiments, although most of them didn't really know Miriam. Friedan, amid her grief, could not but express a mix of admiration and resentment. "She was very proud of me," she said, her voice cracking, as she delivered Miriam's biography to the group. Miriam "was also very cantankerous like me," she said, as though she were her mother's mother.[17]

A new wave of articles and books appeared announcing the failure of feminism. *Good Housekeeping* ran a series of prominent ads featuring "New Traditionalists," a.k.a. women choosing to be housewives. Friedan began using the phrase "a new feminine mystique" to describe the backlash. Thus, when Marcia Cohen's *The Sisterhood: The Inside Story of the Women's Movement and the Leaders Who Made It Happen* was published, depicting Friedan as a disorganized control freak, she ignored it. She was driven to continue the work her mother had inspired her to do. She marched in Washington to protest *Webster v. Reproductive Health Services*, a case in which the Supreme Court ruled that the state of Missouri had the right to deny funding to abortion clinics. Post *Roe v. Wade*, it was a setback. She held a "think tank" session to critique the phrase "the mommy track," inspired by Felice Schwartz, a Harvard Business School professor contending that corporations needed to deal with two tiers of women—caretakers and career women. Friedan called the mommy track "the Mommy Trap" and "retrofeminist."[18] She wrote: "It is dangerous and deplorable for the *Harvard Business Review* and Ms. Schwartz to say that women managers have to make a choice between career and family. At a time when 95 percent of male executives have children but the majority of female executives are childless, it is dangerous to affirm the policies and attitudes that created just that situation. Yet that is what Ms. Schwartz has done by supporting the view that women have to make a choice."[19]

At least her oldest son, Daniel, was marrying a physics teacher from Iceland, one of the most gender-equal countries in the world.

She returned to Aspen to talk about "the cutting edge" in social movements. She was inspired, in part, by Zalman Schachter-Shalomi, the charismatic Lubavitcher turned guru, founder of Jewish Renewal, and feminist who had taught her son Jonathan in Philadelphia. Friedan attended several of Reb Zalman's workshops, gravitating to his idea of "Spiritual Eldering," which encouraged people of all faiths to resist common wisdom about aging as decline. His meditating on the tension between acting and thinking helped her move beyond her sharp-elbowed activism.[20]

Yet no sage could soften her anger at Michael Dukakis for forsaking abortion during his campaign. Or her rage in 1988 at the election of George H. W. Bush, which she feared would further a "symbolic annihilation of women." She redoubled her battles for gender equality, reproductive rights, and the rights of working mothers, even appearing in disheveled finery on an episode of *The Firing Line*, where she refused to back down in the face of the sneering and goading of William F. Buckley and Michael Kinsley. As in earlier eras, some issues she dismissed or ignored made her seem out of touch, such as her failure to address the AIDS epidemic, intersectionality—a new theory of feminism created by legal scholar Kimberlé Crenshaw—or the fear sowed in Israel by the Intifada. But at the Minds for History conference at Arcosanti that year, she explained in public for the first time that she did not include Black women in *The Feminine Mystique* because her editor told her she was already taking too much on.[21]

Out of her frustration at this sterile decade emerged a new attempt at dialogue with her movement daughters. Her review of the so-called manifesto of the third wave, *The Beauty Myth: How Images of Beauty Are Used Against Women*, by twenty-eight-year-old Yale grad Naomi Wolf, signaled a first effort. Published in America in 1991, *The Beauty Myth* traded *The Feminine Mystique*'s blaming of Freud, housework, and Madison Avenue for women's oppression for blaming the cult of beauty. Friedan was divided. She was sensitive to beauty as capital. Part of her believed that feminists did not have to—should not—neglect conventions of feminine beauty. She feared that the media would use lookism to minimize women's fight for equality. In her own life, she compromised, getting her hair done at Vidal Sassoon and wearing feminine clothes but refusing plastic surgery. And yet she was conscious that she had suffered because of the way she looked. Not long after writing the review, she described herself as a young woman—"I don't look that ugly. But I was Jewish." It was a rare, if incomplete, acknowledgment of her pain as a double outsider—Jew and woman. But she does not resolve the tension between those identities—maybe that is impossible. Thus, although her review of Wolf's book for *Allure* magazine began, "The whole question of beauty and feminism is more complex than Wolf paints it," she doesn't tackle the idea fully. Tacking on an idea that could have come out of *Cosmopolitan*, she added, "The better [women] are able to feel about ourselves as people, the more we are able to enjoy being women, the more beautiful we feel and look, and the more we can take delight in celebrating ourselves." But she nonetheless concluded that the "controversy it [the book] is eliciting could be a hopeful sign of a new surge of feminist consciousness."[22]

On most other occasions, though, she reproached third-wave feminists. At the gala for the twentieth anniversary of the National Women's Political Caucus, she lambasted their weak collective activism and asked: "where are the daughters?" She scolded them for using the phrase "I'm not a feminist but . . ." instead of proclaiming "I'm a feminist and . . ."[23]

In the fall of 1991, when she was seventy, Roy Walford, her sixty-seven-year-old sometime boyfriend, entered Biosphere 2, a 3.14-acre research and experimental community built under a geodome in the Sonoran Desert. It was designed to survive a nuclear holocaust. He was the only elderly crew member. When Walford emerged two years later, their relationship flickered then tapered off. They were both busy with their own projects. When they did sleep together in the summer of 1994, he fell out of bed. (His health had deteriorated in the geodome.)

If Friedan mourned the loss of this romance, those sentiments are in the closed section of her papers in Cambridge. In her fourth book, she expressed respect for Walford, citing him as one of a new generation of active elderly people; he likewise held her in esteem, writing that she embodied "the essential liberal attitude, the ability to be open, receptive, unafraid in the face of opinions, temperaments, passions." He singled out Friedan for stoicism, observing that many people he knew whined about aging, but she never did.[24]

For years she had argued that the women's movement should exclude sexual politics from its reckoning. However, in the fall of 1991, she seemed to turn about, publicly criticizing Republicans for their cruel treatment of Anita Hill during the Supreme Court nomination hearings of Clarence Thomas. In Washington, after Republicans attacked Hill for her brave testimony that Thomas had sexually harassed her, Friedan refused to shake the hand of Senator Alan K. Simpson, who had brutally questioned Hill on the stand. "I hope you will be opposed by a woman and defeated by a woman," she said. She accosted Republican Nancy Landon Kassebaum of Kansas, then one of two female senators, and begged her to change her vote. "Nancy, please, please," she implored. Unswayed, Kassebaum voted for Thomas, although she regretted it later.[25]

After the Senate confirmed Thomas, Friedan erupted against the male blind spot and the ability and ease with which the senators blotted out the humanity of Anita Hill—caricatured her. She argued that Thomas's nomination made it more difficult for women to seek redress for sexual harassment. And, about Arlen Specter, another senator who interrogated Hill, she leveled the same scathing language she had reserved for Ronald Reagan and George Bush, saying, "The way he tried to destroy Anita Hill was a declaration of war against women."[26]

Two weeks after Thomas was confirmed, *Backlash: The Undeclared War on Women* by the thirty-two-year-old writer Susan Faludi, was published. Faludi named Friedan as one of the villains responsible for the Republican undoing of second-wave gains, singling out "the mother of feminism," for "yank[ed]ing out the stitches to her own handiwork" in *The Second Stage*. Whereas a decade earlier, Friedan might have lashed out, she regarded her inclusion in Faludi's book as homage. "Faludi put everyone into *Backlash*," she said. What got to her was being left out. Resigned to skipping a NOW twenty-fifth anniversary dinner honoring past presidents because the organization had not formally invited her, she defaulted to her old label when they did finally include her. "I am here as the mother of you all," she said, to a standing ovation.[27]

Such victories were short-lived. Upon reading that the scholar Carolyn Heilbrun had agreed to write Steinem's biography, she worried that it would eclipse any that would be written about her. The USC think tank had diminished in importance. She was having too many conversations with members who thought it should be more inclusive. She was not there to diversify she was there to lead, she told one who dared protest. Still, it is striking to learn how, even after Anita Hill, she refused to include the fight against sexual harassment as central to the platform of liberal feminism. At a think tank session in the spring of 1993, she framed the issue as clearly as she ever had: "Is the feminist focus on sexual harassment part of a general move to empowerment, or is it a diversion from deeper organizational and economic problems?"[28]

Since #MeToo, this will strike many readers as absurd. As will Friedan inviting to this session Frank Gehry, her "dear friend" of twenty-five years, who, while designing the Disney Concert Hall, "had a charge of sexual harassment [against him] that almost went to court." Gehry described one of the lawsuits as occurring because he called an allegedly incompetent employee a "cunt." But Friedan argued that his genius should give him a pass and pointed out that the experience had hurt him, too. Adamant that women accusing men was unproductive, she tried to shift the think tank's outrage against one misogynist man to outrage against misogynist Hollywood, joking that she would file a class-action sexual harassment suit against the producers of the movie *Indecent Proposal*, in which a character played by Robert Redford offers Demi Moore's character's husband a million dollars to sleep with her. She quoted a *Ms.* magazine poll finding that "sexual issues were of less consequence than work and family." She even conceded that it was critical to not put up with sexual harassment, although she worried that it might usher in a culture of censorship. "What are we going to become, the Soviet Union or Nazi Germany?"[29] she asked, but she came back to her old idea that focusing on sexual harassment distracts from unsexy issues like equal pay and political representation: "The sexual issues catalyze the rage that is caused by many things and is very sexy to deal with. . . . I wish that sexual harassment had removed Clarence Thomas from the Supreme Court, but I think we as feminists in leadership roles have to guard against our own seduction by relatively cheap issues that are easy to solve."[30]

Not long after that think tank, in the first week of May 1993, Friedan went on a hike with some friends in Yosemite, including the publisher and philanthropist Sara Miller McCune and Jeremiah Kaplan, president of Simon and Schuster, with whom she had had an affair and "still had a great crush" on. She was visibly ill. According to McCune, she was abusing her prescription inhaler, a dangerous practice at high altitudes. The morning after the hike, Friedan called her doctor from McCune's house, and shouted at him over the phone. Nonetheless, the group started out on another hike. This time, Friedan collapsed, they returned to the car, and McCune drove her friend to a medical center. From there, an ambulance rushed her to Good Samaritan Hospital in Los Angeles. "I really thought everyone was kind of overreacting," she wrote.[31]

As the orderlies wheeled her into the operating room for

aortic valve heart replacement surgery, she began reciting the Shema. It turned out that her body would not accept the first replacement heart, made from a pig's bladder, about which she later joked: "My Jewish heart rejected the pig valve." She had to call in a favor to get a human heart, and her second replacement surgery, on May 21, used one that belonged to a teenage boy. That seemed to transform her. She started calling wait staff, whom she had been known to attack, "honeybunch," said the activist Robin Morgan. Letty Cottin Pogrebin recounted that, "in the middle of a blizzard, she gave a talk at my mother-in-law's assisted living facility and never said 'you owe me one.'" Her energy and drive remained high. Instead of recuperating, over Memorial Day weekend, she flew to Miami for the American Booksellers Association convention to promote her forthcoming book on the third age. Rolling onstage in a wheelchair, she garnered a standing ovation from breakfasters at a meeting in the vast Fontainebleau Hotel ballroom. Her publisher planned an eighteen-city tour that fall. But back in New York, rehospitalized for a spinal infection and in terrible pain, she wondered whether *The Fountain of Age* would be published posthumously. She finished writing her will and felt calm.[32]

Published nearly thirty years after *The Feminine Mystique*, *The Fountain of Age* aimed to change the paradigm around aging. Bulkier than her first book, weighing in at six hundred pages, it challenges received wisdom about growing old, critiquing hormone replacement therapy (then wildly popular) and the medicalization of menopause. As in *The Feminine Mystique*, Friedan tells funny stories about herself, including many about her rafting and rappelling Outward Bound trip for the fifty-five-plus set in the Appalachian Mountains. Her doctor: "are you out of your mind?" Another remarkable moment tells of how the death of her ex-husband's brother, Mark, whom she adored, made her rest easier with her own mortality. Besides being entertaining (at times), *The Fountain of Age* includes many memorable interviews with accomplished and vital older people, giving special emphasis to scientists such as E. O. Wilson and Stephen Jay Gould. In her push to discover the real limits of aging (as opposed to those imposed upon us), Friedan poses questions such as whether living longer was "an accidental byproduct or an evolutionary breakthrough." She singles out the work of several "maverick" gerontologists whose work shows that science does not mandate that old people deteriorate. But her strongest evidence of elderly men and women who reinvented themselves is anecdotal. The writer Bel Kaufman threw dance parties for herself. Friedan's friend Joe Wilder, a workaholic surgeon, after operating on Zero Mostel, returned to an old love—painting. She tells inspiring tales of those who flourished despite disease. Samuel Atkin, a psychoanalyst with Parkinson's and other late life ailments, continued practicing. Although the book is marred by inaccuracies, sloppy citations, and it focuses on healthy wealthy white people, it still makes stirring observations about how aging changes our dreams in the context of our mortality. One chapter, "Intimacy Beyond the Dreams of Youth," starts with a nightmare in which Friedan buries a version of herself: "In my house, against the wall, pushed out of the way, was something quite large, all wrapped up in a rug. Like a mummy. And I said, what is wrapped up in that rug? No one was paying any attention to it, it didn't really get in the way. But I didn't want something wrapped up, hidden like that in my house. I insisted on slitting it open. . . . There was a woman wrapped up in the rug and she was still alive. . . . How could I let her out without her exploding with rage."[33]

A more upbeat moment pays homage to Zalman Schachter-Shalomi's spiritual frankness, noting how, in his first book, *The First Step: A Guide for the New Jewish Spirit*, he describes presenting yourself to God—"Here I Am! This Is Me! This Is How I Am!" At seventy-two, Friedan appreciated Zalman's radically direct approach to meeting the divine. After years of trying to make society more gender equal and years of defending traditional views, she wanted to forgive herself.[34]

All in all, *The Fountain of Age* differed from *The Feminine Mystique* in two central ways: Its critique swaps housewifery for the medical profession. Also, whereas the first book attacked mothers, this one, finally, celebrated daughters: "Mary Catherine Bateson started out in rebellion against her famous mother, Margaret Mead, who subsumed three husbands and her daughter's upbringing to the demands of her anthropological fieldwork. Bateson went on to write *Composing a Life*, which is about how women's lives don't 'fit that single-minded linear career path.'"[35]

*The Fountain of Age* concludes with a commemoration of her break with the women's movement. Aging granted her freedom from its "power politics," she wrote. She wanted her legacy to include her whole life.[36]

The book received mixed reviews, with some writers applauding Friedan for tackling the "aging mystique" and others expressing qualms about how she did it. In the *New York Times*, Nancy Mairs asked: "Who better than Betty Friedan to chronicle an adventure of such magnitude and significance?" But in the *Los Angeles Times*, Diane Middlebrook argued that some of her memoir-ish "preening" trivialized the very issues Friedan was trying to illuminate. *The Fountain of Age* resulted in far less conversation—and less action—than the monumental bestseller *The Feminine Mystique*. Other issues included the long memories of many feminists Friedan had alienated and the thinness of some content. Then too, Friedan had published a book about aging the year that she had had two open-heart surgeries. And yet if her ill health was a poor advertisement for *The Fountain of Age* physically, her surgeries seemed to have diminished her rage. Now, when she started to lash out, she felt her heart beating and checked herself.[37]

* * *

She would begin dating Michael Curtis, a British professor of political science at Rutgers whose first wife had recently died and whose friend, Princeton professor of Middle Eastern Studies, Bernard Lewis, she admired. Curtis took her to jazz clubs and taught her about the great American songbook. But the affair ended abruptly.

In the summer of 1994, she moved into an airy seven-room apartment in the Wyoming, a Beaux-Arts building in Kalorama Triangle. She had loved Washington from the NOW days, since the time Bill Clinton was elected and she wanted to be near the president whose gender-equal marriage she saw as proof that the changes she had brought about stuck. She started co-chairing "the New Paradigm" at the Woodrow Wilson International Center seminar with the economist Heidi Hartmann to combat the backlash against women brought on by the economic downturn.

She was elated by Ruth Bader Ginsburg's nomination to the Supreme Court. And though chagrined by the hostile response to Hillary Clinton's infamous remark about not just wanting to stay home and bake cookies, she approved of the powerful new kind of first lady. Yet she was disappointed when the version of the Family and Medical Leave Act signed during Clinton's first term only offered workers twelve weeks per year of unpaid leave and counted pregnancy as a disability. She worried about the dystopian scene in Robert Putnam's *Bowling Alone.* She herself kept a busy social calendar, holding court at the Cosmos Club, attending a writers' luncheon at the Women's National Democratic Club, where she, often the only woman at the table of journalist and historian heavy hitters, wore a Nina Ricci coat bought in Paris and drank Bloody Marys with an extra shot. She frequented her favorite restaurant, Nora's. But she refused to wear glasses and could barely see.

She convened Women, Men, and Media symposia, focusing on topics as diverse as coverage of Hillary Clinton and the dearth of women on the front page of the *New York Times.* She believed her "Geiger counter," the interior ticking that alerted her to the feminine mystique decades earlier, signaled "The New Paradigm," the Woodrow Wilson International Center working group she co-chaired aiming to end political polarization. She saw how the Gingrich Revolution had redistributed power in Congress, giving over fifty seats to the Republicans, and threatening the advances she made.

At seventy-four, determined that the United Nations Fourth World Congress on Women demonstrate the universality and longevity of the revolution she started, she protested again. Held from September 4 to 15, 1995, in Beijing, it attracted 40,000 women, four times as many as Nairobi. It was more global than Nairobi too, with women from all over the world weighing in on female poverty, infanticide, global violence against women, and stalled progress in women's equality. Beijing would be the first UN-sponsored conference to conclude without the "Zionism as Racism" rhetoric. Yet China's human rights violations overshadowed these achievements.

Friedan put herself in the middle of it all. In June, the Chinese had arrested Harry Wu, a dissident journalist who had recently returned to China after years away. Although she deplored China's human rights violations, she publicly insisted that the conference be held. "Certain powers . . . want to use the Harry Wu thing to keep American women out of the World Congress of Women in China," she told *Newsweek*'s David Alpern in a radio interview.[38]

Upon arriving in China on September 1, amid a countrywide media blackout, she announced that there was no women's movement there. She drew a crowd: 120 women packed into a space designed for 30 to listen to her talk about higher minimum wage, shorter work weeks, and the renewed danger for women as scapegoats. But in a reprise of Mexico City, the Chinese government had physically separated the official conference from the NGO, holding the former in Beijing and the latter in

Huairou, a rural town an hour away. It was "a sea of mud," griped Friedan, who now walked with a slight limp and had trouble navigating the narrow paths between tents. Her critics were quick to judge her. Robin Morgan reports seeing her asleep at a talk. Anne Applebaum writes that she checked her watch while Inuit women were speaking.[39]

For Friedan, the highlight was Hillary Clinton's twin efforts fending off conservative critics discrediting the conference and criticizing China's human rights record. The phrase from one of Clinton's speeches echoed her slogan from *The Second Stage*—"women's rights are human rights and human rights are women's rights." Friedan asked a reporter, "Do you know what the word 'kvel' means?" She noted that Clinton "appeared not as the wife of the president but as her own woman." And "For me what is most magnificent is the new sense of woman in a public space." But she had only heard about it. During a torrential rainstorm, the Chinese government downsized Clinton's venue. Friedan was one of a group trapped in a crowd outside. Still, back in the States, she downplayed the dissent and the chaos and celebrated the conference, telling the *Los Angeles Times* that Beijing proved "the coming to maturity of the women's movement as a global force of great power."[40]

# 13

## *Life So Far*

On the afternoon of Sunday, February 4, 1996, a group of dear friends held a seventy-fifth birthday party for Friedan at Marlene Sanders's apartment on West End Avenue and 93rd Street. The place was packed. Notables like J. Anthony Lukas, the journalist Linda Wolfe, the correspondent Betty Rollin, the writer Anne Roiphe, and her old friend the sociologist Si Goode attended the joyous event. The celebrants mentioned Betty's passion, her indignation, and her tenacity. Among the many memorable roasts, Robert Caro repeated a story his wife, Ina, had told him about swimming with Betty at Barcelona Neck, Queens, across a slender inlet through which barges cruised. When Caro asked his wife if she was careful, she replied, yes, "I look out for the boats." And Friedan?

"Betty feels the boats have to look out for her," recounted Caro, laughing.[1]

When Friedan finally spoke, she was moved. She only wanted to talk about love.

But she had legacy on her mind too. A year earlier, Daniel Horowitz, a scholar whose wife, the historian Helen Lefkowitz Horowitz (from the think tank), had turned down Friedan's request to be her biographer, sent her a draft of an article he was working on about her. He needed her permission to quote from the unpublished papers. When she returned from Beijing, she finally read a draft and found herself unrecognizable. Horowitz argued that she had covered up her years as a Popular Front journalist and was less of a housewife than she claimed. Enraged, Friedan denied Horowitz access to her papers and threatened to sue him, ostensibly for fair use and copyright infringement.

Published in *American Quarterly* soon after her birthday party, "Rethinking Betty Friedan and *The Feminine Mystique:* Labor Union Radicalism in Cold War America" did not initially impel Friedan to publicly rebut Horowitz; *au contraire*, months after his essay appeared, she emphasized anew her labor roots. In October, she spoke at "The Fight for America's Future," a teach-in at Columbia University aiming to unite a reenergized labor movement with academic stars including Cornel West, Richard Rorty, and Michael Lind. "We must take on the culture of corporate greed to defend and extend democracy to revitalize our vision of the common good that places the highest priority on people's lives and not on . . . the corporate bottom line," she said to an audience of over 1,500 at Low Library before she celebrated the election of John Sweeney to the presidency of the CIO.[2]

Yet at a talk in Washington not long after that, Friedan publicly belittled Horowitz, albeit without mentioning his name. "Some historian recently wrote some attack on me in which he claimed that I was only pretending to be a suburban housewife," she said. Until this moment, she had largely ignored the takedowns of her work. Horowitz's article needled her. For even as she was going after him, she seemed to be embarking on an apology campaign for her early excesses. At a celebration for Kate Millett, she conceded that part of her contribution had been to acknowledge the "many ways of loving." But also, at a moment when a new wave of "momism" threatened to undo feminism, she openly celebrated being the mother of the movement. At a party for the thirtieth anniversary of the founding of the National Organization for Women, Friedan confessed for the first time that she had no regrets about neglecting her offspring for the women's movement. "Much as I feel for my children and grandchildren, this is the most exciting thing I have done," she said.[3]

On September 17, 1997, over three years after her aortic valve had failed the first time, it failed again. This time, doctors replaced it with an artificial one. "I have risen from the dead," she bragged to a *Washington Post* reporter eight days after surgery. She immediately began directing a research project at Cornell University, "Women, Men, Work, Family, and Public Policy," where she identified "problems that had no name" as privatization, deregulation, and outdated employment models. She dubbed these problems "new" and convened a conference on them at Bellagio, the elegant Italian writers' colony on the shores of Lake Como. She steamed ahead on her memoir, which she hoped would provide a fuller explanation of her past than any biographies. She steamed ahead as well in her personal life. One suitor, Dr. Irving Schwartz, was the widower of Felice N. Schwartz, whose idea about "the mommy track" Friedan had derided.[4]

Debating conservative women writers piggybacking on Newt Gingrich's Republican counterrevolution—Christina Hoff Sommers and Danielle Crittenden, for example—on C-Span, Friedan demolished their argument that she had succeeded so well that there was no need for more revolution. Since women had flooded white-collar professions, become business owners, and made huge legal and social advances, feminism was over. But Friedan did not just hit her adversaries intellectually. She cast them in the worst role she knew of: ungrateful daughters. "These women are beneficiaries of the women's movement," she told the *Boston Globe.*[5]

She tried to incorporate some of the objections of these bad daughters into her last polemic, *Beyond Gender: The New Politics of Work and Family.* Published at the end of 1997, *Beyond Gender* was based on conversations held at the Woodrow Wilson Center, where she had been a fellow. It returns to ideas of her youth even as it tries to address challenges the women's movement faced as it limped to the end of the twentieth century. The book both defends other oppressed groups and eschews identity politics. In a way, Friedan is more optimistic than she was in 1976 or 1981, although she rants about the endurance of the usual bad suspects: Black anti-Semitism; Rush Limbaugh calling her a "feminazi." She wistfully recalls one book that inspired NOW, Hannah Arendt's *On Revolution,* quoting it: "The participation in the making of history, the movement itself, was the real reward." She asks readers for new approaches to the problems hindering women from achieving true equality. But the strongest part of the book is where she attributes feminism's greatest obstacle to "the culture of corporate greed," the disappearance of solid middle-class jobs, and "the sharply increased income inequality between the very rich . . . and the rest of us." She warns of wealth inequality and worries that the increasing difficulty all Americans—except the richest men—endure would make "scapegoats of women again."[6]

*Beyond Gender* received less attention than Friedan's earlier books, partly because third-wave feminists found it—her—outdated. Also, shortly after the book was published, Friedan supported Bill Clinton after his affair with Monica Lewinsky. She, along with Gloria Steinem and other second-wavers, argued that the legislative advances benefitting women made during his presidency were more important than any private transgression. In the *Guardian*, Friedan wrote that, with women only earning seventy cents on the dollar, it was immoral for the media to emphasize Clinton's sex life: "Enemies are attempting to bring him down through allegations about some dalliance with an intern." She feared "sexual McCarthyism," reasoning that if such investigations became the norm, no one would run for public office.[7]

Yet she remained hopeful due to women "electing the president of the United States," Madeleine Albright becoming secretary of state, and the media coverage of women "transforming the American political landscape" in a way that was far more equitable than in 1970. Still, late-life jabs stung, especially those evoking the hurts of her youth. In 1999, having decided she did not like the stern portrait that editor and painter Byron Dobell had completed, she would only pay him if he destroyed it. Instead, he contrived to have the portrait hang in the Century Association in Manhattan, where Alan Fern, then director of the National Portrait Gallery, saw it and asked Dobell to donate it. Friedan also continued to try to quash one of the two unflattering biographies endangering her legacy: Daniel Horowitz's 1998 *Betty Friedan and the Making of The Feminine Mystique*, an expansion of his article arguing that Friedan had covered up her Popular Front journalism. Nor had she exactly cooperated with Judith Hennessee, whose *Betty Friedan: Her Life*, published a year later, dwelled on its subject's so-called "second rate" character. Most reviews of these books either repeated their claims or further dismissed Friedan. The political scientist Alan Wolfe contended that *The Feminine Mystique* should be ejected from the canon because the thinkers it goes after—Mead, Alfred Kinsey, Bruno Bettelheim—had themselves been discredited. "The faults of the book loom large," he wrote.[8]

* * *

In 2000, on the edge of her eighth decade, Friedan published her memoir, *Life So Far.* She had been working on it for years, most recently with her assistant and the ghostwriter Linda Bird Francke. But she had been afflicted with both a severe case of writer's block and her own diminishing abilities. Thus the slight memoir only revealed a few new biographical details about her Communist youth and her Jewish childhood, which she portrayed as less assimilated than she had let on. In Peoria, she writes for the first time, her mother spoke German, her father spoke Yiddish, and she tutored a refugee from Hitler's Germany. She tries to correct Daniel Horowitz's ideas about her Popular Front past by casting herself as a detective, as she had in *The Feminine Mystique:* "My experience with Communist dogma had given me a healthy distrust of all dogma that belied real experience, while Smith had given me the conceptual ability to take on the feminist mystique, and my training by the psychological giants of the day plus my training as a hands-on reporter gave me a third ear to hear pieces of new truth behind denials and defenses and rigidity. That ability to follow leads, clues from many different fields, was invaluable once I truly committed myself to solve this mystery."[9]

*Life So Far* failed—and not because of the specter of radical politics. Much of it dictated, the book omitted significant events in both Friedan's life and the women's movement. It did contain apologies for some imprecisions of *The Feminine Mystique*, such as the comparison of concentration camps and suburban women. But her self-portrait as a woman of Rabelaisian appetites (she liked "not just the clitoral orgasm," she announced, as if she were still arguing with women's liberationists in 1968) bothered reviewers, as did her score-settling, forty years after what many regarded as her major accomplishments. It is marred by horrible errors. However, what attracted the biggest noise was the old accusation that Carl had battered her—and her shame about it. "I was a disgrace, really, to the women's movement by being such a worm. How could I reconcile putting up with being knocked around by my husband while calling on women to rise up against their oppressors?"[10]

Friedan's confession revived sexist and ageist attempts to discredit her and the movement. John F. Kennedy Jr.'s *George* magazine, which would fold the following year, published an advance excerpt with a lurid title, "Battling for Women While Beaten at Home." Carl rallied to protest his innocence in *Time* magazine, calling his ex-wife's account a "complete fabrication" and dredging up the story from the 1960s about how she once came at him with a knife. He launched a website (no longer extant) to recount his version of their marriage, which included being the victim of marital violence. Friedan, seemingly responding to her ex-husband, retreated to her defense from years earlier. On C-Span she used the word "Rashomon" to cast doubt on the authority of her own memoir. And she told the *New York Times* the violence went two ways: "We were both hot tempered people." This did not assuage Carl, with whom she had largely reconciled, and who had married a third time, to Donatella Pes, thirty-five. He had flown to Los Angeles to be with Friedan when she had the heart valve transplant. She had attended his eightieth birthday party at Sardi's the previous fall. But now he railed against her portrayal of him as an abuser: "Never in my life have I ever gratuitously struck anyone," he wrote in a letter to the *Times*.[11]

Here the question is why Friedan revisited the painful story of her turbulent marriage after so long. Some friends attribute it to her mental deterioration. A more elaborate theory is that though she feared since the late 1960s that conservatives would discredit the women's movement because of her private life, she was angry about being ostracized. So, she did the work for the movement's enemies by exposing herself as a victim. Another part of the puzzle has to do with generativity. In *Life So Far*, she explains that her pain created something positive, namely sparking Emily's involvement in anti-domestic violence efforts. She did apologize to Carl, saying she had no idea that the media would fasten on the abuse story. On *Good Morning America* she recanted, asserting that she was "no passive victim of a wife beater" and retreating to the claim that the marriage was like a bad chemical reaction. But to feminists taking domestic abuse more seriously than they had in 1963, her explanations looked like equivocating.[12]

Although most reviews of *Life So Far* excoriated it, a few thoughtful evaluations appeared. Laura Miller lamented that the women's movement had never achieved the status of civil rights and described Friedan as having "a tragic, Lear-like inability to handle her own power." The activist Stephanie Gilmore wrote that "what may seem to be liberal in that [*sic*] such women as Friedan . . . pursued change within existing social and political systems is actually radical in that such change transforms society, politics, law, economics, and more." In the *New York Times*, Wendy Steiner recognized the double standard about female leadership that Friedan embodied. Steiner quotes one of Friedan's wise sentences about its challenges: "I don't think it's a requirement to be sweet to be an effective leader or activist." Still, Steiner makes the point that forty years after *The Feminine Mystique*, people often unfairly expect women to comport themselves in a likeable way in order to earn trust: "To read this memoir is to grasp the labor and pain and sacrifices of one's mother without necessarily loving her for her efforts." Steiner concludes: "She leaves us in a sad bind, aware of the public good that came of her 'mothering' but unable to feel that her struggle was truly carried out on our behalf." But Friedan's friends argued that Steiner didn't go far enough in her gender analysis. As one put it, echoing Friedan years earlier, no one asks whether Martin Luther King Jr. was "truly carrying out his struggle on our behalf." Even Carl conceded that his ex-wife was a "real visionary . . . I would just advise a person not to marry one," he said.[13]

Her last article for *Allure* magazine, "The Bootylicious Mystique: Is Beyoncé Knowles a Role Model for Post Modern Feminism?," seems initially like a glib adulation of a pop star. But published in 2002, the article circles back to Friedan's writing about women balancing work and family even as it anticipates fourth-wave feminism. Celebrating Beyoncé's work ethic, Friedan cemented multicultural, intersectional femininity to her second-wave secular Jewish-influenced utopian humanism. "When women are not dependent on men for their identity, the whole picture changes," she wrote. She saw in Beyoncé an ability to lead. The *Allure* article represents a late-life response to longtime criticism about her race myopia, and it leapfrogged over the second-wave radicals who shunned her to ally herself with the next generation.[14]

When she summered in Sag Harbor, she attended services at Temple Adas Sag Harbor, a Reform synagogue—the oldest one on Long Island—but she often fell asleep in the pews. She also attended the Conservative Synagogue of the Hamptons in Bridgehampton once or twice. In 2003, Jan Uhrbach, then a young rabbi there, hosted Friedan at Shabbat dinner. Friedan could not hear well, but she asked Uhrbach what it was like to be a woman rabbi. Had she experienced sexism? What did she do when she encountered it?

I take control, Uhrbach said.

Good for you! Friedan replied, adding that if Uhrbach had been a single man, the synagogue would have provided help for the dinner. "I'm gonna tell the board, she said."[15]

On April 25, 2004, in Washington, D.C., the March for Women's Lives protested President George W. Bush's singular threat to Planned Parenthood, reproductive rights, and *Roe v. Wade*. It was the first NOW-sponsored event Friedan had appeared at in decades. On the Mall, she joined hundreds of thousands of protesters of all ages, but she did not address the crowd. She had started using a motorized golf cart to get around and she maneuvered it around to the back of the White House. She seemed depressed. But then, as Rebecca Traister—the only journalist to mention her by name—wrote in *Salon*, millennials swarmed her. Her old pal Carole De Saram said, "she lit up and became Betty."[16]

A few months later, after selling her apartment in the Wyoming, Friedan schlepped her ancient furniture, a portrait of her painted by her sister, Amy, and photos of her with the Clintons and her siblings to the Georgetown, an assisted living complex on Q Street, where Eugene McCarthy also resided. She would not be alone for long. Gabrielle Wellman, whose father, Sid, lived there too, met Betty on her first day. "I thanked her for her life's work, and she waved that aside and told me that she was just being moved in by her 3 adult children and was none too pleased to be there," Wellman recalled.[17]

Soon afterward, Friedan gave her last *public* talk at the Library of Congress, "The Revolution Is Not Over." "Women don't yet have a voice," she said, reminding her audience that although women comprised 51 percent of the population, they still constituted only 12 percent of Congress. She complained: "Nobody talks about the poor anymore," and "the discrepancy between the haves and have-nots is increasing, and that is not good."[18]

That summer, she returned to Sag Harbor for the last time. Sometimes she repeated herself or forgot what she was saying mid-sentence. Her friend Alida Brill, years younger, recalls her asking her for the first time "*What are YOU going to do about this*"—this being George W. Bush—instead of the usual plural "we." Occasionally, she still seemed full of energy. She whizzed around in her golf cart, deaf to the trucks zooming behind her, as she drove the short distance from her house to eat lunch at the Dockside Bar & Grill. Lucy Komisar, a colleague from NOW who had been writing exposés of the corruption in offshore banking, visited her on Labor Day weekend. "She was very glad to see me," said Komisar. They sat down, and Friedan asked what she was working on. "Betty listened and asked questions about corruption and offshore banking," she said. "She commented: 'we did not challenge the system enough.'"[19]

When she returned to the Georgetown in the fall, she started a romantic relationship with Sid Wellman. "My Dad had absolutely no idea who Betty was nor anything about her status in the women's movement," Gabrielle Wellman recalled. On Armistice Day 2005 (also Sid's birthday), Wellman and her partner, Caren, drove the elderly couple to his favorite restaurant, the Olive Garden. They borrowed a local friend's two-door Chevy Chevette. Caren drove and Sid, with his bad knees and shrunken six-foot frame, squeezed in the front passenger seat. Friedan and Gabrielle were smushed in the back. Gabrielle remembered: "There was a bit of struggle getting out of the car. Betty didn't have the leg strength to extricate herself out of the back seat. She weathered the indignity with aplomb and appeared to enjoy my dad's holding the door of the restaurant open for her and pulling out her seat at the table."[20]

Not long after that, Friedan's mental state worsened. She began to repeat herself. Then, in December 2005, Carl died of cancer. Afterward at age eighty-four, she still joked about remarrying. On the phone with Harry Jr.'s wife, she asked, "Why can't you find me a nice man—like my brother?"[21]

In her lucid moments, Friedan advised her smart Jewish daughters to call for justice and take risks, even if it meant standing alone. She cared more about them carrying on than she did about her own well-being. She slowly succumbed to her many ailments, including late-onset diabetes and heart problems but she kept drinking and eating sugar until the end, refusing to do anything that others told her to do, as she had for her whole life.

At the beginning of February 2006, Betty's niece Laurie (Harry Jr.'s daughter) flew to Washington to join Emily, Jonathan, Daniel, and their old friends, Steve Slon and his wife, Estelle, at her bedside. It seemed that the end was near. Good-byes were said and Friedan asked to call her good friend of forty years, the writer and editor Natalie Gittelson.

They sent out for Chinese food and Friedan said she didn't feel well. She never got back up. At 2:50 p.m. on the afternoon of February 4, the end came. She died on her birthday, like Moses. The writer Emily Bazelon, a relative on her mother's side, recalled, "there was a lot of sorrow." The official cause of death was congestive heart failure.

On Monday, February 6, at the funeral service at Riverside Memorial Chapel in New York, the three-hundred-plus mourners were a who's who of the women's movement. Kim Gandy, then president of NOW, Marlene Sanders, Phyllis Chesler, Letty Cottin Pogrebin, Kate Millett, the women's health expert Barbara Seaman, Congresswoman Elizabeth Holtzman, and Alix Kates Shulman, author of *Memoirs of an Ex-Prom Queen*. Amitai Etzioni also attended. According to some of Friedan's friends, Gloria Steinem was not there.

Rabbi Joy Levitt presided. Muriel Fox, who had known Friedan since 1963, spoke first: "She was not only the most important woman of the twentieth century but of the second millennium." Etzioni, who initially met Friedan in 1974, talked about how, before she changed the world, "women knew that they should not be heard too often." Liz Holtzman said, "the impact of Betty's work has forced ayatollahs here and around the world to recognize the equality of women." The journalist Marlene Sanders spoke about her fun side. Then the children and grandchildren had their turn. Jonathan recalled his mother telling them to go outside to play while she was writing *The Feminine Mystique* ("I can't concentrate!"). And he read a poem he had written about her. One line confessed—or was it joked—that his family had had more psychotherapy than any in America. Emily offered her own variety of wisdom and grief. Asked to make sense of her mother, she told a reporter: "You don't . . . She made so many connections and yet was exquisitely lonely . . . the ultimate contradiction was that Betty just didn't fit into this world. That was her curse, and yet she started a revolution." Rafael Friedan, her grandson, then twenty-three, talked about how she could scare busboys and about her generosity.[22]

Six of Friedan's nine grandchildren went with the plain pine box with a Star of David carved on it out of Riverside Chapel. The family drove to Sag Harbor, where they buried the mother of feminism in the Sag Harbor Jewish cemetery, on a densely wooded hill about a five-minute drive south of the village. Rabbi Jan Uhrbach officiated. She was reading about the exodus from Egypt in the Torah and in her remarks, she connected that to Friedan's role as a leader and liberator. "Look if it wasn't for her, I wouldn't be here," she said.[23]

Newspapers all over the world published tributes. The page-one *New York Times* obituary said *The Feminine Mystique* "ignited the feminist movement" and called it "one of the most influential nonfiction books of the 20th century," even though it then explained how she became "outmoded." Eleanor Smeal, former president of NOW, offered pure laudation. "She was a giant in the 20th century for women," she said. Hillary Rodham Clinton told a reporter: "She defined the problem, and then she had the courage to do something about it." Even Marian Wright Edelman, though noting her temperament, wrote in the *Chicago Defender:* "Her strong voice was in the forefront . . . and will be sorely missed."[24]

The tartest obituary, by Germaine Greer, criticized her

grandiosity: "She thought she was the wave." But that sour assessment was the exception. Other second-wavers produced Bettyisms, such as the one by her friend and colleague Karen DeCrow. At a NOW meeting at DeCrow's house in Syracuse, there were arguments and Friedan stormed out to get a taxi. Except that there were none. After forty-five minutes, she came back. Third-wave feminists contributed sober pieces wondering how young women would continue without Their Mother. The writer Susan Jacoby expressed concern about "how much explanation is required" to introduce Friedan to young women who benefitted immeasurably from her achievements. In the Jewish press, one writer observed that she was "used to doing battle." Even those she disagreed with mourned the loss of an icon, notably Kate Millett. "She was supposedly the mother of us all," Millett said at a ceremony that August going on to remark that Friedan actually seemed to lack those qualities. "She was not maternal, comforting, easy. She was an organizer."[25]

Over three years later, on the morning of July 25, 2009, Friedan's children provided their tribute, a headstone designed by the Japanese sculptor Mashiko. Rabbi Uhrbach officiated over the unveiling of the headstone, which was shaped like a wave. "All of us women owe her a debt," Uhrbach said. Lines etched on the back of the stone evoke branches blowing in the wind or Friedan's unruly mane of hair. On the front, Mashiko inscribed the last sentence of Rabbi Hillel's exhortation to action in English and Hebrew. "If not now, when?"[26]

# *Epilogue: "Not Your Grandfather's Patriarchy"*

At a celebration for the fiftieth anniversary of *The Feminine Mystique* at the Radcliffe Institute, the scholar Stephanie Coontz said that Friedan's most important accomplishment was making our world into "not your grandfather's patriarchy . . . or your father's privilege." She was arguing that without Friedan, women would be much farther from equal rights than they are. It is true, as the historian Christine Stansell once wrote, that at the time of *The Feminine Mystique*, "'Woman' was an identity bleached of any political significance." And yet the phrasing consigns Friedan to the past, which is incomplete. Yes, we no longer believe that women need only be housewives. But that was barely the beginning of her contribution. A more complete point of view is to regard Friedan's story as a parable about a woman who, in remaking the world more gender-equal, ultimately could not live the life some of her daughters were able to enjoy. Or her story could be seen as a moral tale about what it really takes to make society equal for women. She is the fighter who hardly won all of her battles, the Jewish activist whose origins in a mid-century Midwestern Reform Jewish family propelled her and held her back. Which is not to minimize either the contribution of *The Feminine Mystique* or her phenomenal and phenomenally messy efforts organizing women. The National Organization for Women, the National Women's Political Caucus, and other less known groups were key to securing many of the equal rights women do have today. And they are key to understanding the distance that remains until women have equality.[1]

Friedan led women a long way and many things about her command admiration: her resistance to her mother and her esteem for her grandfather, her early academic success, her commitment as a labor journalist, her tenacity in the world of women's magazines, and her insistence on bringing forward the traditional experiences of wife and mother into the 1960s revolution. These pieces, added to less admirable ones, contributed to the creation of *The Feminine Mystique*, a magnificent if flawed volume whose sum is greater than its parts. But her ostracism in the 1970s and her reinvention in the 1980s are part of Friedan's story too. The degree to which she continued to fight for women's rights—the dedication with which she tried to fix the world—even after radicals pushed her aside is extraordinary. It must have taken a lot of courage to keep moving forward.

She was no saint. She would be cancelled today. But her impact should be studied. From the late 1960s, she worked tirelessly, first to make sure women would be able to fulfill themselves outside the home, then to ensure they had equality in the workplace, legally, in terms of controlling their own bodies, in politics and in religious life. In every arena, she succeeded to the extent that she did because of her energy and drive, because of her insistence on wedging herself in, of starting something, no matter how outlandish it sounded—sometimes because of her ability to be monstrous. She would not back down, which could set others against her. Yet even when she was wrong, she was right. As she said at a talk at Arcosanti in 1990, "The cutting edge has to embrace life." And she did. If her brusque manner could alienate her sisters and daughters, she always tried to use it to drive women forward. She never flinched; she barreled on to gather together the ones who were always being told to wait. As Friedan often said, since women's equality was not a given in every sector of American culture, what was crucial is that the conversation continue. And that is still true today.[2]

So many of her dreams have not come to pass. Legislation to financially support caregivers—most of whom are women, as Friedan observed—stalls in Congress. Men still skimp on the housework. Women still have not achieved economic equality in the workplace—notably in the supposedly utopian atmosphere of the tech industry. Nor have they achieved equality in political representation. Friedan would find it concerning that a new trend appears to be so-called "heteropessimism"—the conceit that young men and women are having difficulty finding each other. One of the biggest recent developments in feminism, #MeToo, she would find a distraction, and even if you disagree it is difficult to ignore that identity politics has not secured women's equality as she named it. She would be enraged that the choice for women between working and having a family continues to be fraught largely because the political system has failed to address systemic inequalities. The Supreme Court assault on women's reproductive rights, the overturning of *Roe v. Wade*, she would find cataclysmic. Friedan would also surely be dismayed at young women's abandonment of feminism, their focus on sexual politics, and the extent to which the media still drives a largely gendered conversation about women and work. She would be angry at Planned Parenthood's replacement of the phrase "pregnant woman" with "pregnant people" and interested in *New York Times* columnist Michelle Goldberg's recent reporting on a new anti-feminist backlash. "Feminism is particularly given to cycles of matricide," Goldberg writes.[3]

Friedan was a prophet who, in showing us how to try to repair the world, showed us that doing so was not just messy but destructive. No one thanks you for it. She did so because she could not be in the world any other way. She was an idealist, a transformer, a fortuneteller, and a pragmatist who continues to enrage enemies and inspire daughters to this day. She was also, especially in the second half of her life, a giving friend and mentor who made extraordinary efforts to help women she cared about find their "participation in modern life." Her friend the writer and editor Alida Brill calls her "generous of spirit." Mahnaz Afkhami, the professor and activist who hosted her in Iran in 1974, remembered her advice. After Afkhami emigrated to the United States a few years later, she met Friedan one time for coffee. When she confessed that, as an Iranian woman, she could not disassociate herself from her past, Friedan replied: "Disassociate yourself from your own past? I would not think of it. As exiles, you have to own who you are. Like I did."[4]

In 1999, at a Festschrift at the National Arts Club in New York, Friedan described herself years earlier starting NOW with the phrase "ordinary-extraordinary." The choice of words shows that she believed both in her own exceptionalism and, despite flares of *hauteur*, in her humbleness. She rejoiced when women from many different milieus joined her in the struggles that she considered both exalted and unassuming. Fourteen years after her death, her project, to gather "ordinary-extraordinary" women, remains unique, as does her groundbreaking and courageous book, *The Feminine Mystique*, which continues to generate conversation and opposition and draws attention to the gender inequality that we should have put behind us long ago.

# NOTES

## Introduction

1. Daphne Merkin, "Sister Act," *New Yorker*, June 14, 1999, 78. Daniel Horowitz, *Betty Friedan and the Making of The Feminine Mystique: The American Left, the Cold War, and Modern Feminism* (Amherst: University of Massachusetts Press, 1998), for example, 165. Elisabeth Bumiller, "Gloria Steinem: Everyday Rebel," *Washington Post*, October 12, 1983, B1.

2. Friedan quoted in Judith Hole and Ellen Levine, *Rebirth of Feminism* (New York: Quadrangle Books, 1971), 92.

3. Email from Daniel Friedan, February 16, 2016.

## Chapter 1. A Prophet in Peoria

1. *St. Louis Globe Democrat*, January 23, 1892, 7. *Chicago Tribune*, March 20, 1897, 14. James Montgomery Rice, *History of Peoria County, A Record of Settlement*, volume 2 (Peoria, 1912), 259, Google Books.

2. "Had to Come to New State for Legal Reasons," *Buffalo Courier*, August 8, 1896, 5, documents how Sandor and Bertha went to New York State to get married because it was the nearest state where they could do so as cousins. The first newspaper item about Sandor's having moved to Peoria is in 1904. Then there is an item documenting his move back to St. Louis, *Jewish Voice*, November 23, 1906, 2. *Jewish Voice*, October 29, 1909, 7. *Washington University Medical Alumni Bulletin*, 1917. https://digitalcommons.wustl.edu/med_bulletins/19/. US Census, 1910.

3. Friedan first talked about her Peoria "roots" in "We Don't Have to Be That Independent," *McCall's*, January 1973, 147. Sam Hodes, "History of the Jewish People of Peoria," unpublished paper, 1937, BUSC. See *Decatur Herald*, April 25, 1916, 6. *Decatur Herald*, April 26, 1916, 3. James Montgomery, *Peoria City and County, Illinois: A History of Settlement* (1912), 256–60. Quote about Horwitz, Herman Eliossof, *Jews of Illinois, Their Religious and Civic Life*, 372. #9, HathiTrust Digital Library. Friedan talks and writes several times about her grandfather's work eradicating VD in the red-light district.

4. Miriam is first listed as a student at Bradley in the *Polyscope* Yearbook 1914, 750. *Polyscope* Yearbook 1915, *Polyscope* Yearbook 1916, *Polyscope* Yearbook 1917, 75, 107. Thanks to Linda Aylward for helping me with the yearbooks. Horwitz family movements documented in *Jewish Voice*, August 13, 1915, 7. *American Israelite*, August 17, 1916, 3. *Jewish Voice*, July 20, 1917, 3; *Jewish Voice*, November 30, 1916, 3. *Jewish Voice*, November 30, 1917, 7.

5. Cheryl Kay Fogler, unpublished master's thesis, "The Plight of Wage-Earning Women in Peoria," Illinois State University, 2018, argues that in the twentieth century, Peorian women could not make enough money to live by themselves. I am basing my timeline on *Leshnik's 1918 Directory*, 849, which shows Miriam living with her parents while working as a stenographer at Newman Stratton. *Leshnik's 1919 Directory*, 861, shows her working at JW Franke, also while living at home, *Leshnik's 1920 Directory*, 618, shows her as married and living with Harry at the Jefferson Hotel. In *Life So Far*, Betty writes that her mother worked for the *Peoria*

*Journal* or the *Star*, but the *Journal* started in 1931 and the *Star* started in 1946. Miriam's obituary says that it was the *Journal Evening Transcript*, a predecessor paper. However, there is no record of this in any city directory nor could I find her bylines. Sandor was a lieutenant colonel in the army reserves. *Washington University Alumni Medical Quarterly* January–April 1948. https://digitalcommons.wustl.edu/cgi/viewcontent.cgi?article=1040&context=med_alumni_quarterly.

6. *Jewish Voice*, May 23, 1919, 8, suggests that Ben Goldstein and Sandor Horwitz met at a talk for veterans at Anshai Emeth in St. Louis. In the 1930 Census, Harry Goldstein lists his immigration date as 1896. Friedan, *Life So Far*, 18. Ferber never lived in St. Louis though Hurst did.

7. It's possible Harry Goldstein arrived in Peoria as early as 1896. But *Franks' 1899 City Directory* shows he was living there by that year. "Diamond ones" quoted in many places, including Barbara Mantz Drake, "Liberty's Champion," *Peoria Journal Star*, February 21, 1999. "A Well-Organized Storekeeping Built Up This Business," *Jewelers' Circular*, 75, no. 2 (January 30, 1918), 100, Google Books; *Jewelers' Circular*, 75, no. 1, 1920. *Ashton Gazette*, January 21, 1909. "The Story of a Good Girl," *Jewish Voice*, June 23, 1911.

8. Illinois County Marriage Records, November 7, 1910. Judith Hennessee, *Betty Friedan: Her Life* (New York: Random House, 1999), 4. Edna died of leukemia. But according to *Pantograph*, December 13, 1911, 3, it was typhoid fever. City Records 1912–17 give Harry M. Goldstein's address as the Jefferson Hotel. For example, *Leshnik's 1916 Directory*.

9. Miriam may have done more in the store than Betty gave her credit for. She made at least one trip with Harry to Chicago to check out other jewelry stores in November 1920. *Jewelers' Circular* 81, no. 3 (November 3, 1920), 133, Google Books. Honeymoon detail thanks to *Jewelers' Circular* 80, no. 2 (February 11, 1920), 1, Google Books. Lisa Hammel, "The 'Grandmother' of Women's Lib," *NYTimes*, November 19, 1971, 52.

10. Miriam quoted in Merle Shaine, "Mom's Lib," *Maclean's*, November 1, 1971, 46.

11. Harry quote from phone interview with Esther Cohen, May 1, 2017. Miriam quoted in Shaine, "Mom's Lib," 46.

12. Harry Goldstein Jr. interview. Federal Census, 1930, shows two servants living at 105 Farmington Road, Ella Vantine and Hazel Burnett. Friedan, "We Drove the Rackets Out of Our Town," *Redbook*, August 1955, 36.

13. Friedan quoted in Joyce Antler, *The Journey Home: Jewish Women and the American Century* (New York: Schocken Books, 1997), 263.

14. Friedan quoted in "B.G." 1, 1941, "Smith College. Highlander Folk School writer's workshop," 1941: notes, draft of article, "Highlander Folk School: American Future," and story, "The Scapegoat," correspondence, printed material. Papers of Betty Friedan, 1933–1985, Box: 16, Folder 276, Schlesinger Library, Harvard Radcliffe Institute, Cambridge, Mass. (hereafter cited as PBF). Copyright © Betty Friedan. Reprinted by Permission of Curtis Brown, Ltd. All rights reserved.

15. Betty Friedan interview, Marcia Cohen Papers, 1967–1987. Box 1, Schlesinger Library, Harvard Radcliffe Institute, Cambridge, Mass. (hereafter cited as PMC). Amy Goldstein interview, Box 1, PMC. Amy quoted in Marcia Cohen, *The Sisterhood: The Inside Story of the Women's Movement and the Leaders Who Made It Happen* (New York: Simon and Schuster, 1988), 58, 61.

16. Esther Menaker and William Menaker, *Ego in Evolution* (New York: Ecco Press, 1963), 102–4. The character they call "B" is likely Betty, according to Daniel Horowitz. "Information on Friedan's Therapy," note, n.d., Box 1, Daniel Horowitz Papers, College Archives, CA-MS-01123, Smith College Special Collections, Northampton, Massachusetts. Friedan, *Life So Far*, 30.

17. Harry cited in Milton Meltzer, *Betty Friedan: A Voice for Women's Rights* (New York: Puffin Books, 1986), 8. Friedan, *Life So Far*, 19; Cohen, *The Sisterhood*, 56–57.

18. Miriam quoted in Shaine, "Mom's Lib," 46.

19. Miriam quoted in Lynn Tornabene, "The Liberation of Betty Friedan," in Janann Sherman, ed., *Interviews with Betty Friedan* (Jackson: University Press of Mississippi, 2002), 28.

20. Betty Friedan, *It Changed My Life: Writings on the Women's Movement, With a New Introduction* (Cambridge, Mass.: Harvard University Press, 1998), 296.

21. Harry Jr. quoted in Harry Goldstein interview.

22. *Daily Times,* Friday July 18, 1913. Sandor Horwitz, "The Science of Medicine from Jewish Lore Gathered from Biblical and Talmudic Sources," 1931. Courtesy of the American Jewish Historical Society.

23. Friedan quoted in Antler, *The Journey Home,* 262. Friedan, *Life So Far,* 18. On the mortgages, see Horowitz, *Betty Friedan and the Making of The Feminine Mystique,* note 9, 262. Betty Goldstein, "Through a Glass Darkly," April 3, 1938. "Peoria High School. High school autobiography, 1938," PBF. Box: 14, folder 248.

24. Interview with Esther Cohen.

25. Friedan quoted in "Jewish Roots: An Interview with Betty Friedan," *Tikkun,* Jan.–Feb. 1988, 25. Antler, *Journey Home,* 262.

26. Friedan quoted in *Jewish Roots,* 25.

27. Amy quoted in Cohen, *The Sisterhood,* 58; Friedan quoted in Hennessee, *Betty Friedan,* 7, 8. Harry Jr. said she threw a glass and that he still had the scar.

28. Hodes, "History of the Jewish People of Peoria," 137; Friedan, "Jewish Roots," 25; Cohen, *The Sisterhood,* 56. Mary Walton, "Can Betty Friedan Rescue the Women's Movement?" *Philadelphia Inquirer,* November 1, 1981, 10.

29. Betty Friedan cited in Paul Wilkes, "Mother Superior to Women's Lib," in Sherman, ed., *Interviews with Betty Friedan,* 7.

30. In *Life So Far,* Friedan misremembers this trip as being on her eighteenth birthday, impossible given the play's dates in Chicago. "Review of Stage Year . . ." May 24, 1936, *Chicago Daily Tribune.* "*Saint Joan* will open June 8 at the Grand Opera Theatre." Betty was fifteen. In her autobiography, she writes that only her mother accompanied her. George Bernard Shaw, *Saint Joan: A Chronicle Play in Six Scenes and an Episode,* 1924. Gutenberg.net.au. Heilbrun quoted in Robin Blaetz, *Visions of the Maid: Joan of Arc in American Film and Culture* (Charlottesville: University of Virginia Press, 2001), 78. Shaw was incensed at the Catholic Church's at-

tempts to censor his play, and it's possible that Betty was aware of this.

31. Betty Goldstein, "Cabbages and Kings," *Peoria Observer*, April 30, 1937, May 14, 1937. April 9, 1937. Thanks to Jo Grewell at Peoria High School.

32. Friedan quoted in Hennessee, *Betty Friedan*, 15. Kenneth Phillips Britton and Roy Hargrave, *Houseparty* (New York: Samuel French, 1929), 141. Cohen, *The Sisterhood*, Notes, 3. Drake, "Liberty's Champion." Friedan, *Life So Far*, 24.

33. Charlotte Brontë, *Jane Eyre* (Penguin Classics Deluxe Edition, 2010), 111.

34. "Victoria Regina Will Open in December 27, 1937 at the Erlanger," *Chicago Daily Tribune*, September 5, 1937.

35. *Peoria Journal Star*, March 14, 1938. *Warrior's Husband*, clipping, n.d. Peoria Players Scrapbook, Bradley University Special Collections.

36. Goldstein, "Through a Glass Darkly," 1938, PBF. Box: 14, folder 248.

37. Betty's bad temper cited in Horowitz, *Betty Friedan and the Making of The Feminine Mystique*, 19. Antler, *The Journey Home*, 263. Betty cited in Hennessee, *Betty Friedan*, 8.

38. Betty Friedan Oral History, April 17, 1973. Friedan, Betty Goldstein 1971–5, Box 67–9: Folder 17–18. Smith Centennial Oral History Project Records, 1971, College Archives, CA-MS-00090, Smith College Special Collections, Northampton, Massachusetts. Copyright © Betty Friedan. Reprinted by permission of Curtis Brown, Ltd. All rights reserved. She uses the word "freak" five or six times in this interview.

## Chapter 2. "Split at the Root"

1. Eleven percent cited in Horowitz, *Betty Friedan and the Making of The Feminine Mystique*, note 12, p. 268. Eleven percent also in an unpublished history thesis by Helene J. Sinreich, "Merit Based Admissions to Kosher Kitchens: 1887 to Present Day 1997," Smith College, 1997. But Judith Hennessee, *Betty Friedan*, 21, says the quota was 8 percent. Tarlow quoted in *Life So Far*, 35. Justine

Blau, *Betty Friedan: Feminist, Woman of Achievement* (New York: Chelsea House, 1990), 28. Professors cited in Hennessee, *Betty Friedan*, 29–30.

2. "Scripts," n.d. "Smith College. English: other fiction, scripts, articles," PBF, Box: 16, folder 271.

3. Friedan, *Life So Far*, 43. No one at the Heinz Historical Society could find a record of a Jim Lynch, who Betty writes was a Heinz relative. "Oral History Interviews with Friedan, February 27–April 24, 1992 and December 11, 1993." Tape One, Side One, Betty Friedan Audio Collection, 1963–2007 T-97; T-125; Phon-7, T-125.98. Schlesinger Library, Harvard Radcliffe Institute, Cambridge, Mass. (hereafter cited as ACBF). Copyright © Betty Friedan. Reprinted by permission of Curtis Brown, Ltd. All rights reserved.

4. Friedan quoted in Amy Stone, "Friedan at 55," *Lilith*, Fall 1976, 11.

5. "Jean Forbes Is New Weekly Editor," *Smith College Associated News*, March 15, 1939, 8 (hereafter cited as *SCAN*). Student publications and student publications records, College Archives, Smith College Special Collections, Northampton, Massachusetts. Betty Goldstein Transcript, Classes of 1941–1950 records, College Archives, CA-MS-01016, Smith College Special Collections, Northampton, Massachusetts.

6. Nicholai Evreinov, *The Theatre of the Soul*. https://archive.org/details/theatreofsoulmonooevreuoft/page/8/mode/2up.

7. *SCAN*, October 25, 1939, 2. Transcript of Sally Gavin, Box 5, Folder 3. Permission granted by Judith Hennessee Papers, David M. Rubenstein Rare Book & Manuscript Library, Duke University (hereafter JHP). Program, "The Theatre of the Soul," November 2, 1939, Dramatics Records, Box 3044, Smith College Archives (SCA), Smith College Special Collections, Northampton, Mass.

8. Friedan quoted in Alida Brill, *Dear Princess Grace, Dear Betty: The Memoir of a Romantic Feminist* (Tucson, Ariz.: Schaffner Press, 2016), 160. Betty Goldstein, Poem, November 1939, "Smith College. Miscellaneous printed, ca. 1940–1974." PBF, Box: 21, folder 310. Betty Goldstein, "Poems for the present," 5. "Smith College.

Miscellaneous printed, ca. 1940–1974." PBF, Box: 21, folder 310. Opinion, March 1940. *SCAN*, March 13, 1940.

9. Smith College. English: paper, "The Isolated Ego," 1942, PBF, Box: 16, folder 266. Horowitz, *Betty Friedan and the Making of The Feminine Mystique*, note 43, p. 280. She also said she learned of penis envy at Berkeley; Horowitz, *Betty Friedan and the Making of The Feminine Mystique*, 96.

10. Friedan, "Jewish Roots," *Tikkun*, 26.

11. Oral History Interviews with Friedan, February 27–April 24, 1992, and December 11, 1993. Tape 2, Side 1. ACBF.

12. Friedan, *Life So Far*, 54.

13. Ibid., 49.

14. *Bulletin of Smith College*, 1938–1942, SCA. Horowitz, *Betty Friedan and the Making of The Feminine Mystique*, 55, n14, 273.

15. "Burst my lung": *Life So Far*, 35.

16. *SCAN* October 29, 1940, 1, 4; "Bettye Goldstein Will Be New Editor," *SCAN*, March 11, 1941, 1; "This Is What We Believe," *SCAN*, March 14, 1941, 2. *SCAN*, May 2, 1941. Sondra Henry and Emily Taitz, *Betty Friedan: Fighter for Women's Rights* (New York: Enslow Publishers, 1990), 27. Friedan, *Life So Far*, 35.

17. BG to James Dombrowskie [*sic*], June 18, 2, 1941, Betty Goldstein Folder, Highlander Research and Education Records, Wisconsin Historical Society, Madison, Wisconsin (hereafter cited as BGF). Copyright © Betty Friedan. Reprinted by permission of Curtis Brown, Ltd. All rights reserved. Bettye Goldstein, typescript, "The Writer's Workshop," n.d. "Smith College. Highlander Folk School writer's workshop, 1941: notes, draft of article, 'Highlander Folk School: American Future,' and story, 'The Scapegoat,' correspondence, printed material." PBF, Box: 16, folder 275.

18. Bettye Goldstein, "Learning the Score," 2, 1941, PBF, Box: 16, folder 274.

19. Bettye Goldstein, Smith College. English 328a: paper, "The Scapegoat," 1941, PBF, Box: 16, folder 271, 10/1/1941. BGF. BG to colleagues at *SCAN*, October 5, 1941. Bettye Goldstein, "The Scapegoat," *Smith College Monthly*, October 1941, 5, 26–28. "Smith College. *Scan, Opinion, Smith College Monthly* and *Focus* con-

taining contributions by Bettye Goldstein, 1939–1942 (BG on editorial staff)." PBF, Box: 21.

20. "Memorial Minute," Harold Edward Israel Faculty File, Faculty and staff biographical files, College Archives, SC-MS-01008, Smith College Special Collections. *SCAN*, October 28, 1941, 4.

21. *SCAN*, October 3, 1941. Cited in Hennessee, *Betty Friedan*, 26. *SCAN*, October 21, 1941.

22. "Behind a Closed Door," *SCAN*, October 3, 1941. "The Red Menace," *SCAN*, October 14, 1941, 2, "The Right to Organize," *SCAN*, October 21, 1941, 2. "The Tatler Suspension," *SCAN*, November 7, 1941, 2.

23. "Dean Hallie Flanagan Davis Asks SCAN to Tell Her About Students at Smith," *SCAN*, December 9, 1941, 4.

24. Hennessee, *Betty Friedan*, 25. "Declaration of Independence," *SCAN*, December 5, 1941, 3. "Epilogue of Failure," *SCAN*, March 10, 1942, 2.

25. Cited in Cohen, *The Sisterhood*, 62.

26. Friedan (and Harry Sr.), *Life So Far*, 58. Communist Party of the United States of America Records do not contain a record of her joining.

27. Stone, "Friedan at 55," 11; Friedan, "Jewish Roots," *Tikkun*.

28. Amy Adams, November 20, 1993, in *50th Reunion Book, Class of 1944*, Box 2124: Folder 21, Classes of 1941–1950 records, College Archives, CA-MS-01016, Smith College Special Collections, Northampton, Massachusetts. "Bully at 16, Now Is Pastor," *Press and Sun Binghamton*, March 11, 1948, 3, Hennessee, *Betty Friedan*, 34; JHP, Harry Goldstein Jr. interview. "Mr. and Mrs. Adams Win Tufts Degrees," *Portsmouth Herald*, February 20, 1945, 3. Conversation with Tufts Alumni Office August 4, 2020. Tufts Combined Catalogs, Bulletins, and Course Announcements, 1943–44.

29. Friedan, *Life So Far*, 69.

30. Ibid., 61.

31. Erik Erikson's Jewish background from Marshall Berman, "The Man Who Invented Himself," *NYTimes*, March 30, 1975. Some details about the women come from Horowitz, *Betty Friedan*

*and the Making of The Feminine Mystique*, 95, and from fn 19. Frenkel-Brunswik killed herself in part because she had not received the recognition she deserved. Betty Friedan, *The Feminine Mystique* (1963; New York: W. W. Norton, 2001), 181.

32. Biographical, including clippings. FBI files. FBI file, 1978, p. 2, PBF, Box: 1, folder 67. Friedan, *Life So Far*, 59. Cited in Hennessee, *Betty Friedan*, 36. Horowitz, *Betty Friedan and the Making of The Feminine Mystique* 92–93.

33. Romance documented in F. David Peat, *Infinite Potential: The Life and Times of David Bohm* (New York: Basic Books, 1997), 49. Friedan, *Life So Far*, 55. Kai Bird, *American Prometheus: The Triumph and Tragedy of J. Robert Oppenheimer* (New York: Random House, 2006), 187. Lomanitz is from Shawn Kristian Mullet, "Little Man: Four Junior Physicists and the Red Square Experience," unpublished Ph.D. dissertation, Harvard University, 2008, 46. Interview of G. Rossi Lomanitz by Shawn Mullet on July 29, 2001, Niels Bohr Library & Archives, American Institute of Physics, College Park, MD. https://www.aip.org/history-programs/niels-bohr-library/oral-histories/24703-3. I date Betty's involvement with Bohm to fall semester because of Miriam's comment about analysis in *Maclean's*. Betty's quotes from "Oral History Interviews with Friedan, February 27–April 24, 1992 and December 11, 1993." Tape 2. ACBF. University of California, Berkeley, graduate work. Correspondence, 1942–1943. Note from M. M. Bromberg to BF January 29, 1943. PBF, Box: 22, folder 320.

34. Friedan cited in Hennessee, *Betty Friedan*, 35. Friedan quoted in Henry and Taitz, *Betty Friedan*, 31. Miriam quoted in Shaine, "Mom's Lib," 46.

35. Friedan cited in Henry and Taitz, *Betty Friedan*, 32.

36. Smith College. Centennial study: interview with Friedan, 1975; re: lawsuit against Smith College for discrimination in hiring practices. "Smith autobiography, 1973" PBF, Box: 22, folder 315. Hennessee, *Betty Friedan*, 35, writes that she took several lovers, pursuing them "coldly." Henry and Taitz, *Betty Friedan*, 33. But according to Friedan in *It Changed My Life*, 12, she was "virtually a virgin" when she arrived in New York. Oral History Inter-

views with Friedan, February 27–April 24, 1992, and December 11, 1993. Tape 2 ACBF, reveals that "the boy" is Loevinger.

37. Friedan, *The Feminine Mystique*, 94–95.

38. Friedan cited in Horowitz, *Betty Friedan and the Making of The Feminine Mystique*, 98.

## Chapter 3. "My Roots Are in My Moving"

1. Betty Friedan, "My Roots Are Not in Any Place, But Grow From Passion, Pain, Struggles Shared," *McCall's* January 1972, 38. According to US Census Bureau, only 20 percent of the population moved in 1948. Eleanor Roosevelt quoted in "The People Must Carry on for FDR, Mrs. Roosevelt Says," *Federated Press*, April 2, 1946, Federated Press Records, Rare Book and Manuscript Library, Columbia University Library (hereafter cited as *FP*).

2. Betty's precise start date at *FP* is difficult to ascertain. New York City White Pages, reel 57–58 1943, '44. (According to another source, it is Aloise Buckley, Priscilla's older sister, whom she roomed with in the Village.) Hennessee, *Betty Friedan*, 84.

3. Robert Schrank, *Wasn't That a Time? Growing Up Radical and Red in America* (Cambridge, Mass.: MIT Press, 1999), 201.

4. Friedan quoted in Cohen, *The Sisterhood*, 64.

5. Friedan, *It Changed My Life*, 12.

6. Friedan, *Life So Far*, 102. Interview with John Krich, May 5, 2016. Aron M. Krich, *Sweethearts: A Novel* (New York: Crown, 1983), 203.

7. Biographical, including clippings. Autobiographical notes, pre 1969. Friedan quote n.d. "Biographical Notes." PBF, Box: 1, folder 62. Betty Goldstein, "Pretty Posters Won't Stop Turnover of Women in Industry," *FP*, October 26, 1943. Betty Goldstein, "Miners' Wives Wear Silver Foxes, Bosses Insist," *FP*, November 12, 1943, 3. Friedan quoted in Horowitz, *Betty Friedan and the Making of The Feminine Mystique*, 108.

8. Betty Goldstein, "The Rich Certainly Have Their Troubles," *FP*, October 15, 1943, 3. Betty Goldstein, "Negro's Problem Same as Any Other Worker's, Only Worse, Ottley Says," *FP*, Octo-

ber 7, 1943, 2. Betty Goldstein, "Negro Parents Fined $10 Each for Keeping Children Out of Jim Crow School," *FP*, October 1, 1943, 1.

9. BG-DS, "War on Race Hatred Starts as Nazi Slogans Appear," *FP*, November 3, 1943, 4. BG-DS, "All Labor Asks Palestine as Haven for Jews," *FP*, November 8, 1943. Betty Goldstein, "Monied Interests Are the Real Fascists Here, Says Seldes in New Book," *FP*, December 7, 1943, 1. BG-RT, "NYC Probes Anti-Jewish Outbreaks," December 30, 1943. January 17, 1944. BG-RT, "Official Report Charges Christian Front Behind Anti-Jewish Outbreak in New York," January 11, 1944. BG-RT, "Native Fascist Group Will Protect Gentiles for $100," *FP*, February 28, 1944, 1.

10. Betty Goldstein, "Well-Heeled 'White Collar' League Seen as Disguised Native Fascist Threat," *FP*, March 16, 1944, 1.

11. Betty Goldstein, "Rich Losing Monopoly on T-Bone Steak," "Wartime Living," *FP*, September 27, 1943, 3; Betty Goldstein, *FP*, October 29, 1943; October 20, 1943. Betty Goldstein, "Women Needed on the Job," "Wartime Living," *FP*, August 28, 1944, 4; "Wartime Living," *FP*, September 25, 1944, 4. "Wartime Living," *FP*, October 9, 1944, 4.

12. Friedan quoted in JHP, transcript of Betty Friedan interview, Box 5: Folder 3. Betty Goldstein, "Workers Flock to Newly Opened Jefferson School," *FP*, March 22, 1944.

13. Friedan, *Life So Far*, 121. "Some interesting dreams": Oral History with Betty Friedan, February 27–April 24, Tape 3, Side 1, ACBF. Bettye Naomi Goldstein Smith College transcript. "Magic File" Smith College Archivist Reference Files, CA-MS-01213. Smith College Archives. In the summer of 1946, she sent her transcript to a number of schools, including Columbia, UCLA, and the University of Chicago. In 1959, she would send it to herself.

14. Schrank, *Wasn't That a Time?*, 203. Friedan, *It Changed My Life*, 12.

15. "The Diaper Mystery," *FP*, January 25, 1945. "New Southern Party Uses Hitler Slogans," *FP*, February 9, 1945. "Inaugurate Black Book of Crimes Against Jews," *FP*, February 16, 1945. "Two Navy Yard Unionists Fired for Anti-Semitic Leaflets," *FP*, April

27, 1945. "Expose School Quotas Barring Minority Groups," *FP*, February 9, 1945. "Political Activity Saved Labor Men From Insanity in SS Camps," *FP*, April 26, 1945. "Wartime Living," *FP*, April 30, 1945.

16. Betty Goldstein, "Workers Mourn for Roosevelt, the Greatest Friend," *FP*, April 16, 1945. Lillian Stone in Horowitz, *Betty Friedan and the Making of The Feminine Mystique*, 300. *The New Masses*, October 23, 1945.

17. She moved into the studio in spring 1945. Manhattan White Pages r58 spring 1945. In his fictionalized version of their affair, Mike Krich says that in her Village apartment, she slept in the living room. In her 2000 memoir, Friedan says that she did so because she wanted to have sex. But Gladys Carter tells Judith Hennessee that her friend wanted to have sex even before that. Carter transcript. JHP.

18. Betty Goldstein, "Post War Living," *FP*, January 23, 1946.

19. Betty Goldstein, "Strikebreaking Days Are Over, Bergoff Mourns," *FP*, January 29, 1946. "Atom Scientists Appeal to Labor," *FP*, March 8, 1946. "Plot for Army Control of Atomic Energy Would Endanger World Peace," *FP*, March 15, 1946.

20. "The People Must Carry on for FDR, Mrs. Roosevelt Says," *FP*, April 2, 1946. "Family Day on the Westinghouse Picketline," *FP*, April 23, 1946.

21. *Federated Press* Grievances, 1945–46 Box 35: Folder 35, Newspaper Guild of New York Records, Tamiment Library/ Robert F. Wagner Labor Archives, New York University (hereafter cited as FPG). Early career: journalist writings. Federated Press: Newspaper Guild: script for radio show, "The news and what to do about it," February 1944. Typed fragment of note from BG, April 26. PBF, Box: 23, folder 332. Also see Horowitz, *Betty Friedan and the Making of The Feminine Mystique*, 117–20. Marc Stone cited in BG letter to Newspaper Guild, May 23, 1946, FPG. BG to Jack Ryan, May 22, 1946, FPG.

22. Betty Goldstein, "Joliot-Curie—a Pioneer of the Atom Age," *FP*, June 13, 1946.

23. Meltzer, *Betty Friedan*, 23.

## Chapter 4. "It Was Almost as Good as Having a Baby"

1. Dating based on transcript of Carl Friedan interview, Box 5: Folder 3, JHP. Miriam's address in the City Directory, Peoria, 1944 and 1946 was the Jefferson Hotel. Thanks to Linda Aylward for this detail. Thanks to Elizabeth Nguyen at the American Gem Society for information on Miriam visiting HQ in 1946. Miriam started changing her life shortly after her husband died. Ruth McKay, "White Collar Girl: Perfect Gems," *Chicago Tribune*, May 2, 1944, 15.

2. "News of the Theatre," *NYHT*, May 13, 1946, 12A. *NYTimes*, June 1, 1946, 21. Also Lakeside Theater programs, thanks to Marty Kane at the Lake Hopatcong Historical Museum.

3. Transcript of Carl Friedan interview. Box 5, Folder 3, JHP. Friedan cited in Horowitz, *Betty Friedan and the Making of The Feminine Mystique*, 132. Friedan quoted in Cohen, *The Sisterhood*, 66. Miriam quoted in Shaine, "Mom's Lib," 1971.

4. Letter cited in Hennessee, *Betty Friedan*, 47.

5. Friedan, *Life So Far*, 68. Miriam Katz, *City Directory*, Peoria, 1948, Peoria Historical Society / Special Collections / Bradley University (hereafter cited as PHS). Thanks to Linda Aylward. In 1946 Miriam is still listed as Goldstein in the City Directory, Peoria. She married Katz on February 4, 1946, in Florida.

6. Betty Goldstein, *UE News*, August 9, 1947, 8–9. https://digital.library.pitt.edu/collection/united-electrical-radio-machine-workers-america-ue-records.

7. Details about Belfrage in Horowitz, *Betty Friedan and the Making of The Feminine Mystique*, 133.

8. Gladys Carter Transcript, JHP. Margaret Mead: "Dilemmas The Modern Woman Faces," *NYTimes*, January 26, 1947, BR18.

9. Losing her wallet, *Life So Far*, 81. I'm not sure what Friedan means here. The New Theatre League was most active before 1942. Friedan quoted in transcript of Carl Friedan interview, Box 5: Folder 3, JHP. Hudson Guild /New Theatre *Waiting for Lefty*. *NYTimes*, February 13, 1948. Myra McPherson interview, JHP. 1947 season Lakeside Theatre program, author's copy.

10. Transcript of Carl Friedan interview, JHP. Friedan, *Life So Far*, 30.

11. Friedan, *Life So Far*, 70.

12. Friedan cited in Kirsten Fermaglich, "Perpetrators, Bystanders, Victims: Jewish Intellectuals and the Holocaust in Post-War America," Ph.D. dissertation, New York University, 2001, 194. Betty Goldstein, "In Defense of Freedom: The People Vs. the UnAmerican Committee," *UE News*, November 7, 1947, 6–7. UE Records, University of Pittsburgh Special Collections.

13. Friedan, *It Changed My Life*, 8. "Carl Friedan Has Allied West Newbury's Residents with the Stage," *Boston Sunday Globe*, August 1, 1948, 48.

14. Betty Friedan, "The Lady Looks Like an Angel—But She's Dynamite in the Fight for Progress," *National Guardian*, January 31, 1949, 2, https://archive.org/details/sim_guardian_1949-01-31_1_16/page/2/mode/2up.

15. NYC White Pages 1949 show Carl Friedan still living on West 86th Street. Friedan quoted in Henry and Taitz, *Betty Friedan*, 40.

16. Thanks to Linda Aylward for the tidbits about Elmore S. Katz. Announcement of funeral services, *LATimes*, December 16, 1948, 27. City Directory, Peoria, 1950, lists Miriam H. Katz. Peoria Historical Society Collection, Bradley University (PHSC). Miriam Goldstein wedding announcement, *Chicago Tribune*, May 19, 1950. City Directory, 1952, lists Miriam Oberndorf, Chicago, PHSC.

17. Horowitz, *Betty Friedan and the Making of The Feminine Mystique* dates Friedan's move to Parkway Village to 1950. Hennessee, *Betty Friedan*, 55, dates it to 1951.

18. Perhaps she had talked to Aloise Buckley, who made a stir about radicalism at Smith, as her brother recently had about Yale. Sylvie Murray, *The Progressive Housewife: Community Activism in Suburban Queens* (Philadelphia: University of Pennsylvania Press, 2003), 144, 146.

19. Betty Friedan, *UE Fights for Women Workers*, June 1952. https://digital.library.pitt.edu/islandora/object/pitt%3A31735047451178/viewer#page/1/mode/2up.

20. Cited in Horowitz, *Betty Friedan and the Making of The Feminine Mystique*, 151–52.

21. Pre–*The Feminine Mystique* writing; notes, background material, typescript drafts; includes issues of newsletter *The Parkway Villager*, 1949–1953. "They found out Americans aren't so awful after all" (re: Parkway Village), Article, n.d., Parkway Village, 1952. PBF. Box: 27, folder 384.

22. Menaker quoted in Friedan, *The Feminine Mystique*, 145.

23. Betty Friedan, "How to Find and Develop Article Ideas," *The Writer*, March 1962, 13.

24. Betty Friedan, "We Built a Community for Our Children," *Redbook*, March 1955, 42–45, 62–63. Betty Friedan, "Happy Families of Hickory Hill," *Redbook*, February 1956, 39, 87–90. According to Horowitz, *Betty Friedan and the Making of The Feminine Mystique*, 189, n. 21, she also explored Frank Lloyd Wright's community Usonia, New York.

25. Friedan, "How to Find and Develop Article Ideas," 12. Friedan, "We Drove the Rackets Out of Our Town," 86.

26. Interview with Daniel Friedan. Cited in Kirsten Fermaglich, "Perpetrators, Bystanders, Victims," 200–201. Pre–*The Feminine Mystique* writing. "Draft for TV play on suburban conformity," n.d. 2, 7, PBF. Box: 36, folder 463. Only in 1990 did Friedan go public with her opinion that Snedens was anti-Semitic, telling *New York* magazine that a neighbor who "had a play on Broadway one year" did not get invited to join the tennis club, implying that he was banned because he was Jewish.

27. Robin Blaetz, *Visions of The Maid: Joan of Arc in American Film and Culture* (Charlottesville: University of Virginia Press, 2001), 147.

28. Friedan, *Life So Far*, 91.

29. Description of Ivies in Terry Talley, *Gems on The Hudson: The Grand Views* (New York: Magic Angel Books, 2006), 124–25. Interview with Anne Bell, March 14, 2021. The Victorian sofa is $25 elsewhere.

30. Transcript Jonathan Friedan, JHP.

31. Interview with Daniel Friedan, May 3, 2016. Catherine

Breslin, "Chatelaine Drops in on Betty Friedan," *Chatelaine*, February 1965, 69.

32. Pre–*The Feminine Mystique* writing. Smith College class of 1942, "15th reunion questionnaire. Draft questionnaires, 1957." PBF. Box: 31, folder 416. "15 years later, Anonymous Questionnaire," 1942, Magic File, Smith College Archivist reference files, CA-MS-01213. Smith College Archives.

33. Brockway story first cited in Wilkes, "Mother Superior to Women's Lib," in Sherman, ed., *Interviews with Betty Friedan*, 17.

34. Friedan, *Life So Far*, 134.

35. Ibid., 92. "County Draws on Its Talented . . ." *Journal News*, October 8, 1958, 1. "Resource Pool Planned," *Journal News*, June 21, 1960, 1.

36. "New Notes, Classroom and Campus," *NYTimes*, July 3, 1960, E8. "Classes Taught by Intellectuals," *NYTimes*, November 7, 1960, 37.

37. In his 1950 bestseller, *The Lonely Crowd*, David Riesman warned that Americans were sinking into passivity ("other directed," as he called it). Friedan quoted in Breslin, *Chatelaine*, "Chatelaine Drops in on Betty Friedan," 72. "Biographical, including clippings. Awards, 1941–1978." "It was almost . . ." "Biographical Notes." PBF. Box: 1, folder 62. Friedan, *The Feminine Mystique*, 62; Betty Friedan, "Introduction to the Tenth Anniversary Edition," *The Feminine Mystique*, 36.

## Chapter 5. "The Problem That Had No Name"

1. Friedan, *The Feminine Mystique*, 44.

2. Ibid., 96. Joanne Meyerowitz, "Beyond *The Feminine Mystique:* A Reassessment of Post-War Culture," *Journal of American History*, 79, no. 4 (1994): 1455–82. Grace Paley, "Mom," *Esquire*, December 1975, 85–86. Nathan Glazer and Daniel Moynihan's *Beyond The Melting Pot: The Negroes, Puerto Ricans, Jews, Italians, and Irish of New York City*, published in 1963, blamed Black matriarchs for ruining their families.

3. Sheila Rowbotham, *Women's Consciousness, Man's World* (New York: Penguin Books, 1973), 5. On p. 4, Rowbotham refers

to the thriller-like quality of *The Feminine Mystique*, as does Rachel Bowlby, "The Problem with No Name: Rereading Friedan's *The Feminine Mystique*," *Feminist Review*, September 1987, 61.

4. Friedan, *The Feminine Mystique*, 65.

5. Ibid., 115.

6. Ibid., 117, 118.

7. Ibid., 127, 129, 131.

8. Ibid., 135.

9. Ibid., 280, 226, 222.

10. Ibid., 229.

11. Ibid., 258, 266.

12. Ibid., 295.

13. Ibid., 325, 329. Kirsten Fermaglich, "The Comfortable Concentration Camp: The Significance of Nazi Imagery in Betty Friedan's *The Feminine Mystique*," *American Jewish History*, 91, no. 2 (June 2003): 163, 177, 180. The historian Jennie Eagle has found similar attempts to link Black and white women in drafts. Jennie Eagle, "Betty Friedan and Juliet Mitchell: Critiques of Ideology and Power," unpublished MA thesis, CUNY, 2018, 14–15.

14. Friedan, *The Feminine Mystique*, 359.

15. Friedan, *The Feminine Mystique*, 395.

16. Burton Beals to BF, October 9, 1962. Friedan, 1963 file, W. W. Norton and Company Records, Rare Book and Manuscript Library, Columbia University Library (hereafter cited as WWN). Lillian Smith, *How Am I To Be Heard? Letters of Lillian Smith*, ed. Margaret Rose Gladney (Chapel Hill: University of North Carolina Press, 2018), 138. Letter from BF to AM, M4405, 1/21/63. Abraham Maslow Papers, Drs. Nicholas and Dorothy Cummings Center for the History of Psychology, University of Akron. Letter from AM to BB 1/28/63, M4405, Abraham Maslow Papers, Drs. Nicholas and Dorothy Cummings Center for the History of Psychology University of Akron.

17. The Feminine Mystique. Correspondence, re: promotion and publicity, 1959. "Letter, Carl to BF, n.d." PBF. Box: 57, folder 710. Cited in Tania Grossinger, *Memoir of an Independent Woman:*

*An Unconventional Life Well Lived* (New York: Skyhorse Publishing, 2013), 119.

18. Cited in Stephanie Coontz, *A Strange Stirring: The Feminine Mystique and American Women at the Dawn of the 1960s* (New York: Basic Books, 2012), 19–20, 84.

19. Cited in Coontz, *A Strange Stirring*, 126. Gerda Lerner, letter to BF, February 6, 1963, widely reprinted. Jessie Bernard, "Review of *The Feminine Mystique*," *Marriage and Family Living*, 25, no. 3, August 29, 1963, 381–82.

20. Grossinger, *Memoir of an Independent Woman*, 114.

21. Carson spot, *Journal Herald*, August 14, 1963, 52. "Came out swinging" quoted in *Montreal Star*, May 10, 1963, 15. Virginia Graham, *There Goes What's Her Name: The Continuing Saga of Virginia Graham* (New York: Prentice, 1965), 89, 172. *TV Guide* schedules show BF first appearing on *Girl Talk* on March 8, 1964. Friedan, *Life So Far*, 141. Quoted in Grossinger, *Memoir of an Independent Woman*, 116. Grossinger quoted in Wilkes, "Mother Superior to Women's Lib," in Sherman, ed., *Interviews with Betty Friedan*, 17.

22. Mannes cited in Hennessee, *Betty Friedan*, 84. Smith, "Too Tame the Shrew," *Saturday Review*, February 23, 1963, 46, 34. Lucy Freeman, "The Feminine Mystique," *NYTimes*, April 7, 1963, 39. At the time when Friedan was working on *The Feminine Mystique*, Charlotte Perkins Gilman's "The Yellow Wallpaper," and *Women and Economics: A Study of the Economic Relation Between Men and Women as a Factor in Social Evolution* (whose interest in social reforms and use of the word "humanism" Friedan would echo, as she did Gilman's repudiation of Freud) had been out of print for years. In her papers, I found no evidence that Friedan read Gilman.

23. Diane Ravitch, "Mama in Search of Herself," *New Leader*, April 15, 1963, 29. In 1980 Sandra Dijkstra, "Simone de Beauvoir and Betty Friedan: The Politics of Omission," *Feminist Studies* 6, no. 2 (1980): 291–303 called it "deradicalized." Dijkstra would become Susan Faludi's agent. Friedan quoted in George Cotkin, *Existential America* (Baltimore: Johns Hopkins University Press, 2005), 254.

24. Ravitch, "Mama in Search of Herself," 29. Cited in Horowitz, *Betty Friedan and the Making of The Feminine Mystique*, 213. Hennessee, *Betty Friedan*, 82–84. Philip Rieff cited in Oral history interviews with Friedan. February 27–April 24, 1992 and December 11, 1993. Tape Six, ACBF.

25. The Feminine Mystique Correspondence: Editor Burton Beals 1958–1969. "Letter from Tania Grossinger to Burton Beals, April 10, 1963," PBF. Box: 57, folder 709.

26. WWN, Carl Friedan to Mr. Storer, May 22, 1963. F Folder.

27. The Feminine Mystique Correspondence: "letters describing genesis of the book, 1959–1962." "Letter from Betty Friedan to nd," PBF. Box: 57, folder 708.

28. The Feminine Mystique Correspondence: George Norton re: disagreement over *The Feminine Mystique* promotion, draft, 1967, n.d. "Letter from Betty Friedan to Burton Beals," n.d. PBF. Box: 57, Folder 714. "'Mystique' View, Backed by Many, Author Finds," *NYTimes*, March 12, 1964, 30.

29. Friedan cited in Tornabene, in Sherman, ed., *Interviews with Betty Friedan*, 33.

30. Interview with Harry Goldstein Jr.

31. Quote found in several sources. *The Feminine Mystique*. Correspondence: editor Burton Beals, 1958–1969. "Letter from Burton Beals to BF, October 7, 1963." PBF. Box: 57, folder 709, to date her leaving Norton. Numbers, *Hennessee*, 78.

32. Schlesinger Library exhibit commemorating the fiftieth anniversary of *The Feminine Mystique*. https://www.radcliffe.harvard.edu/schlesinger-library/exhibition/it-changed-my-life-feminine-mystique-50.

33. Robbie Terman, "From the Archives: To Volunteer or Not to Volunteer? the Betty Friedan Conundrum," *Jewish Women's Archive*, https://jwa.org/blog/from-archives-to-volunteer-or-not-to-volunteer-betty-friedan-conundrum. "Hillel Alumni Hosts Brunch . . ." *B'nai B'rith Messenger*, June 26, 1964. "Conservative Women to Discuss Mystique," *American Jewish World*, February 28, 1964. Julius J. Nodel, "Is the Feminine Mystique a Feminine Mistake?"

quoted in Fermaglich, "The Comfortable Concentration Camp," 225. Letter, I. B. Stransky, *St. Louis Jewish Light*, October 30, 1963, 4.

34. "Philco Presents the World Over: The World's Girls," October 25, 1963, The Paley Archive at the Paley Center for Media, New York City. "Angry Battler for Her Sex: Betty Friedan Attacks the Feminine Mystique," *Life*, November 1, 1963, 84.

35. Editorial correspondence. Agents: Marie Rodell and Joan Daves, Inc., 1953–1963; includes rejection letters for early chapters of *The Feminine Mystique*. Letter, Marie Rodell to BF, December 3, 1961, PBF. Box: 154, folder 1937. Letter, Marie Rodell to Alan Collins, November 3, 1963, WWN.

## Chapter 6. The "NAACP for Women"

1. Friedan spoke of Kennedy in her talk at Harvard in February 1966. Friedan, *It Changed My Life*, 218. However, several scholars write that JFK associated this phrase with political demagoguery.

2. Friedan, *It Changed My Life*, 70. Paperback numbers, Wilkes, 17; Tornabene, 31 in Sherman, ed., *Interviews with Betty Friedan.*

3. Friedan quoted in John G. Stewart, "When Democracy Worked: Reflections on the Passage of the Civil Rights Act of 1964," *NYLS Law Review*, 2014–15, 59, 162.

4. Carl quoted in Carl Friedan Transcript, JHP.

5. Carl quoted in Hennessee, *Betty Friedan*, 92.

6. Friedan, *The Fountain of Age* (New York: Simon and Schuster, 2006), 14; Friedan, *Life So Far*, 156; Friedan, *It Changed My Life*, 75.

7. Judy Klemesrud, "Women's Movement at Age Eleven . . . ," *NYTimes*, November 15, 1977, 63. Muriel Fox interview, June 2020. Jon Sloan interview.

8. Raphael quoted in "Betty Friedan Remembered," February 3, 2007. ACBF.

9. Betty Friedan, "Working Women 1965, The False Problems and the True," *Cosmopolitan*, January 1965, 48.

10. Letter from Betty Friedan to Alva Myrdal, June 11, 1965. From the personal archives of Alva and Gunnar Myrdal, Refer-

ence code 405/3/1/4/17. Swedish Labor Movement Archive and Library. Murray cited in Toni Carabillo, *Feminist Chronicles: 1953–1993* (New York: Women's Graphics, 1993), 15. Edith Evans Asbury, "Protest Proposed on Women's Jobs," *NYTimes*, October 13, 1965, 32. Pauli Murray, *Song in a Weary Throat: Memoir of an American Pilgrimage* (New York: Liveright, 2018), 476–80.

11. Correspondence. Friedan's letters re: Jane Crow, 1965–1967. Letter n.d. to PM. PBF, Box: 143, Folder 981. Friedan, *It Changed My Life*, 95. The phrase "NAACP for women" has been attributed to Pauli Murray, Muriel Fox, Dorothy Robinson, and Friedan herself. In "How NOW Began," she writes that she had been asked "hundreds of times" why she did not start one. "How Now Began: Background Memorandum on NOW from Betty Friedan," n.d., "Presidential Reports, Letters, etc. 1966–76," Records of the National Organization for Women, MC 496, Box 43: Folder 1, 3, 14. Schlesinger Library, Harvard Radcliffe Institute, Cambridge, Mass. (hereafter cited as RNOW).

12. India trip, 1966: correspondence with Indira Gandhi, 1966, 1971. Letter from BF to Esther Peterson, March 5, 1966. PBF. Box: 78, folder 906.

13. "Women—Dare We Not Discriminate," February 18, 1966, Part One. https://www.youtube.com/watch?v=gK4EkUOO4fs&ab_channel=TheHarvardLawForum.

14. Friedan quoted in "Women—Dare We Not Discriminate." Linda McVeigh, "Betty Freidan [*sic*]," *Harvard Crimson*, February 24, 1966. https://www.thecrimson.com/article/1966/2/24/betty-freidan-pwhen-the-other-law/.

15. Interview with Muriel Fox. Friedan, *It Changed My Life*, 95, 100. Letter from PM to BF, n.d., Pauli Murray Papers 1927–1985 MC 412, Box: 95, folder 1681. Schlesinger Library, Harvard Radcliffe Institute, Cambridge, Mass. Permission to reprint granted by the Charlotte Sheedy Literary Agency as agent for the author. Copyright © Pauli Murray Foundation (hereafter cited as PPM).

16. "Remarks," June 28, 1966, Lyndon Baines Johnson White

House Files, LBJ Presidential Library. Friedan, *It Changed My Life*, 102.

17. Some details of this event are from Sides One and Two, "Series VII Audiovisual Material." "Phone Conversation with Nancy Knaack, September 16, 1976," Papers of Toni Carabillo and Judith Meuli 1890–2008, MC 725, Schlesinger Library, Harvard Radcliffe Institute, Cambridge, Mass. The story about Friedan's tantrum is repeated in Cohen, *The Sisterhood*, 135. Hennessee, *Betty Friedan* 100. Flora Davis, *Moving the Mountain: The Women's Movement Since 1960* (Champaign: University of Illinois Press, 1999), 54. The words that get italicized differ.

18. Sides One and Two, "Series VII Audiovisual Material." "Phone Conversation with Nancy Knaack, September 16, 1976," Papers of Toni Carabillo and Judith Meuli 1890–2008, MC 725, Schlesinger Library, Harvard Radcliffe Institute, Cambridge, Mass. Friedan, *It Changed My Life*, 103. Italics in original.

19. Hole and Levine, *Rebirth of Feminism*, 84.

20. NOW Statement of Purpose widely available. There have been many accounts of this historic moment. For example, Rosalind Rosenberg, *Jane Crow: The Life of Pauli Murray* (New York: Oxford University Press, 2017), 299–300.

21. Correspondence, General, 1966. Letter BF to DH, June 20, 1966. PBF. Box: 143, folder 1795.

22. Letters to civil rights leaders from Friedan, on and around July 12, 1966, widely available including NAACP Papers, Proquest Historical Vault. University of Chicago. A fuller list includes Thurgood Marshall, Stokely Carmichael, Whitney Young, Roy Wilkins, and Bayard Rustin. Betty Friedan, "The National Organization for Women's 1966 Statement of Purpose," 1996. http://www.now.org/history/purpos66.html. Report of the Legal Committee of the National Organization for Women 1967, https://feminist.org/resources/feminist-chronicles/part-iii-the-early-documents/report-of-the-legal-committee-of-the-national-organization-for-women-1967/.

23. This figure comes from an interview with Sonia Pressman

Fuentes, who writes that of 42 founders she queried, 6 were Jewish. Interview with Sonia Pressman Fuentes, March 14, 2016. Altogether, there were 49 founders, but she did not query all of them. Friedan quoted in Stone, "Friedan at 55," 11.

24. Friedan quoted in "Minutes, Founding Conference, Washington, DC, October 29–30, 1966," RNOW, Carton 23. Biographical including clippings. Resumes, biographies, 1951–1980; includes job application Judy Michaelson, *New York Post*, November 29, 1966, PBF. Box: 1, folder 61.

25. Cited in Dorothy White Austin, "NOW Top Officer Is Wisconsinite," *Milwaukee Journal*, October 31, 1966.

26. Most of the actions listed in this section are listed in the November 21, 1966, NOW press release, Dorothy Kenyon Papers, Sophia Smith Collection, Smith College, Northampton, Mass., Box 10 (hereafter cited as DKP). Writ of mandamus cited in Gail Collins, *When Everything Changed: The Amazing Journey of Women from 1960 to the Present* (New York: Little, Brown, 2009), 85–86.

27. Friedan, *It Changed My Life*, 138. Kennedy quoted in Sherie M. Randolph, *Florynce "Flo" Kennedy: The Life and Times of a Black Feminist Radical* (Chapel Hill: University of North Carolina Press, 2018), 112–13. According to Randolph, this was the first meeting of New York NOW, but Muriel Fox says it was the second. Friedan, *Life So Far*, 187. Muriel Fox remembers NAACP being more supportive.

28. Correspondence. General, 1968; includes Coretta Scott King. PBF, Box: 144, folder 1802. NOW. Correspondence. Coretta Scott King, 1967, 1969. Letter from BF to CSK. PBF, Box: 22, folder 1985. Friedan, *Life So Far*, 187. She makes this claim years earlier, in *It Changed My Life.* Friedan cited in Charlotte Hale, "Should Women Revolt?" *Atlanta Journal and the Atlanta Constitution*, May 28, 1967, SM8. Thanks to Casey Westerman for this citation. Also, "NOW to Discuss Women's Rights Under New Law," *Atlanta Constitution*, June 1, 1967, documents the NOW office opening shortly after that talk. Email from Jane Bond Moore, October 8, 2016. Several women told the story about Stokely Carmichael's line being a joke. NOW being asked to join the Leadership Con-

ference on Civil Rights: Dorothy Haener Papers, NOW Acts, Box 22: Folder 7, Walter Reuther Library, Wayne State University. Friedan repeats the Carmichael quote in *Life So Far*, 186–87.

29. "11 Picket Times Classified Office," *NYTimes*, August 31, 1967. "Bunnies of the air" is quoted in several newspapers, for example, *Daily News*, September 13, 1967, 683.

30. Friedan, *Life So Far*, 242. Hennessee, *Betty Friedan*, 112. This story is also backed up by Carl.

31. Myrdal quoted in Robert McEowen, "Is A Woman's Place In The Home?" *Vancouver Sun*, September 9, 1969, European trip to Prague, Stockholm, Germany, Paris, 1967: arrangements, correspondence, 1965–1967. BF to Hanus Papousak, December 7, 1967, 1. PBF, Box: 80, folder 917. European trip to Prague, Stockholm, Germany, Paris, 1967: arrangements, correspondence, 1965–1967. Letter to Ulla Aaltonen, Nov 7, 1967. PBF. Box: 80, folder 917. Birgitta Wistrand, Skype interview, May 19, 2021.

32. "President's Report to NOW, Washington, DC, 1967," cited in Friedan, *It Changed My Life*, 127–28. The activist Morag MacLeod Simpson wrote to Friedan saying that it was not Black activists but someone from the Anti-Defamation League/B'nai B'rith who said the women did not belong under the umbrella of civil rights. Letter from Morag MacLeod Simpson to BF, February 8, 1968, Dorothy Haener Collection, Box 22: Folder 8, Walter Reuther Library, Wayne State University.

33. Friedan, *It Changed My Life*, 130. "Minutes of National Conference of NOW, RNOW" Carton 23: Folder 2. Document II, "The Right of a Woman to Determine Her Own Reproductive Process." National Conference Report, 1967, RNOW. Alice Echols, *Daring to Be Bad: Radical Feminism in America* (Minneapolis: University of Minnesota Press, 1989), 167–69.

34. https://350fem.blogs.brynmawr.edu/1967/11/19/national-conference-of-now-minutes/National Conference, Call to Conference, agenda, minutes, 1967. RNOW, Carton 23: Folder 2. Sue Ellen Browder, *Subverted, How I Helped the Sexual Revolution Hijack the Women's Movement* (San Francisco: Ignatius Press, 2015), 70. Browder's take on this conference is that Friedan forced abortion

onto the bill of rights although the membership vote did not support her.

35. Interview with Ti-Grace Atkinson, March 24, 2017. Menaker, *Ego in Evolution*, 102. Brill, 169. Friedan quoted in Judith Hill Paterson, *Be Somebody: A Biography of Marguerite Rawalt* (Fort Worth: Eakin Press, 1986), 182. Email with Paterson, 2018.

36. Marilyn Bender, "The Feminists are on the March Once More," *NYTimes*, December 14, 1967, 78. European trip to Prague, Stockholm, Germany, Paris, 1967: arrangements, correspondence, 1965–1967. BF to Bob Rimmer, December 7, 1967, PBF. Box: 80, folder 917.

## Chapter 7. "Our Revolution Is Unique"

1. Letter from BF to George Meany 2/68, Box 3: Folder 9, National Organization for Women New York City Chapter Records, Tamiment Library/Robert F. Wagner Labor Archives.

2. Friedan quoted in "Sees Woman in 'Negro' Phase," *Des Moines Register*, April 3, 1968, 10. Friedan quoted in *San Francisco Chronicle*, May 5, 1968, 45. Friedan quoted in *NOW Acts* Winter/Spring 1969, 8, Dorothy Haener Records, Box 22: Folder 7, Walter Reuther Library, Wayne State University.

3. Dolores Alexander, "NOW to Try Four Prong War Against Bias," *Newsday*, May 7, 1968, 94. Friedan, *It Changed My Life*, 209.

4. Charlotte Curtis, "White House Candidates Let the Women Down," *NYTimes*, May 7, 1968, 40.

5. Betty Friedan, "Up from the Kitchen Floor," *NYTimes*, March 4, 1973, 8. Anne Koedt, "The Myth of the Vaginal Orgasm," *Notes from the First Year* (New York: New York Radical Feminists, 1968).

6. Marilyn Bender, "Valeria Solanis a Heroine to Feminists," *NYTimes*, June 14, 1968, 52. Memo from Mary Eastwood to BF, June 15, 1968, Dolores Alexander Papers, Sophia Smith Collection, Smith College, Northampton, Mass. (Hereafter cited as DAP.)

7. Friedan cited in Breanne Fahs, *Valerie Solanas: The Defiant Life of the Woman Who Wrote SCUM and Shot Andy Warhol* (New

York: The Feminist Press at CUNY, 2014), 182. Notes, New York NOW membership meeting, June 20, 1968, DAP.

8. Friedan, *Life So Far*, 179. Carl tells a version of the knife story in 2000. Other sources include Ti-Grace Atkinson and Mary Jean Tully in JHP. I'm dating it to 1968 because Atkinson "had nearly no contact" with Betty after the end of 1968. Also, the divorce was finalized in May 1969. According to Atkinson, Betty lacked shame about chasing Carl, blade in hand, but worried that witnesses might tell a judge what they saw and adversely impact a ruling on any divorce settlement. Interview with Ti-Grace Atkinson. Email Atkinson, September 26, 2016.

9. Women and the '68 election, "1968: typescripts." "Violence and NOW," handwritten note, 1. PBF. Box: 81, folder 926, dating based on "mailed to Ivy Bottini 7/24/68."

10. Letter from BF to KC, August 18, 1968, "Correspondence of Betty Friedan, President, 1967–69," Box 74. Aileen C. Hernandez Papers, Sophia Smith Collection, SSC-MS-00730, Smith College, Northampton, Mass. (hereafter ACH). Betty Friedan, "An Opinion: Betty Friedan on the Conventions: We Are the Invisible 51% in the Politics of Sex," *Mademoiselle*, October 1968, 22.

11. Carolyn Jay, "GOP to Get 'Bill of Rights' for Women," *Miami News Service*, July 30, 1968, 15. Bill of Rights for Women Republican Convention. https://uindy.historyit.com/item.php?id=313701. "A Bill of Rights for Women," Democratic National Convention Records, Box 2, Folder 30, Special Collections, Chicago Public Library. Friedan, *Life So Far*, 207–9. Friedan, *Mademoiselle*, 220.

12. Phone interview with Noreen Connell, May 12, 2016. Friedan, *Life So Far*, 211.

13. "Women Launch Boycott of Colgate Palmolive," *Lexington–Herald Leader*, September 16, 1968, 2.

14. Elizabeth Shelton, "Feminism Faces a Backlash," *Washington Post*, October 23, 1968, C2.

15. Letter, BF to Wilma Scott Heide, November 8, 1968, ACH, Box 74, Sophia Smith Collection, Smith College, Northamp-

ton, Mass. Friedan, *It Changed My Life*, 138. Shelton, "Feminism Faces a Backlash." Friedan, "Our Revolution Is Unique," December 6, 1968, President's Report to NOW, *It Changed My Life*, and many other places. In 1968, Coretta Scott King dialed back her involvement in NOW. Although she was invited to the 1968 Atlanta NOW National Board meeting, she sent her sister, Edythe Scott Bagley, in her stead. The subject of Bagley's talk was how Black women have "suffered more deeply than any of her other fellow human beings." NOW Minutes, National Conference 1968 (December 7–8) Carton 23: Folder 7, RNOW, SL.

16. Lynne Powell, "U.S. Women Treated as Objects," *National Guardian* 20, no. 5 (1967): 7. Friedan, "Our Own Revolution Is Unique," in Friedan, *It Changed My Life*, 143. Barbara Seaman also referred to her this way. As late as 1985, introducing her at Temple Sinai in Los Angeles, the rabbi would use King's language: she "had a dream."

17. Friedan and Hacker quoted in Sheila Tobias, Ella Kusnetz, and Deborah Spitz, *Selected Proceedings of the Cornell Conference on Women* (Ithaca, N.Y.: Know, Incorporated, 1969), 5–6.

18. Friedan, *It Changed My Life*, 145. Friedan quoted in Tobias et al., *Selected Proceedings*, 8–9.

19. Friedan quoted in Tobias et al., *Selected Proceedings*, 3, 8, 9, 10, 16. Friedan, *It Changed My Life*, 146.

20. Interview with Muriel Fox.

21. Cohen, *The Sisterhood*, 21. Gloria Steinem, "After Black Power, Women's Liberation," *New York*, April 7, 1969, 8.

22. Friedan, *It Changed My Life*, 157, 156, 160. "Friendly Skies Thunder with Gals Protest," *Chicago Tribune*, February 15, 1969, 5.

23. Rosalind Rosenberg, *Divided Lives: American Women in the Twentieth Century* (New York: Hill and Wang, 2008), 205–6. Steinem, "After Black Power, Women's Liberation," 8.

24. Friedan quoted in Tornebene in Sherman, ed., *Interviews with Betty Friedan*, 32. Senate testimony May 5, 6, 7, 1970.

25. Friedan quoted in Stone, "Friedan at 55."

26. Interview with Nydia Leaf, March 27, 2022.

27. Peter Hellman, "The Consequences of Brownstone Fever,"

*New York*, March 31, 1969, 26; Jo Roman, *Exit House: Choosing Suicide as an Alternative* (New York: SeaView Books, 1980), 47–49. Thomas W. Ennis, "City Plans to Sell West Side Houses," *NYTimes*, November 5, 1967, R1. Thomas W. Ennis, "Group of Friends Rebuild and Combine Old Brownstone Into a Coop," March 2, 1969, and "9-G Co-Op," *Forum*, July/August 1969, Box 3, Folder 7, 9G Cooperative, Judith Edelman Architectural Collection, Ms1997-010, Special Collections and University Archives, Virginia Tech, Blacksburg, Va. JHP, and Nydia Leaf interview. Friedan, *It Changed My Life*, 269.

28. Maryann Barakso, *Governing NOW: Grassroots Activism in the National Organization for Women* (Ithaca, N.Y.: Cornell University Press, 2004), 46. Dolores Alexander: Voices of Feminism Oral History Project, Sophia Smith Collection, 20. https://findingaids.smith.edu/repositories/2/archival_objects/89244.

29. Telephone interview with Michael Murphy, May 27, 2016.

30. Cited in Hennessee, *Betty Friedan*, 129. Dolores Alexander transcript, JHP. Email from Joan E. Winter, June 6, 2016. Phone interviews March 2022. *LATimes*, July 13, 1969, 124.

## Chapter 8. Sexual Politics and the Women's Strike for Equality

1. Kate Millett, *Sexual Politics* (Champaign: University of Illinois Press, 1970; 2000), 18.

2. Friedan, "Some Days in the Life of the Most Influential Woman of Our Time," *McCall's*, June 1971, 36. Friedan quoted in Hole and Levine, *Rebirth of Feminism*, 221.

3. Friedan, *It Changed My Life*, 173. The scholar Jo Freeman complained that the First Congress was "fraught with dissention, backbiting." https://www.jofreeman.com/socialmovements/polorg.htm. "Women's Rights Group Asks for the Moon," *Shreveport Journal* (AP), December 8, 1969, 3; Sidney Abbott and Barbara Love, *Sappho Was a Right-On Woman: A Liberated View of Lesbianism* (New York: Stein and Day, 1972), 112.

4. Daniel Horowitz, "Rethinking Betty Friedan and *The Feminine Mystique:* Labor Union Radicalism in Cold War America,"

*American Quarterly* 48, no. 1 (1996): 28. European trip to Prague, Stockholm, Germany, Paris, 1967: arrangements, correspondence, 1965–1967. BF to Robert Rimmer, December 7, 1967. PBF, Box 80, folder 917.

5. William O'Neill, *Everyone Was Brave: The Rise and Fall of Feminism in America* (New York: Quadrangle Books, 1969), 342.

6. Friedan telegram to Nixon quoted in Vera Glaser, "Women Unite to Challenge Court Nominee," *Miami Herald*, January 24, 1970, 2. Echols, *Daring to Be Bad*, 8. FBI File National Organization for Women 1 of 3, 6/19/69 vault. FBI.gov. Ivy Bottini Interview, May 3, 2016.

7. Friedan quoted in Committee on the Judiciary Senate, Nomination of George Harrold Carswell, Proquest Congressional Database, January 27–29, February 2–3, 1970, 88.

8. Ibid., 92.

9. Muriel Fox interview. Several people have said that Friedan did not like Alexander because she "crossed" her. Hennessee, *Betty Friedan*, 132–34, argues that Friedan was mad that she was not nominated to the board. BF letter to Sylvia Hartman, February 14, 1970. Women's History Research Center Collection, Box 23: Folder 14, American Heritage Center, University of Wyoming. Copyright © Betty Friedan. Reprinted by permission of Curtis Brown, Ltd. All rights reserved. Friedan quoted in Leslie Bennetts, "On Aggression in Politics: Are Women Judged by a Double Standard?" *NYTimes*, February 11, 1979, B3.

10. Muriel Fox interview. Figures in Judith Hennessee, *Betty Friedan*, 127.

11. Susan Brownmiller, "Sisterhood Is Powerful," *NYTimes*, March 15, 1970, 230. Friedan, *Life So Far*, 231. Cynthia Fuchs Epstein said the idea for the strike started at the commune.

12. "Feminist Friedan: Action, But Only One Battle Plan," *San Francisco Chronicle*, April 9, 1970, 28. Friedan, *It Changed My Life*, 178. Shirley Bernard, "The Women's Strike: August 26, 1970," unpublished doctoral dissertation, 1975, 2, SL.

13. Friedan quoted in Bernard, "The Women's Strike," 31, 32.

14. Ibid., 32. Clendinen Dudley and Adam Nagourney, *Out*

*for Good: The Struggle to Build a Gay Rights Movement* (New York: Simon and Schuster, 1999), 90.

15. Friedan quoted in *Philadelphia Inquirer*, May 8, 1970, 2. https://www.newspapers.com/image/179949341/?terms=betty%20friedan&match=1. Friedan, *It Changed My Life*, 243. Interview with Jonathan Slon.

16. Friedan, "Some Days in the Life of the Most Influential Woman of Our Time," *McCall's*, June 1971, 34. Natalie Gittelson interview, May 26, 2016.

17. Cited in Hennessee, *Betty Friedan*, 225. Friedan, *Life So Far*, 272.

18. Interview with Catharine Stimpson, February 9, 2016. Interviews with Friedan's friends and colleagues who wished to remain anonymous.

19. Friedan quoted in "Lib Holds Fund-Raising Party," *Newsday* (AP), August 10, 1970, 83. Berman quoted in *NYTimes*, July 26, 1970.

20. Jill Johnston, *Admission Accomplished: The Lesbian Nation Years* (London: Serpents Tail Press, 1998), 6–7.

21. Charlotte Curtis, "Women's Liberation Gets into the Long Island Swim," *NYTimes*, August 10, 1970, 32, 36.

22. "Liberation Now." Copyright © Betty Friedan. Reprinted by permission of Curtis Brown, Ltd. All rights reserved. Radicals accused her of trying to profit from the song.

23. Friedan, *It Changed My Life*, 188.

24. Friedan quoted in "Feminist Calls for Strike to Mark Women's Suffrage," *Boston Globe*, August 24, 1970, 15. Also, groups of women in Europe celebrated the day. Friedan, *Life So Far*, 241.

25. Friedan quoted in "The Lib Ladies Give This Town What For," *New York Daily News*, August 27, 1970, 74.

26. Friedan, "Up From the Kitchen Floor," 1973; Dorothy Kenyon letter to BF November 20, 1970. DKP, Box 10. Judy Klemesrud, "Coming Wednesday," *NYTimes*, August 23, 1970. "Leading Feminist Puts Hairdo Before Strike," *NYTimes*, August 27, 1970, 30.

27. "Leading Feminist," *NYTimes*, 1970. Cited in Cohen, *The*

*Sisterhood*, 283. Another paper told how, at lunchtime in the (formerly) men-only room at Whyte's, a restaurant in the financial district, Friedan ate crabmeat, drank whiskey sours, and, when asked if her lunch companions were secretaries, replied, "They're security analysts!" pounding the table. Bernard, "The Women's Strike," 35. Friedan quoted in *Newsday*, August 26, 1970, 4.

28. Estimates range between 20,000 and 50,000. Jonathan quoted in Emily Bazelon, "The Mother of Feminism," *NYTimes*, December 31, 2006, Section 6, 43.

29. Bryant Park events cited in many sources. Eleanor Holmes Norton quote, Bernard, "The Women's Strike," 220.

30. Betty Friedan, "Women in the Firing Line," *NYTimes*, October 28, 1984, 626.

31. Abbott and Love, *Sappho Was a Right-On Woman*, 118. *Liberation News Service*, August 29, 1970, 13, 14. Pacifica Radio, Women's Liberation, August 26, 1970. https://archive.org/details/pacifica_radio_archives-BB2603.

32. There are several different figures for NOW membership in 1970. As Shirley Bernard writes, NOW closely guarded numbers in those years. Ruth Rosen, *The World Split Open: How the Modern Women's Movement Changed America* (New York: Penguin Books, 2000), 93. Bernard, 21. Maggie Doherty, "Feminist Factions Filled the Streets for This Historic March," *NYTimes*, August 26, 1970. Friedan quoted in "Women on the March," *NYTimes*, August 30, 1970, 125.

33. "Strange" in "Woman and Jews: The Quest for Selfhood," *Congress Monthly*, 1984. Midge Decter, "The Liberated Woman," *Commentary*, October 1970, 35–44. https://www.commentary.org/articles/midge-decter-3/the-liberated-woman/. Trude Weiss-Rosmarin, "The Unfreedom of Jewish Women," *The Jewish Spectator*, October 1970, 2–6. Greenberg quoted in Mark Oppenheimer, "Pushing for Change, Within the Bounds of Orthodoxy," *NYTimes*, July 6, 2013, 12.

34. Friedan quoted in Transcript of McGovern Committee Hearing, September 30, 1970, 1148. *off our backs*, November 8, 1970, 11.

35. "Women's Teach In Schedule," *The South End*, October 20, 1970, 2. Walter P. Reuther Library, Wayne State University. Dorothy Sue Cobble, *The Other Women's Movement* (Princeton: Princeton University Press, 2004), 192–93.

36. Wilkes, in Sherman, ed., *Interviews with Betty Friedan.*

37. Friedan, *Life So Far*, 129. "Critique of Sexual Politics: An Interview with Betty Friedan," *Social Policy* 1 (November/December 1970): 38–40.

38. "Feminist Marchers Brave Icy Rain," *NYTimes*, December 12, 1970, 66. Judy Klemesrud, "The Lesbian Issue and Women's Lib," *NYTimes*, December 17, 1970, 47. "Winter Kills NYC March for Abortion," *Boston Globe*, December 13, 1970, 22. Friedan, *It Changed My Life*, 201.

39. Kate Millett, *Flying* (New York: Random House, 1974), 474.

## Chapter 9. "I've Been More of a Jewish Mother to the Movement Than I Have to My Own Children"

1. Myra McPherson, "The Former Mr. Betty Friedan Has Scars to Prove It," *Washington Post*, February 7, 1971, L1. Friedan quoted in Jane Gregory, "It's Betty's Turn; Carl, Are You Listening?" *Boston Globe*, March 16, 1971, 25.

2. Betty Friedan, "What's the Point of Making It If You Can't Celebrate Being 50?" *McCall's*, August 1971, 59.

3. Claudia Dreifus, "The Selling of a Feminist," *Nation*, June 7, 1971, 728.

4. "In New York City, You Really Gotta Know Your Line," *off our backs*, 1, no. 22, May 27, 1971, 10–11.

5. Corso, Mailer, quoted in Israel Shenker, "Norman Mailer vs. Women's Lib," *NYTimes*, May 1, 1971, 19. Also quoted in D. A. Pennebaker, "Town Bloody Hall," 1979. Cohen, *The Sisterhood*, 291. Peter Manso, *Norman Mailer, His Life and Times* (New York: Washington Square Press, 2008), 522.

6. Friedan quoted many places, for example Pennebaker and in Mary Breasted, "Among the Combatants: Mailer vs. Women's Lib," *Washington Post*, May 3, 1971, D1.

7. A spring 1972 issue had an article by Jane O'Reilly about

housework, ostensibly Friedan's old subject. "McCarthy Has Words for Dem '72 Outlook," *New York Daily News*, February 8, 1971, 68. Friedan, *It Changed My Life*, 230.

8. Bella Abzug, *Bella! Ms. Abzug Goes to Washington* (New York: Saturday Review Press, 1972), 161. "Those Who Have Been Approached By Betty Friedan and Have Agreed To Serve As Conveners of the Caucus" from Patsy Mink Collection, Box 563, Folder One, Library of Congress. *The Spokeswoman*, June 1, 1971, 1. Eileen Shanahan, "Women Organize for Political Power," *NYTimes*, July 11, 1971, 1.

9. Onka dekkers, "National Women's Political Caucus," *off our backs*, December 1971, 19. Friedan, *It Changed My Life*, 214.

10. Cited in Julie Gallagher, *Black Women and Politics in New York City* (Bloomington: University of Illinois Press, 2012), 180. Shanahan, "Women Organize for Political Power," *NYTimes*, July 11, 1971.

11. "Women's Caucus Target of White House Jokes," *NYTimes*, July 14, 1971, 17.

12. Friedan, *It Changed My Life*, 226. Elsa Goss, "Lessons in Liberation," *Philadelphia Inquirer*, December 10, 1972, 449.

13. It's possible Friedan remembered Steinem's comment in Paul Wilkes's 1970 profile. "She has undertaken the immense job of bringing up the status of women so that love can succeed. Hopefully so that her own emotional needs as a woman can eventually be fulfilled." Friedan quoted in Curt Suplee, "Betty Friedan: Her Brave New World," *Washington Post*, October 19, 1983, B1, B15. Friedan quoted in Sydney Ladensohn Stern, *Gloria Steinem: Her Passion, Politics, and Mystique* (New York: Birch Lane Press, 1997), 226.

14. Memo BF to All Conveners of the NWPC, NOW chapters, State Commissions on Women, and Other Sisters, August 10, 1971, LaDonna Harris Papers and American Indian Opportunity Records, MSS 826 (Box 67, Folder 7), Special Collections/Center for Southwest Research, University Libraries, University of New Mexico. Copyright © Betty Friedan. Reprinted by permission of Curtis Brown, Ltd. All rights reserved.

15. Cited in Kay Mills, *This Little Light of Mine: The Life of*

*Fannie Lou Hamer* (New York: Dutton, 1993), 286–87. Also Owen Taylor, *Delta Democrat Times*, October 28, 1971, 10.

16. Betty Friedan, "Betty Friedan's Notebook: Do I, Of All People, Still Have a Double Standard About Sex?" *McCall's*, November 1971, 50.

17. Merle Shain, "Mom's Lib," *Maclean's*, November 1971, 46.

18. "My Roots Are Not in Any Place . . ." Betty Friedan's Notebook, *McCall's*, Jan 1, 1972, 119. Miriam told one journalist, "Betty has now matured a great deal," Lisa Hammel, "The 'Grandmother' of Women's Lib," *NYTimes*, November 19, 1971; and another, "Betty always excelled at everything, but she never felt she did well at anything," Shaine, "Mom's Lib," 46.

19. Rita Mae Brown wrote that Friedan's maid wore a white apron and cap. Robin Morgan told a student reporter that Friedan "did not give her black maid the day off on International Women's Day." *And Ain't I a Woman*, July 2, 1971, 12. Carl told Judith Hennessee that she fired "at least 40 of them" and "treat[ed] them like dirt." Carl Friedan, JHP. Brownmiller quoted in Cohen, *The Sisterhood*, 188.

20. According to several sources, it was "more than 500" people. "Shirley Chisholm Makes It Formal: She's a Candidate," *Washington Post*, January 26, 1972, A5. Friedan quoted in Unsigned, "Politics in Black: Lady Chisholm Is at Center Stage," *New York Amsterdam News*, February 5, 1972, A10.

21. Correspondence. Liz Carpenter, Shirley Chisholm, 1971–1972. Shirley Chisholm to BF, May 12, 1972, PBF, Box: 144, folder 1810. "The 1972 Campaign," *NYTimes*, June 8, 1972, 38. Friedan, *It Changed My Life*, 223.

22. Laurie Johnson, "Dream for Women: President Chisholm," *NYTimes*, February 14, 1972, 19. Friedan quoted in Patricia Stewart, "Woman Activist Backs Candidacy of Chisholm," *Hartford Courant*, February 8, 1972, 21. Morris Kaplan, "U.S. Court Eases Rules . . ." *NYTimes*, February 11, 1972, 1.

23. Friedan quoted in Shirley MacLaine, "Women, the Convention, and Brown Paper Bags," *NYTimes*, July 30, 1972, SM14. Transcript of Barbara Lamont interview, Box 5, Folder 4, JHP.

24. Chuck Andrews, "Watermelon for the Natives," *New York Amsterdam News*, July 1, 1972. Bayard Rustin, "Black Women Aren't Fooled By Women's Movement," "Politics in Black," *New York Amsterdam News*, July 15, 1972, A7. The traveling watermelon story is recounted in several places in JHP, including transcripts of interviews of Lois Gould, Martha McKay, Gloria Steinem, Jacqui Ceballos, and Ludwig Gelobter. Martha McKay says it was made up.

25. Transcript of interview of Jacqui Ceballos, Box 4: Folder 2, JHP. Transcript of interview with Bob and Lois Gould, Box 5: Folder 3, JHP. Natalie Gittelson, "Which Ms. Has the Movement?" *Harper's Bazaar*, July 1972, 80.

26. Germaine Greer, "McGovern, The Big Tease," *Harper's*, October 1972, 3.

27. Nora Ephron, "Miami," *Crazy Salad: Some Things About Women and Scribble Scribble: Notes on the Media* (New York: Vintage, 1978), 52, 56. Theodore White, *The Making of the President* (New York: Harper Collins, 1972), 222.

28. Friedan quoted in Ephron, *Crazy Salad and Scribble Scribble*, 58. Friedan quoted in Sally Bixby Defty, "Women Get Day Care Plank," *St. Louis Post-Dispatch*, August 21, 1972, 1. Lynn Sherr, "Democratic Women," *Saturday Review*, August 7, 1972, 7.

29. Walsh quoted in Ellen Goodman, "Abortion Plank: A Family Feud," *Boston Globe*, July 13, 1972. Shirley MacLaine quoted in "Democratic Delegates Defeat Abortion," *Montreal Gazette*, July 13, 1972. Carol Richards, "Women Delegates Cry Foul," *Press and Sun Bulletin*, July 13, 1972, 4. Friedan quoted in Ephron, "Miami," 54, 60.

30. "Betty Friedan's Notebook: What Have Women Really Won?" *McCall's*, November 1972, 74, 76, 78, 172; Myra McPherson, "Sisters v. Sisters: Abortion Battle Turns Bitter," *Washington Post*, July 12, 1972, A1, A20. Lectures, conferences, TV and radio talks. Democratic National Convention, 1972: McGovern's abortion plank. "Abortion," fragment, n.d., 18. PBF, Box: 104, folder 1213; Ellen Goodman, "Abortion Backers: Sore Losers," *Boston Globe*, July 12, 1972, 22 Friedan quoted in Nan Robertson, "Democrats Feel Impact of Women's New Power," *NYTimes*, July 15, 1972, 1. There are discrepancies as to the exact number of votes by

which abortion lost. Judith Hennessee says 466. The *New York Times* has it at 472 and the *Boston Globe* puts the difference at 471 votes.

31. Friedan, *It Changed My Life*, 225. Betty Friedan, "Beyond Women's Liberation," *McCall's*, August 1972, 135. "Betty Friedan—Bi Chauvinism: Pigs vs. Boors," *Washington Post*, July 19, 1972, B3.

32. Frank Swertlow, "Friedan, Steinem Air Split," *Boston Globe*, July 20, 1972, 27. "Beyond Women's Liberation," *McCall's*, 1972, 134–36. Deirdre Carmody, "Feminists Scored by Betty Friedan," *NYTimes*, July 19, 1972, 43.

33. The kids calling their mom "Betty" predates *The Second Stage*.

34. Wanda Urbanska, "Following the Feminist Footsteps," *Philadelphia Daily News*, October 28, 1981, 25. Joan Didion, "The Women's Movement," *NYTimes*, July 30, 1972, BR1.

35. Cited in Hennessee, *Betty Friedan*, 178. "GOP Women More Formal," *Austin-American Statesman*, August 21, 1972, 11. "Delegates Tangle with Mrs. Friedan" (*UPI*), August 23, 1972, 2. "GOP Women Shout at Betty Friedan," *Hartford Courant*, August 24, 1972; Otile McManus, "Waiting in the Wings Isn't Mrs. Friedan's Style," *Boston Globe*, August 24, 1972, 12.A.

36. Friedan, *It Changed My Life*, 321.

37. Midge Decter, *The New Chastity and Other Arguments Against Women's Liberation* (New York: Coward, McGann, and Geoghegan, 1972), 55.

38. *Martha Deane Show*, October 5, 1972, PCM. "Aunt Tom" was a phrase she first used in 1968 to attack a radical feminist.

39. Marjorie Spruill, *Divided We Stand: The Battle Over Women's Rights and Family Values* (New York: Bloomsbury, 2018). Schlafly's biographer, Donald T. Critchlow, *Phyllis Schlafly and Grassroots Conservatism: A Woman's Crusade* (Princeton: Princeton University Press, 2008), 230, argues that STOP ERA was not funded either by the insurance industry or the KKK, whereas Spruill thinks that there is something to these allegations. Other books weighing in on this issue do not provide hard evidence that the insurance industry or the KKK was behind the failure of the ERA. Friedan quoted in "Who's Paying to Fight Rights Amendment," *Democrat and Chronicle* (UPI), February 18, 1973, 8. "Women's Lib Leader

Urges Feminists to Free Men From Sex Stereotype," *Post-Dispatch News Service*, February 19, 1973, 2.

40. Betty Friedan, "Up From the Kitchen Floor," *NYTimes*, March 4, 1973.

41. Laurie Johnston, "Mrs. Friedan's Essay Irks Feminists," March 8, 1973, *NYTimes*, 52. "Friedan Responds," March 25, 1973, *NYTimes*, 16. Press release March 6, 1973, author's personal collection.

42. Quoted in Lolita Driver, "Lots of Discord, Often in Unison," *Pantograph*, May 2, 1973, 8.

43. Quoted in "Betty Friedan Labels Opponent an 'Aunt Tom,'" *Galesburg Register-Mail*, May 2, 1973, 15. Georgene Curry, "Schlafly, Friedan, Differ on ERA," *Vidette*, May 3, 1973, 1, 9. Lolita Driver, "Lots of Discord, Often in Unison," *Pantograph*, May 2, 1973, 8. "Notes on People," *NYTimes*, May 3, 1973, 49. "Schlafly, Friedan Meet in Debate," *Decatur-Herald*, May 3, 1973, 11.

## Chapter 10. "It Changed My Life"

1. Friedan quoted in Patricia Hill Burnett, *True Colors: An Artist's Journey from Beauty Queen to Feminist* (Troy, Mich.: Momentum Books, 1995), 84. Friedan quoted in Stone, "Friedan at 55." Interview with Alice Shalvi, March 8, 2016.

2. Betty Friedan, "Woman and Jews: The Quest for Selfhood," *Congress Monthly*, February/March 1985, 8. Correspondence. Dorit Padan-Eisenstark re: women in Israel, 1973–1974. BF to Dorit Padan-Eisenstark, January 9, 1974, 1–2, PBF, Box: 147, folder 1860. Judy Peres, "Israel Still Trapped in Feminine Mystique," *Jerusalem Post*, June 19, 1973, 3. Friedan quoted in Judy Klemesrud, "Betty Friedan as College Professor," *NYTimes*, November 11, 1974, 25.

3. Paul Kurtz, "Feminism and Humanism, An Interview with Betty Friedan and Jacqueline Ceballos," *The Humanist*, May/June 1974. "The World through Humanist Eyes," *Tampa Bay Times*, August 20, 1988, 74–75.

4. Quoted in Barbara Walters, "'Not for Women Only,' Famous Parents and Their Daughters," April 23, 1974.

5. Quotes are from Friedan, "Coming Out of the Veil," *Ladies' Home Journal*, June 1975, 71, 98–101. Greer's first piece was "Women's Glib," *Vanity Fair*, June 1988, 32; the second was in the *Guardian* three days after Betty's death. Germaine Greer, "The Betty I Knew," *Guardian*, February 7, 2006.

6. Georgia Dullea, "A Feminist Think Tank Sets Its Sights on Reshaping the American Economy," *NYTimes*, May 16, 1974, 46. Interview with Warren Farrell.

7. Friedan quoted in *Miami Herald*, August 23, 1974, 31. Friedan, *It Changed My Life*, 442.

8. Friedan quoted in Judy Klemesrud, "Feminists Recoil at Film Designed to Relate to Them," *NYTimes*, February 26, 1975, 29. Friedan, *It Changed My Life*, 6, 305–6, 309.

9. When she was in Iran, she likely read pieces of *Urban Design and Women's Lives*, a critique of the official redesign of Tehran then in progress by the young architect Moira Moser-Khalili, wife of the architect Nader Khalili. Moser-Khalili argued that the official plan neglected the role of women and working-class people. Robert Joffe, "Aspen Where the Designers Go to Let Their Crazies Out," *Washington Post*, June 30, 1974, G4. Aspen Seminar 1975 Sides 1 & 2, ACBF. Jane M. Thompson, "World of the Double Win," *Feminist Art Journal* 5, no. 3 (1976): 16. *The Second Stage* (Cambridge, Mass.: Harvard University Press, 1998), 163–66.

10. Cited in Jocelyn Olcott, *International Women's Year: The Greatest Consciousness Raising Event in History* (Durham: Duke University Press, 2017), 119.

11. Olcott, *International Women's Year*. According to Mahnaz Afkhami, Princess Ashraf donating money to the UN women's festival had nothing to do with Friedan. Numbers at the Tribune vary. These are from Olcott, p. 266, n. 9.

12. Though she acknowledged having worked for a CIA-financed foundation in the late 1950s and early 1960s, Steinem denied any continuing involvement in the organization. Chesler cited in Jessica Lancia, "Gloria Steinem: The Transnational Life of an American Feminist," MA thesis, University of Florida, 2015, 139.

Stern, *Gloria Steinem*, 298. Ingrid Hedley Stone, "I Wanted to Ask Gloria Steinem a Question," *Majority Report*, August 9, 1975, 3.

13. Cited in Stern, *Gloria Steinem*, 257.

14. The three most prominent conference officials were men—Kurt Waldheim, Luis Echevarria, president of Mexico, and Pedro Ojeda Paullada, Mexican attorney general. Marlise Simons, "UN Conference Arouses Feminists' Anger," *Washington Post*, June 22, 1975, A12. Maxine Hitchcock, "Report on 'The Tribune Speak-out:' June 19–July 2, 1975," 1. Friedan quoted in Judy Klemesrud, "U.S. Group Assails Women's Parley," *NYTimes*, June 22, 1975, 1.

15. Olcott, *International Women's Year*, 125. "The Selling of Women's Year, 1975: UN Is Finding It No Easy Matter," *NYTimes*, June 4, 1975, 45. "Stay Vigilant, Freidan [*sic*] Tells Women," *Miami Herald*, Sunday, June 22, 1975, 18. Wynta Boynes quoted in Carol Kleinman, "Chicanas Disrupt Parley," *Chicago Tribune*, June 22, 1975, 18. Friedan quoted in "US Delegation Draws Fire at Women's Conference," *LATimes*, June 22, 1975, 14. Friedan quoted in "Betty Friedan Fears CIA Movement Role," *NYTimes*, June 23, 1975, 22.

16. James P. Sterba, "Women Find Elusive Unity at Parley," *NYTimes*, June 24, 1975, 3. "Women Bicker During Friedan Address on US," *Austin American-Statesman*, June 24, 1975, 28. "Betty Friedan 'Manipulative,'" *Austin American-Statesman* (AP), June 27, 1975. Hitchcock, "Report on 'The Tribune Speakout,'" 3, quotes Friedan as saying "internal dirty linen," however the AP has it "external dirty linen." Friedan quoted in Carol Kleinman, "Updating the Status of Women: After the Rhetoric Time for a Vote," *Chicago Tribune*, July 2, 1975, 33. Olcott, *International Women's Year*, 126.

17. Friedan, *It Changed My Life*, 458, 440. Olcott, *International Women's Year*, 206. Interview with Carole De Saram, July 19, 2021. Burnett, *True Colors*, 108–9, also supports Friedan's account of events.

18. Friedan, *It Changed My Life*, 458, 453, 459.

19. R. Carroll, "Lib in A Land of Macho," *Newsweek*, July 7, 1975, 28–30. Friedan, *It Changed My Life*, 448. Friedan quoted in "Mrs. Rabin Pleads for Unity: Women Conferees walk out on Israeli PM," *LATimes*, June 26, 1975, 12.

20. Friedan was also angry about bad scheduling and lack of

mimeograph machines. Friedan quoted in Stanley Meisler, "Private Feminists Ask Voice at UN Parley," *LATimes*, June 27, 1975, 1. "A First-Hand Report from Mexico City," *Pandora*, August 1, 1975, 1, 4. Stanley Meisler, "Private Feminists Rebuffed at Parley," *LATimes*, June 28, 1975, a6. Judy Klemesrud, "As the Conference Ends, What Now, For Women?" *NYTimes*, July 2, 1975, 40.

21. Betty Friedan, note, n.d. Gloria Steinem Papers, Box 190, folder 10, Sophia Smith Collection, Smith College, Northampton, Mass. (hereafter GSP). Betty Friedan interview [with Phil Donahue?], discusses Steinem and the CIA 1976 [?], 1976. GSP, Box 224: Folder 70. Friedan, *It Changed My Life*, 436. Gil Troy, *Moynihan's Moment: America's Fight Against Zionism as Racism* (New York: Oxford University Press, 2012), 178.

22. Friedan quoted in Stone, "Friedan at 55"; "Kristallnacht at the United Nations," *JTA*, November 12, 1975, https://www.jta.org/archive/kristallnacht-at-the-united-nations-100000-in-rally-to-protest-against-anti-zionist-resolution-mass. "60 Prominent Women Condemn UN Anti-Zionist Resolution," *JTA*, November 12, 1975. By this time, the Jewish community took her as their own. For example: "Twelve Jewish Women Are Among 50 Most Influential Women Chosen in US," *Jewish Sentinel*, September 25, 1975, 4.

23. Enid Nemy, "Feminists Reappraise Direction and Image," *NYTimes*, November 8, 1975, 1. Enid Nemy, "13 NOW Leaders Form a Dissident 'Network,'" *NYTimes*, November 15, 1975, 57.

24. Friedan, *It Changed My Life*, 387.

25. Friedan quoted in Hennessee, *Betty Friedan*, 218. Friedan used the same phrase to describe Steinem to Marcia Cohen.

26. Stephanie Harrington, "Betty Friedan . . ." *NYTimes*, July 4, 1976, BR2. Christopher Lehmann-Haupt, "It May Not Change Yours," *NYTimes*, August 2, 1976, 23. Memo, n.d. "Chair. Colom. Advisory Committee [correspondence about objections to Betty Friedan's It Changed My Life], 1976." Records of the National Women's Political Caucus 1970–2006. MC 522, Box 30, folder 17, Schlesinger Library, Harvard Radcliffe Institute, Cambridge, Mass. (hereafter cited as RNWPC). Letter to Robert Bernstein, Septem-

ber 28, 1976. "Chair. Colom. Advisory Committee [Correspondence about Objections to Friedan's *It Changed My Life*]," RNWPC, Box 30: Folder 17. Rosen, *The World Split Open*, 241–51.

27. National Jewish Community Relations Advisory Council plenary session on women's rights, June 1976: transcript, pp. 14, 16, 24. BFAP 577 Box: 17, folder 24. *The Sentinel* (see below) says 350 people attended. "Friedan says ERA Is a Jewish Concern," *JTA*, July 2, 1976, 4. https://www.jta.org/archive/njcrac-leader-rejects-criticism-of-jewish-institutional-structure. Joint Program Plan (3 of 3), 1972–1975, Box: 2, folder: 5. National Jewish Community Relations Advisory Council Records, I-172. Courtesy of the American Jewish Historical Society. *UPI*, June 30, 1976, 17. "Says 'Democratizing' Jewish Community May Destroy It," *Jewish Sentinel*, July 15, 1976, 6.

28. Aviva Cantor, "Is Feminism Good for the Jews?" *B'nai B'rith Messenger*, October 8, 1976, 28. Stone, "Friedan at 55," *Lilith*, Fall 1976, 7.

29. Linda Charlton, "Militants Lose in Battle to Require Equal Role," *NYTimes*, July 14, 1976. Correspondence April–June 1974. Letter from Barbara Cox to Eliza Paschall, June 18, 1974. BFP. Box: 148, folder 1877. Friedan quoted in *Sacramento Bee*, July 13, 1976.

30. Martha McKay Oral History. Oral Histories of the American South. https://sohp.org/martha-mckay-1920-2009/. "Toss Up for ERA in Illinois," *In These Times*, April 5, 1978, 4. "Get Tough on ERA: Friedan," *Chicago Tribune*, June 10, 1977, 6. Friedan quoted in "Betty Friedan Sets ERA Tactic Meeting," *Pantograph*, June 10, 1977, 21. Friedan quoted in "Friedan Calls for Stepped Up ERA Effort," *Pantograph*, June 11, 1977, 3.

31. Betty Friedan, "Cooking with Betty Friedan . . . Yes Betty Friedan," *NYTimes*, January 5, 1977, 68. Lit.By.Olar, "Off the Record," *Jewish Sentinel*, July 7, 1977, 33.

32. Program, Arcosanti Festival 77—A Celebration of Health and Healing, October 1–2, 1977. Courtesy of the Cosanti-Foundation, Archives at Arcosanti. Thanks to Hanne Sue Kirsch. Friedan, "Where Are Women in 1978?" *Cosmopolitan*, August 1978, 207.

33. "Letter to My Daughter," *Cosmopolitan*, 1978: handwritten, typescript drafts, some as "Do we have to keep moving?" correspondence. Draft of Letter to my daughter. BFP, Box: 92, folder 1047b. Judy Klemesrud, "Women's Movement at Age 11, Larger, Diffuse, Still Battling," *NYTimes*, November 15, 1977, 63. BF likely meant the Reichstag fire.

34. The figure of 20,000 in attendance, like all crowd numbers, varies. Schlafly quoted in Critchlow, *Phyllis Schlafly and Grassroots Conservatism*, 246.

35. Friedan quoted in Sally Quinn, "The Pedestal Has Crashed: Pride and Paranoia in Houston," *Washington Post*, November 23, 1977, 41. Friedan quoted in Anne Taylor Fleming, "That Week in Houston," *NYTimes*, December 25, 1977, 127.

36. Fleming, "That Week in Houston."

37. Henry and Taitz, *Betty Friedan*, 96. Blu Greenberg interview, April 20, 2016.

38. Friedan, "Where Are Women in 1978?" 211.

39. Betty Friedan NEH Research Grant Application Sheet. Box 10: Folder 190, DAP.

40. Quoted in John Umbers, "Equal Rights Amendment Is Mired In Confused and Emotional Debate," *NYTimes*, May 28, 1978, 1. Betty Friedan, "The ERA: Does It Play In Peoria?" *NYTimes*, November 19, 1978, SM, 10, 39.

41. Phone interview with Laura Geller, August 1, 2016.

42. Betty Friedan, "Women as Jew/Jew as Woman," *Congress Monthly*, February/March 1985, 10.

43. Martin Duberman, *Midlife Queer: Autobiography of a Decade: 1971–1981* (New York: Scribner, 1996), 150.

44. Friedan quotes from phone interview with Judith Garten, August 10, 2017. Phone interview with Zachary Karabell, September 20, 2018.

## Chapter 11. Her Second Stages

1. Friedan quoted in Esther Blaustein, "New Issues Posed by Betty Friedan," *NYTimes*, August 26, 1979, LI 10. Friedan, *The Second Stage*, 72. Betty Friedan, "Feminism Takes a New Turn,"

*NYTimes*, November 18, 19, 1979, 10. Beverly Stephen, "Are All Marriages Alike?" *New York Daily News*, November 23, 1979.

2. Letters to the editor, *NYTimes*, December 16, 1979, 39.

3. "Minutes, November 26, 1979," UJA Federation of New York Collection. Courtesy of the American Jewish Historical Society (hereafter cited as UJAFED). "Federation of Jewish Philanthropies Task Force on The Role of the Jewish Woman in a Changing Society 1979–1981." Additional Papers of Betty Friedan 1941–2006, MC 577, Box: 37, Folder 15, Schlesinger Library, Harvard Radcliffe Institute, Cambridge, Mass. (hereafter APBF MC 577). Copyright © Betty Friedan. Reprinted by permission of Curtis Brown, Ltd. All rights reserved. Friedan, "Woman as Jew/Jew as Woman," 10.

4. Friedan quoted in UJAFED, Box 5: Minutes, May 29, 1980. Courtesy of the American Jewish Historical Society. "Conference on Families Achieves Much Accord," *Washington Post*, June 11, 1980, C1. Carol Horner, "It's a Family Affair, With Nationwide Consensus the Goal," *Philadelphia Inquirer*, June 15, 1980, 142.

5. *Community*, October 31, 1980. Letty Cottin Pogrebin, *Deborah, Golda, and Me: Being Female and Jewish in America* (New York: Anchor Press, 1991), 156, 157, 161. Friedan, *The Second Stage*, 199.

6. Mildred Hamilton, "Trying to Meet in the Middle," *San Francisco Examiner*, July 22, 1980, 45. Mildred Hamilton, "The Link Between Sexism and Racism, San Francisco Examiner, July 24, 1980, 55. Friedan quoted in "The UN Conference: What Has It Done for Women?" *San Francisco Examiner*, July 31, 1980, 57. *Newsweek*, August 4, 1980, 35.

7. Interview with Noreen Connell, May 12, 2016. Friedan quoted in "No Conflict in Feminism, Family," *Jewish Floridian*, December 5, 1980, 1. https://ufdc.ufl.edu/AA00010090/02705/images. Nancy Reagan quoted in *Life So Far*, 302.

8. An announcement for a party for *The Second Stage* at the Jewish Federation read: "A mazel tov was extended by Mrs. Greenberg . . . to . . . Betty Friedan on the upcoming publication of her third book . . . as well as the forthcoming marriage of her son." Minutes, Commission for Women's Equality (CWE), September 16, 1981, Box 5, UJAFED. Courtesy of the American Jewish Historical

Society. Interview with Jonathan Slon. Dates of Jonathan Friedan higher education from office of the registrar, Columbia University.

9. Walton, "Can Betty Friedan Rescue the Women's Movement?" 10. Friedan, *The Second Stage*, 22, xii, 40.

10. Friedan, *The Second Stage*, 3, 20.

11. Ibid., 24, 43. Letter, Eric E. Rofes to BF, October 5, 1981, San Francisco Historical Collection, San Francisco Public Library. Permission Granted by Crispin Hollings and Luis Casillas. Eric Rofes Papers, LGBTQIA Center, San Francisco Public Library. Rofes remembers Friedan critically. Being one of the few feminists at the White House Conference on Families was not enough penance for "the lavender menace," he writes. Yet he nonetheless translated what he characterizes as Friedan's shame about Jews into pride: "Nothing prepared me better for my life as a gay activist than growing up as a Jew in America," he writes.

12. Friedan, *The Second Stage*, xvi, 73.

13. Ibid., 95.

14. Ibid., 128.

15. Ibid., 245.

16. Ibid., 317. See note 39, chap. 9 about whether STOP ERA formally took money from the KKK or the John Birch Society. I could not find documentation of Friedan's timeline. However, one piece of documentation proving that someone in Illinois distributed anti-Semitic leaflets to support anti-ratification is from a 1978 General Assembly meeting in the Illinois House of Representatives. Black Democratic Representative Corneal Davis states, "I hold in my hand here the most scurrilous literature that has ever been distributed in this state, listen to what it says: 'E.R.A. is a plot to wreck Christian homes. The E.R.A. is promoted by anti-Christian Jews who want to destroy this nation. It's promoted by Jews.'" Assembly Book, June 22, 1978, 92.

17. Friedan, *The Second Stage*, 328.

18. John Leonard, "Books of the Times," *NYTimes*, October 30, 1981, 29. Zillah Eisenstein, *The Radical Future of Liberal Feminism;* Ellen Willis, "Peace Now? The Greening of Betty Friedan," in *No More Nice Girls: Countercultural Essays* (Minneapolis: Univer-

sity of Minnesota Press, 2012), 62; Herma Hill Kay, "Do We Suffer from a Feminist Mystique?" *NYTimes*, November 21, 1981, Section 7, 3; "Feminist Leader Wins Grudging Orthodox Tribute," *Jewish Floridian*, March 5, 1982, A1–14 https://ufdc.ufl.edu/AA00010090/02770/images. Carol B. Lundgren, *St. Louis Jewish Light*, December 2, 1981, 32. "Betty Friedan's Second Stage Brings Men into the Fold," *Christian Science Monitor*, December 10, 1981. https://www.csmonitor.com/1981/1210/121014.html. Judith Stacey, "The New Conservative Feminism," *Feminist Studies*, Fall 1983, 562.

19. Correspondence, transcripts, clippings, galleys of Friedan's talk. Press release, Mankind 2000, March 31, 2. 1982: APBF MC 576. Box: 55, folder 535. Haifa conference, "Mankind 2000, 1982: correspondence, transcripts, clippings, galleys of Friedan's talk. Press Release, Mankind 2000, April 2, APBF MC 576, Box: 55, folder 535. Haifa conference, "Mankind 2000," 1982: correspondence, transcripts, clippings, galleys of Friedan's talk. Transcript of "The Future of Women," 4, 16, APBF MC 576, Box: 55, folder 535.

20. Email from Lennart Levi, April 23, 2017.

21. Cited in Hennessee, *Betty Friedan*, 236. T. Morgenthau, "Politics in a Post ERA Era," *Newsweek*, July 12, 1982, 33. Cited in Richard Reeves, *Spokane Chronicle*, July 3, 1982, 8.

22. Betty Friedan, "Thoughts on Becoming a Grandmother," *Ladies' Home Journal*, July 1983, 58, 60–63, 141–44.

23. Friedan, *The Fountain of Age*, 368.

24. Friedan, "Women in the Firing Line," *NYTimes*, October 28, 1984. Memo from Phil Baum to Advisory Committee, February 10, 1984. "20th Annual America–Israel Dialogue," *Woman as Jew, Jew as Woman: An Urgent Inquiry*, American Jewish Congress, Jerusalem, Israel, July 30–August 2, 1984; includes correspondence, press release, brochure, clipping, typed speech for session "Women in the Family." Papers of Blu Greenberg, MC 599, Box: 51, folder 5, Schlesinger Library, Harvard Radcliffe Institute, Cambridge, Mass.

25. Cynthia Ozick, "Torah as the Matrix for Feminism," *Lilith*, Winter/Spring, 1985, 47–48. Anne Roiphe, "Four Days and a Cause," *Congress Monthly*, September/October 1984, 5, 7; James Feron, "A Spirited Israeli Dialogue Opens in Jerusalem," *NYTimes*,

August 1, 1984, C2. Betty Friedan, "Women and Jews: The Quest for Selfhood," *Congress Monthly*, 52, no. 2 (February–March 1985): 8, 9.

26. Friedan, "Women and Jews: The Quest for Selfhood," 10, 11. Feron, "A Spirited Israeli Dialogue Opens in Jerusalem." "Women's Movement Can Energize Israel," *Jewish Floridian*, August 24, 1984, A-5.

27. Rochelle Furstenberg quoted in *Congress Monthly* 52, no. 18 (February–March 1985). Also Furstenberg, "Points of Conflict," *Jerusalem Post*, September 26, 1984, A15.

28. Dating of theater piece, *Congress Monthly* (February–March 1985), 27. Emails Gabriella Lev, 2020 and April 2 and 3, 2022.

29. Skype/Zoom Interviews with Naamah Kelman, 2020, February 13, 2022. Friedan, "Women in the Firing Line," *NYTimes*, 1984.

30. Roiphe quoted in *Congress Monthly*, September/October 1984. Ozick quoted in "Torah as The Matrix for Feminism," Winter/Spring 1985. https://lilith.org/articles/from-torah-as-the-matrix-for-feminism/. James Feron, "Israeli Women Seek New Role," *NYTimes*, August 5, 1984, 49. Phone Interview with Alice Shalvi, March 8, 2016. Friedan would later ask for the written version of the prayers. American Jewish Congress, "Dialogue on Women," Israel, August 1984: correspondence, notes, arrangements. Letter, August 17, 1984, Janet Sherman to Betty Friedan, BFP MC 576 Box: 59, folder 564a.

31. Interview transcripts: Voice of America, Cooper-Hewitt Museum of Design's Change, 1984. Voice of America transcript, 37. BFAP MC 576, Box: 59, folder 565. BF to AR May 1, 1985, *NYTimes* Company Records. Arthur Hays Sulzberger Papers. Manuscripts and Archives Division, The New York Public Library, Astor, Lenox and Tilden Foundations. Copyright © Betty Friedan. Reprinted by permission of Curtis Brown, Ltd. All rights reserved. Rabinowitz in *Jewish Post*, January 11, 1974, 7. American Jewish Congress 1985–86. Letter from Ted Mann to BF, August 24. APBF MC 577. Box: 59, folder 564a. Raday documented this in a conference paper, which was then published. "The Israeli Perspective,"

in Eve Chava Landau, ed., "The Status of Women at the Dawn of the Twenty-First Century: Proceedings of the Conference Held Under the Auspices of the International Association of Legal Science and the Minerva Center for Human Rights," UNESCO, 2001, 113–44. Frances Kraft, "Women's Network Fights for Sexual Equality In Israel," *Canadian Jewish News Service*, June 25, 1992, 5. Telephone interview Frances Raday, October 19, 2016. Telephone interview Liz Holtzman, September 27, 2016. Subseries C: Commission for Women's Equality (CWE), 1980, 1984–2002. Records of The American Jewish Congress, i–77. Courtesy of the American Jewish Historical Society.

32. Friedan, *The Fountain of Age*, 29. Friedan quoted in Hennessee, *Betty Friedan*, 246. Phone interview with M.G. Lord, March 20, 2016.

33. Newspapers and wire services give different numbers for the size of the group. *The Jewish Floridian*, May 17, 1985, 3–A. https://ufdc.ufl.edu/AA00010090/02937/images/2. Friedan quote in Kirk Alan Kubicek, "A Visit to Germany" (unpublished manuscript in author's possession), 14. American Jewish Congress (AJC) general, 1985–1988. AJC press release nd. APBF MC 577, Box: 628. Letter from Ted Mann May 3, 1985, "American Jewish Congress (AJC) general, 1985–1988." APBF MC 577 box 689. American Jewish Congress (AJC) general, 1985–1988. May 11, 1985, 12; May 27, 1985 Report to UJA-Fed Board. APBF MC 577. Richard Sandomir, "Trip by New York Group Focuses on Holocaust," *Newsday*, May 2, 1985, 2. Wilbert A. Tatum, "A Ceremony in Dachau," *New York Amsterdam News*, May 11, 1985, 12. *Jewish Week*, May 17, 1985. Anna Tomforde, "Jews Enter Bitburg with March on Dachau," *Guardian*, May 4, 1985, 5. Phone interview with Kirk Kubicek, November 10, 2016. Betty Friedan, "A Personal Journey to Nicaragua (Harper's?): handwritten drafts; typewritten and edited drafts," 42. APBF MC 577, Box: 30, folder 566.

34. Minutes, National Women's Committee on Equality, June 3, 1985, Box 632, i–77, American Jewish Congress. Courtesy of the American Jewish Historical Society.

35. *Maclean's*, July 29, 1985. Ruth Seligman, "Her Place Under the Tree," *Forum 85*, July 11, 6.

36. Friedan, draft, "After Nairobi: Women Time Is the World," 100-page typescript, 30. APBF MC577, Box: 13, folder 1.

37. Number of attendees at the forum varies between 10,000 and 15,000. Number of Jewish attendees ranges between 200 and 400. *Wisconsin Jewish Journal*, August 2, 1985, 3. Friedan, "How to Get the Women's Movement Moving Again." Michael Levin, "What Nairobi Wrought," *Commentary*, October 1985. https://www.commentary.org/articles/michael-levin/what-nairobi-wrought/. United Nations Third World Conference for Women, NGO forum, Nairobi, 1985: clippings. Friedan, draft, "After Nairobi, Women Time Is the World: typescript." APBF MC 576, Box: 60, folder 574, 8–9.

38. Sandra Featherman, "Nairobi Forum Raises Hopes," *Jewish Exponent*, August 2, 1985. Personal collection of author. Interview with Featherman, October 8, 2016. Featherman email August 3, 2017. Interview with Featherman, October 8, 2016. Sheila Rule, "At Nairobi Women's Parley, Old Wounds Still Fester, *NYTimes*, July 15, 1985, A3. Liva E. Bitton Jackson, *Jewish Press* magazine, August 9, 1985, n.d. Alice Henry, "Nairobi Women's Conference," *off our backs*, October 1985, 1, 3, 4. United Nations Third World Conference for Women, NGO forum, Nairobi, 1985: clippings. Friedan, draft, "After Nairobi, Women Time Is the World: typescript." APBF MC 576, Box: 60, folder 574, 18. Mary McGrory, "One Woman's Departure from Feminism," *Washington Post*, July 21, 1985.

39. "Women's Forum Consensus Collapses as US Balks on Palestinian Issue," *Washington Post*, July 26, 1985. Blaine Harden and Mary Battiata, "UN Decade Closes Amid Calls for Worldwide Progress," *Washington Post*, July 28, 1985, A18. Elaine Sciolino, "UN Women's Conference Drops Reference to Zionism as Racism," *NYTimes*, July 27, 1. Nadine Brozan, "Maureen Reagan Assesses Nairobi," August 1, 1985, 1. "Assessment of the Nairobi Conference," *JTA*, August 5, 1985, 4. https://www.jta.org/archive/assessment-of

-the-nairobi-conference-a-victory-for-women-worldwide. E. M. Broner, "The Road to Nairobi," *Moment Magazine*, November 1984, 35. E. M. Broner, Shirley Joseph, "The Nairobi Difference," *Moment Magazine*, October 1985, 29. Friedan quoted in "How to Get the Women's Movement Moving Again," *NYTimes*, November 3, 1985.

40. American Jewish Congress. Minutes, November 4, 1985. Commission for Women's Equality. APBF MC 577, Box: 37, folder 7. Betty Friedan, "Anti-Semitism as a Political Tool: Its Congruence with Anti-Feminism," 1985, 41. Author's collection.

## Chapter 12. "Here I Am! This Is Me! This Is How I Am!"

1. Sara Miller McCune, "Publisher's Note," *American Behavioral Scientist* 37, no. 8, August 1994, 1021.

2. According to Transcript of Gloria Goldsmith Interview, JHP, Streisand came to one session. Friedan, *Life So Far*, 340. Phone interview with John Doyle, August 15, 2016.

3. Phone interview with Frieda Caplan, April 28, 2016.

4. Friedan quoted in Tamar Lewin, "Maternity Leave Suit Has Divided Feminists," *NYTimes*, June 28, 1986, 52. Stuart Taylor, "Justices Hear Debate over Pregnancy Leave," *NYTimes*, October 9, 1986, 30.

5. Friedan quoted in James Barron, "Views on Surrogacy Harden After Baby M Ruling," *NYTimes*, April 2, 1987, A1. Friedan quoted in Iver Peterson, "Baby M's Future," *NYTimes*, April 5, 1987, 1. Tricia Crane, "Baby M and Women's Rights, Feminist Betty Friedan Makes a Case Against Surrogate Motherhood," *LA Herald Examiner*, April 19, 1987, 1. Author's personal collection. Friedan quoted in "USC," 9. Box: 27, Folder 20. BFAP, SL. Robert Hanley, "Jersey's Top Court Hears Arguments on Baby M," *NYTimes*, September 15, 1987, B2.

6. Phone interview with Michael Lerner, January 23, 2017. Friedan, *Tikkun*, 27.

7. Bettyann Kevles, "A Feminist in the Late '80's," *LATimes*, May 17, 1987, 8.

8. Notebook, Box 6: Notebook 33, 1980–81, p. 166. Permission granted by Roy L. Walford Papers, History & Special Collec-

tions for the Sciences, UCLA (hereafter cited as RLWP). Note RW to BF, n.d.; letter, BF to RW, August 3, n.d. Box 10, Folder 9, Friedan, RLWP. Box 6, Notebook 37, p. 165, RLWP. Box 6, Notebook 38.5 p. 104. Notebook 41.

9. Interview with Jon Slon.

10. "Friedan and Group Seeking 'A New National Strategy,'" *NYTimes*, August 9, 1987, LI, 21. Phone interview with Bill Pickens, June 14, 2021. Phone interview with Karl Grossman, January 19, 2017.

11. Paul Surlis, "The Sag Harbor Initiative: The Town Hall as Model," *Monthly Review* 40, no. 11 (1989): 31.

12. *Time*, May 18, 1987, 33.

13. Marylouise Oates, "A Feminine Mystery at a Friedan Fete," *LATimes*, January 27, 1988, 61. Tom Gliatto, "Play Mystique for Me," *USA Today*, February 9, 1988, 1D. USC Institute for the Study of Women and Men, 1986–88. SWMS Newsletter, Volume 1, Number 2, APBF MC 576, Box: 27, folder 1. Interview with Emily Levine, July 7, 2016. *MacNeil/Lehrer NewsHour*, February 12, 1988. Paley Media Center.

14. Letter BF to GS, n.d., Box 86, Folder 42. GSP.

15. Friedan quoted in Hennessee, *Betty Friedan*, 259.

16. Goldstein, "Through a Glass Darkly," 19, PBF. Box: 14, folder 248, "Memorial Service for Friedan's Mother, Miriam Goldstein, ca 1988." Side One, ACBF.

17. "Memorial Service." Obituary, Miriam Goldstein, *Peoria Star Journal*, April 6, 1988, D9. Thanks to Linda Aylward.

18. Friedan quoted in Garry Abrams, "Sniping at 'Sisterhood,'" *LATimes*, August 4, 1988, 1, 63.

19. Friedan quoted in Beverly Beyette, "A New Career Flap," *LATimes*, March 17, 1989, 76.

20. Tad Bartimus, "Conventioneers Debate 'Cutting Edge,'" *Arizona Daily Star*, September 1, 1988, 30. "Spiritual Eldering Project 1989–1992," Additional papers of Betty Friedan, 1937–1993, MC 576. Box 72: Folder 712. Schlesinger Library, Harvard Radcliffe Institute, Cambridge. Mass. Copyright © Betty Friedan. Reprinted by permission of Curtis Brown, Ltd. All rights reserved.

21. Arcosanti Minds for History conference digitized archive. Courtesy of the Cosanti Foundation–Archives at Arcosanti.

22. Betty Friedan, "Can a Feminist Be Beautiful?" *Allure*, March 1991, 63, 64, 66.

23. Friedan quoted in "Twentieth Anniversary of NWPC Gala." C-Span, July 11, 1991. https://www.c-span.org/video/?19097-1/national-womens-political-caucus-gala-party. "Claiming the Future: From Mothers to Daughters," C-Span, July 12, 1991. https://www.c-span.org/video/?19096-1/mothers-daughters-politics.

24. Notebook 41, 1989–1990, RLWP, UCLA.

25. John E. Yang, "After the Furor, A Day of Speeches and Anti-Climax," *Washington Post*, October 16, 1991, A1. "Newsmakers," *Chicago Tribune*, October 17, 1991, 28. Judith Weinraug, "Arlen Specter's Rude Awakening," *Washington Post*, October 18, 1991, 76.

26. Friedan quoted in "Senator Bewildered," *Newsday*, October 20, 1991, 20. Susan Faludi, *Backlash: The Undeclared War Against American Women* (New York: Random House, 1991), 318. "History of Feminism," C-Span, November 4, 1996. https://www.c-span.org/video/?76509-1/history-feminism.

27. Beverly Beyette, "Friedan Is 'Off the Barricades' but Not in Retreat," *LATimes*, February 24, 1992, 142.

28. Frank Gehry, B. J. Hately, et al., "The Politics of Empowerment: A Paradigm Shift in Thought and Action for Feminists. New Questions Beyond The Feminist Focus on Sexual Harassment: Is It Helping Us Move from Victimhood to Empowerment or Is It a Diversion?" *American Behavioral Scientist*, 37, no. 8 (1994). I date this in April 1993 because Susan Rose mentions not just the Thomas hearing but the Robin Abcardian articles that ran in the *LATimes* on March 24 and 28, 1993.

29. Quotes from "The Politics of Empowerment," 1126, 1133, 1134.

30. Friedan quoted in Abigail Trafford, "Old Age: Half Empty or Half Full," *Washington Post*, October 26, 1993, G6.

31. Sara Miller McCune, "Betty Friedan, Open Heart Surgery, and Me," February 23, 2014, *Pacific Standard*. https://psmag.com/social-justice/betty-friedan-open-heart-surgery-and-me-53186.

McCune misdates this event, which I date around May 10 because classes ended at USC around May 5 and her surgery was before May 12. The *New York Times* article referred to is Robin Marantz Henig, "Asthma Kills." March 28, 1993. Friedan, *Life So Far*, 312.

32. Interview with Letty Cottin Pogrebin, February 3, 2016. The *Minneapolis Star Tribune*, May 12, 1993, 6, reports that she is in "stable condition." Spinal infection. *Palm Beach Post*, June 5, 1993, 110.

33. Friedan, *The Fountain of Age*, 254.

34. Ibid., 321.

35. Ibid., 245.

36. Friedan, *Life So Far*, 132, 135. Friedan, *The Fountain of Age*, 638. Her assertion is backed up by the archives.

37. Diane Middlebrook, "The Age Mystique," *LATimes*, September 19, 1993, 134. Wanda Howard, "Betty Friedan Shares Thoughts on Retirement," *Daily Record*, April 2, 1995. "Oral History Interviews with Friedan," February 27–April 24, 1992 and December 11, 1993, Tape 7, ACBF.

38. David Alpern, "Newsweek on Air," August 27, 1995. https://archive.org/details/newsweekonair_950827_complete.

39. Sydney Blumenthal, "Voice of the Voice of America," *New Yorker*, September 18, 1995, 41. "Beyond Gender," *Newsweek*, September 4, 1995, 30. "Feminist Fountainhead Friedan Wows Her Followers in Beijing," *Atlanta Constitution* (AP), September 3, 1995, 18. Doris Wolfe, "This Conference Is Going to Have Impact," *Democrat and Rochester* (AP), September 5, 1995, 4.

40. "China's Feet Held to Fire," *Knight Ridder Service*, September 6, 1995, 50. "U.S. Delegation Is All Wet," *San Francisco Examiner*, September 6, 1995, 8. Pamela Bone, "Vision of a New Order," *The Age*, September 8, 1995, 16. "Beijing Meeting Affirms Women's Sexual Rights," *LATimes*, September 16, 1995, 16. Betty Friedan, "Beyond Gender," *Newsweek*, September 4, 1995.

## Chapter 13. Life So Far

1. "Transcript of toasts to Betty Friedan, on her 75th Birthday party," 3. Personal Collection of Ellen Chesler, author's possession.

2. Steven Greenhouse, "Labor and Academia in a Campus

Meeting," *NYTimes*, October 6, 1996, 39. Steve Fraser and Joshua Freedman, "Hope for Labor at the End of History," *Dissent*, October 2021, https://www.dissentmagazine.org/article/hope-for-labor-at-the-end-of-history. Friedan quoted in Horowitz, *Betty Friedan and the Making of The Feminine Mystique*, 15.

3. Friedan quoted in Horowitz, *Betty Friedan and the Making of The Feminine Mystique*, 15. Two other major articles were: Eva Moskowitz, "It's Good to Blow Your Top: Women's Magazines and the Discourse of Discontent: 1945–1965," *Journal of Women's History* 8, no. 3 (Fall 1996): 66–98, and Joanne Meyerowitz, "Beyond *The Feminine Mystique:* A Reassessment of Postwar Mass Culture," *Journal of American History* 79, no. 4 (March 1993): 1455–82. Karen DeCrow, "Fond Memories of Adventures in Feminism," *Chicago Tribune*, December 29, 1996, 258.

4. "Double Bettys," *Washington Post*, September 25, 1997, C3. Friedan, *The Fountain of Age*, 432.

5. Christina Hoff Summers, *Who Stole Feminism? How Women Have Betrayed Women* (New York: Simon & Schuster, 1994). Wendy Shalit, *A Return to Modesty: Discovering the Lost Virtue* (New York: The Free Press, 1999). Danielle Crittenden, *What Our Mothers Didn't Tell Us: Why Happiness Eludes the Modern Women* (New York: Simon & Schuster, 1999). Mary Leonard, "Non-Feminist Authors Going Against the Grain," *Boston Globe*, March 14, 1999, 1.

6. Betty Friedan, *Beyond Gender: The New Politics of Work and Family* (Baltimore: Johns Hopkins University Press, 1997), 69, 114.

7. Betty Friedan, *Guardian*, January 29, 1998, A5.

8. Friedan quoted in "Public Image of Women in Power," C-Span, February 18, 1997. https://www.c-span.org/video/?78974-1/public-image-women-power. Dobell material widely available. Alan Wolfe, *An Intellectual in Public* (Ann Arbor: University of Michigan Press, 2005), 222.

9. Friedan, *Life So Far*, 111.

10. Friedan, *Life So Far*, 69.

11. Carl in Anne Blackmun, "The Friedan Mystique," *Time*, April 23, 2000, http://content.time.com/time/magazine/article/0,9171,43570,00.html. "Life So Far," C-Span, May 9, 2000.

https://www.c-span.org/video/?157026-1/life-far&playEvent. Friedan quoted in Alex Witchel, "At Home With . . . Betty Friedan," *NYTimes*, May 11, 2000, Section F, 1. Carl Friedan, "A Former Husband Responds," *NYTimes*, May 18, 2000, Section F, 10.

12. Friedan on *GMA* cited in Howard Kurtz, "Abuse Report That Smacks of Unfairness," *Washington Post*, June 5, 2005.

13. *Salon* assigned a former editor at *Hustler* to cover Carl's website and headlined the piece, "Was Betty Friedan a Sexpot?"; Laura Miller, "When Feminists Were Divas," *Salon*, June 9, 2000, https://www.salon.com/2000/06/14/divas_4/. Stephanie Gilmore, roundup of feminist memoirs, *NWSA Journal* 14, no 1 (Spring 2002): 207–212. Wendy Steiner, "Hear Her Roar," *NYTimes*, June 25, 2000, Section 7, 10. Cynthia Fuchs Epstein, "The Major Myth of the Women's Movement," *Dissent*, Fall 1999, 5. Carl quoted in *Miami Herald*, June 27, 2000, 4.

14. Betty Friedan, "The Bootylicious Mystique: Is Beyoncé Knowles a Role Model for Post Modern Feminism?" *Allure*, August 2002, 162.

15. Phone interview with Jan Uhrbach, April 8, 2016.

16. Rebecca Traister, "Behind the Scenes at the March for Women's Lives," *Salon*, April 26, 2004. https://www.salon.com/2004/04/26/womens_march/. C-Span, April 25, 2004. https://www.c-span.org/video/?181451-1/march-womens-lives. Carole De Saram interview.

17. Gabrielle Wellman interview, May 9, 2021.

18. Library of Congress, "A Conversation with Betty Friedan." https://www.loc.gov/item/webcast-3675/.

19. Brill, *Dear Princess Grace, Dear Betty*, 210. Lucy Komisar, interview, 2021.

20. Interview with Gabrielle Wellman.

21. Interview with Harry Goldstein Jr.

22. "Visionary Feminist Ignited Change," *New York Daily News*, February 7, 2006, 4. Jacqui Ceballos, "Goodbye Dear Betty," VFA Newsletter, Spring, 2006, 1. Box 44, KDCP. Emily quoted in "Friedan Remembered as Feminist Pioneer, Feisty, Loving Mother," *AP*, February 7, 2006. https://azdailysun.com/friedan-remembered

-as-feminist-pioneer-feisty-loving-mother/article_9d9c8377-6ba6-5090-90cd-21c269e8b6a9.html. Sheelah Kohlkatar, "What Mystique Did Betty Friedan Wield? A Very Powerful One," *New York Observer*, February 13, 2006. https://observer.com/2006/02/what-mystique-did-betty-friedan-wield-very-powerful-one/.

23. Eve Gittelson, "At the Grave of Our Beloved Betty Friedan," *Daily Kos*. https://www.dailykos.com/stories/2006/2/7/185113/-. Interview with Jan Uhrbach.

24. Eleanor Smeal and Hillary Clinton quoted in Hillel Italie, "Her Work Ushered In Modern Feminist Movement," *Fort Worth Star Telegram*, February 5, 2006, 10. Marian Wright Edelman, "Betty Friedan Was More Than a Feminist," *Chicago Defender*, February 23, 2006, 11.

25. Germaine Greer quoted in *NYTimes*, February 12, 2006, C5. Jim McKeever, "Betty Friedan Is Remembered in Syracuse with Smiles," *Syracuse Post*, February 7, 2006, 1. Karen DeCrow Papers. Permission granted by Charles Deering McCormick Library of Special Collections and University Archives, Northwestern University. Susan Jacoby, "Keep the Mystique Alive," *LATimes*, February 7, 2006, 95. Eva Cox, "Betty Friedan: From Desperate Jewish Housewife to Feminist," *Australian Jewish News*, February 10, 2006. Kate Millett Eulogy, August 26, 2006, VFA Website, Box 44, KDCP.

26. Uhrbach quoted in "Friedan's Headstone, for Friends and Readers, Unveiled in Sag Harbor," *Sag Harbor Express*, July 30, 2009, 4. Interview with Jan Uhrbach.

## Epilogue

1. Coontz quoted in Radcliffe Institute, *Fifty Years After The Feminine Mystique*, 2006. YouTube https://www.youtube.com/watch?v=_ecx9qZPMio&ab_channel=HarvardUniversity. Christine Stansell, "Girlie Interrupted," *New Republic*, January 14, 2001, 23–30.

2. Quote from digital images of Friedan's talk at Minds for History conference at Arcosanti, 1990. Courtesy of the Cosanti Foundation–Archives at Arcosanti.

3. Melissa Korn, Lauren Weber, Andrea Fuller, "Data Shows

Pay Gap Opens Early," *Wall Street Journal*, August 8, 2022, A1. Cecilia Kang and Erin Griffith, "What Sheryl Sandberg's Exit Reveals About Women's Progress in Tech," *NYTimes*, June 3, 2022, B1. Michelle Goldberg, Interview with Ezra Klein, *NYTimes*, July 8, 2022.

4. Urbanska, "Following in Feminist Footsteps, *Philadelphia Inquirer*, October 20, 1981. Skype Interview with Mahnaz Afkhami, August 25, 2016. Zoom Interviews with Afkhami, February 16, 2022, March 11, 2022. Brill, *Princess Grace, Princess Betty*, 168.

# ACKNOWLEDGMENTS

My first great debt is to the many people who spoke with me about Betty Friedan, including her family, friends, acquaintances, admirers, and her colleagues in the movement and elsewhere. There are so many people who helped that I cannot list them all, but I single out Muriel Fox and Jonathan Slon as beyond helpful in every way. My second, and equally profound debt, is to my editor, Ileene Smith—first for not giving up on me and then for pushing me to do better. Thanks also to my agent, Jin Auh, for her patience and support, and to her lieutenants, especially Abram Scharf. Thanks to friends for reading drafts or partial drafts, especially Jack Beatty, Jonathan Santlofer, Rishona Zimring, Rina Ranalli, Liesl Olsen, Gioia Diliberto, Jonathan Eig, Eric Banks, Thad Ziolkowski, Abbott Kahler, Sigrid Nunez, Katha Pollitt, and Jodi MacAuliffe. And thanks to a group of friends, too many to name, for discussing Betty with me for years, especially Sebastian Currier, Rachel Saltz, and Alan Edelstein. Thanks also to the many librarians and archivists who helped: especially Jennifer Fauxsmith and Jenny Gotwals at the Schlesinger Library; Nanci Young, Kate Long, and Mary Biddle at Smith; Heather Jagman at Richardson Library at DePaul; Thai S. Jones at Columbia; and Linda Aylward in Peoria. Thanks to Megan Scauri at American Jewish Historical Society. Thanks to Marissa Fenley for letting me borrow her library card. Many assistants helped, especially Yasmin Zakaria Mikhaiel and Nina Ryan. Thanks to Marci Bailey and Max Robbins for spot research at the Schlesinger and Amy Balmuth for her rigorous fact checking. Thanks to Dan Horowitz for his insights and generosity. Thanks to John Culbert, the former dean of the Theatre School at DePaul University, for giving me one or two extra course releases and to DePaul University for giving me a small leave and grant to help with some final pieces of this project. Thanks to Martine Kei Green-Rogers for her help with production expenses. Thanks to Playa Summerlake and the Walter Reuther Library for the Fishman Travel Award. At Yale, thanks to Heather Gold and Eva Skewes. Thanks to Noreen O'Connor-Abel and Joyce Ippolito. Thanks to the editors who let me write about various aspects of Betty and second-wave feminism over the years: Jean Tamarin, formerly at the *Chronicle of Higher Education*, Matthew Fishbane at *Tablet*, Paul Makishima formerly at the *Boston Globe*, Boris Drayluk at the *Los Angeles Review of Books*, and Francesca Donner, then at the *New York Times*. I apologize to anyone I have left out.

# INDEX

*In this index, sublevels use "BF" to refer to Betty Friedan and "Carl" to refer to Carl Friedan.*

Jewish Lives is a prizewinning series of interpretative biography designed to explore the many facets of Jewish identity. Individual volumes illuminate the imprint of Jewish figures upon literature, religion, philosophy, politics, cultural and economic life, and the arts and sciences. Subjects are paired with authors to elicit lively, deeply informed books that explore the range and depth of the Jewish experience from antiquity to the present.

Jewish Lives is a partnership of Yale University Press and the Leon D. Black Foundation. Ileene Smith is editorial director. Anita Shapira and Steven J. Zipperstein are series editors.

PUBLISHED TITLES INCLUDE:

*Rabbi Akiva: Sage of the Talmud*, by Barry W. Holtz
*Ben-Gurion: Father of Modern Israel*, by Anita Shapira
*Judah Benjamin: Counselor to the Confederacy*, by James Traub
*Bernard Berenson: A Life in the Picture Trade*, by Rachel Cohen
*Irving Berlin: New York Genius*, by James Kaplan
*Sarah: The Life of Sarah Bernhardt*, by Robert Gottlieb
*Leonard Bernstein: An American Musician*, by Allen Shawn
*Hayim Nahman Bialik: Poet of Hebrew*, by Avner Holtzman
*Léon Blum: Prime Minister, Socialist, Zionist*, by Pierre Birnbaum
*Louis D. Brandeis: American Prophet*, by Jeffrey Rosen
*Mel Brooks: Disobedient Jew*, by Jeremy Dauber
*Martin Buber: A Life of Faith and Dissent*, by Paul Mendes-Flohr
*David: The Divided Heart*, by David Wolpe
*Moshe Dayan: Israel's Controversial Hero*, by Mordechai Bar-On
*Disraeli: The Novel Politician*, by David Cesarani
*Einstein: His Space and Times*, by Steven Gimbel
*Becoming Elijah: Prophet of Transformation*, by Daniel Matt
*Becoming Freud: The Making of a Psychoanalyst*, by Adam Phillips
*Betty Friedan: Magnificent Disrupter*, by Rachel Shteir
*Emma Goldman: Revolution as a Way of Life*, by Vivian Gornick
*Hank Greenberg: The Hero Who Didn't Want to Be One*, by Mark Kurlansky
*Peggy Guggenheim: The Shock of the Modern*, by Francine Prose
*Ben Hecht: Fighting Words, Moving Pictures*, by Adina Hoffman

*Heinrich Heine: Writing the Revolution*, by George Prochnik
*Lillian Hellman: An Imperious Life*, by Dorothy Gallagher
*Theodor Herzl: The Charismatic Leader*, by Derek Penslar
*Abraham Joshua Heschel: A Life of Radical Amazement*,
by Julian Zelizer
*Houdini: The Elusive American*, by Adam Begley
*Jabotinsky: A Life*, by Hillel Halkin
*Jacob: Unexpected Patriarch*, by Yair Zakovitch
*Franz Kafka: The Poet of Shame and Guilt*, by Saul Friedländer
*Rav Kook: Mystic in a Time of Revolution*, by Yehudah Mirsky
*Stanley Kubrick: American Filmmaker*, by David Mikics
*Stan Lee: A Life in Comics*, by Liel Leibovitz
*Primo Levi: The Matter of a Life*, by Berel Lang
*Maimonides: Faith in Reason*, by Alberto Manguel
*Groucho Marx: The Comedy of Existence*, by Lee Siegel
*Karl Marx: Philosophy and Revolution*, by Shlomo Avineri
*Golda Meir*, by Deborah E. Lipstadt
*Menasseh ben Israel: Rabbi of Amsterdam*, by Steven Nadler
*Moses Mendelssohn: Sage of Modernity*, by Shmuel Feiner
*Harvey Milk: His Lives and Death*, by Lillian Faderman
*Arthur Miller: American Witness*, by John Lahr
*Moses: A Human Life*, by Avivah Gottlieb Zornberg
*Amos Oz: Writer, Activist, Icon*, by Robert Alter
*Proust: The Search*, by Benjamin Taylor
*Yitzhak Rabin: Soldier, Leader, Statesman*, by Itamar Rabinovich
*Walther Rathenau: Weimar's Fallen Statesman*, by Shulamit Volkov
*Man Ray: The Artist and His Shadows*, by Arthur Lubow
*Sidney Reilly: Master Spy*, by Benny Morris
*Admiral Hyman Rickover: Engineer of Power*, by Marc Wortman
*Jerome Robbins: A Life in Dance*, by Wendy Lesser
*Julius Rosenwald: Repairing the World*, by Hasia R. Diner
*Mark Rothko: Toward the Light in the Chapel*, by Annie Cohen-Solal

*Ruth: A Migrant's Tale*, by Ilana Pardes
*Gershom Scholem: Master of the Kabbalah*, by David Biale
*Bugsy Siegel: The Dark Side of the American Dream*,
by Michael Shnayerson
*Solomon: The Lure of Wisdom*, by Steven Weitzman
*Steven Spielberg: A Life in Films*, by Molly Haskell
*Alfred Stieglitz: Taking Pictures, Making Painters*, by Phyllis Rose
*Barbra Streisand: Redefining Beauty, Femininity, and Power*,
by Neal Gabler
*Leon Trotsky: A Revolutionary's Life*, by Joshua Rubenstein
*Warner Bros: The Making of an American Movie Studio*,
by David Thomson
*Elie Wiesel: Confronting the Silence*, by Joseph Berger

FORTHCOMING TITLES INCLUDE:

*Abraham*, by Anthony Julius
*Hannah Arendt*, by Masha Gessen
*Walter Benjamin*, by Peter Gordon
*Franz Boas*, by Noga Arikha
*Alfred Dreyfus*, by Maurice Samuels
*Anne Frank*, by Ruth Franklin
*George Gershwin*, by Gary Giddins
*Herod*, by Martin Goodman
*Jesus*, by Jack Miles
*Josephus*, by Daniel Boyarin
*Louis Kahn*, by Gini Alhadeff
*Mordecai Kaplan*, by Jenna Weissman Joselit
*Carole King*, by Jane Eisner
*Fiorello La Guardia*, by Brenda Wineapple
*Hedy Lamarr*, by Sarah Wildman
*Mahler*, by Leon Botstein

*Norman Mailer*, by David Bromwich
*Louis B. Mayer and Irving Thalberg*, by Kenneth Turan
*Robert Oppenheimer*, by David Rieff
*Ayn Rand*, by Alexandra Popoff
*Rebecca*, by Judith Shulevitz
*Philip Roth*, by Steven J. Zipperstein
*Edmond de Rothschild*, by James McAuley
*Jonas Salk*, by David Margolick
*Rebbe Schneerson*, by Ezra Glinter
*Stephen Sondheim*, by Daniel Okrent
*Baruch Spinoza*, by Ian Buruma
*Gertrude Stein*, by Lauren Elkin
*Henrietta Szold*, by Francine Klagsbrun
*Billy Wilder*, by Noah Isenberg
*Ludwig Wittgenstein*, by Anthony Gottlieb